Homecomings

Program in Migration and Refugee Studies

Program Advisors:
Elzbieta M. Gozdziak and Susan F. Martin, Institute for the Study of International Migration

Books in the Series:
Homecomings: Unsettling Paths of Return, edited by Fran Markowitz and Anders Stefansson
The Cape Verdean Diaspora in Portugal: Colonial Subjects in a Postcolonial World, by Luis Batalha
Refugee Women, 2nd ed., by Susan Forbes Martin
The Refugee Convention at Fifty: A View from Forced Migration Studies, edited by Joanne Van Selm, Khoti Kamanga, et al.
Migration and the Externalities of European Integration, edited by Sandra Lavenex and Emek M. Uçarer
After Involuntary Migration: The Political Economy of Refugee Encampments, by Milica Z. Bookman
Premigration Legacies and Immigrant Social Mobility: The Afro-Surinamese and Indo-Surinamese in the Netherlands, by Mies van Niekerk
Communication and Identity in the Diaspora: Turkish Migrants in Amsterdam and Their Use of Media, by Christine Ogan

Forthcoming:
New Immigrant Communities: Facilitating Immigrant Integration, edited by Elzbieta M. Gozdziak and Micah Bump
Transnational Migration to Israel in Global Comparative Context, edited by Sarah S. Willen
Catching Fire: Containing Complex Displacement in a Volatile World, edited by Nicholas van Hear and Christopher McDowell
The Uprooted: Improving Humanitarian Responses to Forced Migration, by Susan F. Martin, Patricia Weiss Fagen, et al.

Homecomings

Unsettling Paths of Return

Edited by Fran Markowitz
and Anders H. Stefansson

LEXINGTON BOOKS
Lanham • Boulder • New York • Toronto • Oxford

LEXINGTON BOOKS

Published in the United States of America
by Lexington Books
An imprint of The Rowman & Littlefield Publishing Group, Inc.
4501 Forbes Boulevard, Suite 200, Lanham, Maryland 20706

PO Box 317
Oxford
OX2 9RU, UK

Copyright © 2004 by Lexington Books

All rights reserved. No part of this publication may be reproduced, stored in a retrieval system, or transmitted in any form or by any means, electronic, mechanical, photocopying, recording, or otherwise, without the prior permission of the publisher.

British Library Cataloguing in Publication Information Available

Library of Congress Cataloging-in-Publication Data

Homecomings : unsettling paths of return / edited by Fran Markowitz and Anders H. Stefansson.
   p. cm.
   Includes bibliographical references and index.
   ISBN 0-7391-0830-1 (cloth : alk. paper) — ISBN 0-7391-0952-9 (pbk. : alk. paper)
   1. Return migration. I. Markowitz, Fran. II. Stefansson, Anders H., 1969–
JV6217.5.H65 2004
304.8—dc22   2004019918

Printed in the United States of America

∞™ The paper used in this publication meets the minimum requirements of American National Standard for Information Sciences—Permanence of Paper for Printed Library Materials, ANSI/NISO Z39.48-1992.

Contents

Part I	Introduction	1
1	Homecomings to the Future: From Diasporic Mythographies to Social Projects of Return *Anders H. Stefansson*	2
2	The Home(s) of Homecomings *Fran Markowitz*	21
Part II	Homecomings of Immigrants and Refugees	35
3	Tigrayan Returnees' Notions of Home: Five Variations on a Theme *Laura Hammond*	36
4	Sarajevo Suffering: Homecoming and the Hierarchy of Homeland Hardship *Anders H. Stefansson*	54
5	*Extra Hungariam Non Est Vita?* The Relationships between Hungarian Immigrants and Their Homeland *Éva V. Huseby-Darvas*	76

Part III Blurried Homes, Blurred Diaspora-Homeland Boundaries — 91

6 Homecoming to the Diaspora: Nation and State in Visits of Israelis to Morocco — 92
   André Levy

7 From the Centers to the Periphery: "Repatriation" to an Armenian Homeland in the Twentieth Century — 109
   Susan Pattie

8 When Home Is Not the Homeland: The Case of Japanese Brazilian Ethnic Return Migration — 125
   Takeyuki (Gaku) Tsuda

9 Promised Land, Imagined Homelands: Ethiopian Jews' Immigration to Israel — 146
   Lisa Anteby-Yemini

Part IV Contentious Homecomings — 165

10 Transatlantic Dreaming: Slavery, Tourism, and Diasporic Encounters — 166
    Bayo Holsey

11 Leaving Babylon to Come Home to Israel: Closing the Circle of the Black Diaspora — 183
    Fran Markowitz

12 While Waiting for the Ferry to Cuba: *Adio Kerida* and the Goodbye That Isn't a Farewell — 199
    Ruth Behar

Index — 211

About the Contributors — 215

I
INTRODUCTION

1

Homecomings to the Future: From Diasporic Mythographies to Social Projects of Return

Anders H. Stefansson

> In spite of the wandering habits of Nuer, persons born and bred in a village have a nostalgia for it and are likely to return to it and make their home there, even if they have resided elsewhere for many years.
>
> —E. E. Evans-Pritchard (1940: 115)

"I have returned to spend the last part of my life at home," explained several elderly Bosnians in Banja Luka, a town in the northern part of Bosnia and Herzegovina. Others declared that the main reason why they had decided to give up refugee status and economic entitlements in Western Europe was their wish to return to die at home. Certainly it would have been presumptuous of me, the anthropologist, to question their assertion of homecoming as the natural end of refugee life, indeed of life itself. Yet it was hard for me, if not for them, to forget that although these Bosnian Muslims, or Bosniacs, still regarded Banja Luka as their hometown, during the recent war it had been a place of terror from where they were "ethnically cleansed" by radicalized Bosnian Serbs. In 2003, several years after the end of that war, Banja Luka remained a less than welcoming place for returning ethnic minorities. Nevertheless, my elderly informants defiantly insisted that they belong there and expressed a sense of satisfaction and empowerment of having returned to live once again, "under my own sky" (*podneblje*).

As these defiant Bosnian homecomings suggest, the desire to return can be compelling for diasporic people, and their will to act upon longings for home, homeland, and homecoming even under unfavorable conditions upsets conventional wisdom (Borneman and Peck 1995; Uehling 2002).

Arguing that it is high time to analyze the continuing attractive force of homecoming in an era of globalization, this *Homecomings* volume explores the forces and motives that drive immigrants, refugees, exiles, and their descendants back to places of origin as well as analyzes their often dramatic experiences once they are back in these lands.

The decisions of elderly Bosniacs to return to watch the sunset a few last times at home and then be buried in their native soil arguably represent an extreme case of homecoming. Yet in its extremity, this case illustrates one of the central points of this book: Despite recent notions of postmodernism and antiessentialism and the claim that the bond between people(s), culture, and territory has withered away, place and home, often in the shape of localized homelands or nation-states, continue to be of vital importance to individuals and communities as sources of identity, livelihood, legal rights, and social relations (Gupta and Ferguson 1997; Kibreab 1999; Olwig 1998; Oxfeld and Long 2004: 2). *Homecomings* demonstrates that the "homing desire" of diasporic peoples (Brah 1996: 193) is not merely a defensive and nostalgic reaction to the hardships of displacement and the stigma of ethnic minority status, but it regularly becomes a "charter for new social projects" (Appadurai 1996: 6) that lead them on unsettling, but also potentially relieving, paths of return.

Yet return movements across time and space have largely been ignored in anthropology and migration research, and despite mass dislocations and repatriation efforts of the late twentieth century the theme of homecoming still sits on the periphery of such studies. Today the possibility of "de-diasporization" (Van Hear 1998: 48) or "deglobalization" (Hannerz 1996: 18; Olwig 2003) seems to run counter to the dominant paradigms of our era, which is supposedly characterized by increasing global mobility and cultural hybridity. From such a perspective favoring movement and the creation of what has been termed a counterhegemonic, "delocalized *transnation*" (Appadurai 1996: 172), "going home" to the local community or nation-state from which one migrated or was displaced appears antiprogressive, illogical, and illusory (Chambers 1994; Rapport and Dawson 1998; Warner 1994). Writing against such dissipated theories, or perhaps rather visions, of carefree borderless belongings, *Homecomings* contributes ethnographic case studies to an under-studied phenomenon while challenging a current theoretical master narrative that structures the ways in which researchers perceive and write about social processes (Bruner 1986).

This critique of antiessentialism, however, does not put *Homecomings* on the path toward an antiquated model of essentialism or cultural holism. Rather, paraphrasing Geertz (1984), our argument is voiced in the spirit of a future-oriented "anti-antiessentialism" that we think will better allow social scientists to pay attention to the interplay between mobility and fixity, between change and continuity, and between deterritorialization and (re)territorialization.

Homecomings, we posit, have unsettling consequences for social science as well as for returnees and populations who have stayed behind in their homelands. In the course of protracted absence home develops, and so too do the people living away from home. Because of such transformations of place and identity, homecoming often contains elements of rupture, surprise, and, perhaps, disillusionment, besides the variety of practical problems that returnees usually confront in their "new/old place" (Casey 1993: 294). "De-diasporization" can thus lead to rediasporization. In a similar vein, "deglobalization" may in fact turn out to be globalization in new disguise, as returnees bring with them new habits, resources, and identities that increase cultural complexity in the homelands, and then sometimes leave those places of origin to travel back to their diasporic homes.

Notwithstanding the disenchanting aspects of return, the volume shows that homecomings are often feasible projects that include encouraging experiences. These homecomings, rather than aiming at resurrecting a golden but lost past, are primarily oriented toward creating better, more satisfying future lives. *Homecomings* thus challenges the often rather pessimistic accounts of homecoming found in the existing return migration research, which tends to focus on the "problems of return" (Chimni 2000: 13) and on the illusory dream among diasporic peoples to return to a place and a community frozen in time, which according to some scholars in this field turns homecoming into an impossible project (Chambers 1994: 5; Warner 1994). Taken as a whole, the chapters show that there is no singular process of return; the processes of homecoming are characterized by considerable complexity and ambivalence that provide rich examples of cultural creativity and inventiveness.

Through ethnographic analyses of a wide range of homecoming experiences *Homecomings* moves beyond some of the basic assumptions of much return migration research. This volume is the only one of its kind in that it includes repatriations of war refugees and political exiles as well as the "return" of people who, acting out the yearnings of diaspora discourse, uproot themselves from the only homes they ever knew to resettle in their people's homeland. The volume's arrangement reflects a categorization of homecomers based on the extent of "temporal distance" from the homeland and incorporates what has been termed "ancestral return" (King 1986: 6) in its scope.[1] *Homecomings* also goes beyond studies of return migration by not restricting its analyses to return movements aimed at permanent settlement in places of origin. Several chapters reveal how people negotiate and enact homeland-bound returns through long- and short-term visits, pilgrimages, "roots tours," medical "tourism," temporary work contracts, cash donations, and political activity. Diversity is thus a central feature of *Homecomings*, showing the variety of ways in which homecomings are imagined, motivated, practiced, and experienced.

Altogether, *Homecomings* sheds new light on the study of return by analyzing homecomings as future-oriented social projects that are based on continuous emotional attachment to natal or ancestral homelands, and which result in complex, dramatic encounters with institutions, social conditions, and cultural traditions in these places. These themes are discussed in greater detail in the remaining part of this introduction, which first addresses the history of return migration's invisibility in migration research and then presents several central themes and findings of the volume.[2]

A HISTORY OF HOMECOMINGS: INVISIBILITY COMING FULL CIRCLE

Homecoming as a project that leads into social action is a theme conspicuously absent from much of anthropology and migration research. For the better part of the 20th century returns of immigrants, refugees, and exiles were hardly noticed by scholars, or at least not seen as phenomena of much academic interest. When return slowly started to gain ground as a subject of analysis a few decades ago, it was usually either treated in terms of a myth or a source of symbolic belonging and later as part of ongoing global mobility among "transmigrants." Because of the structural invisibility of return migration, it has been termed "the great unwritten chapter in the history of migration" (King 2000: 7). We suggest that this analytical neglect has been caused by the fact that the conceptual and practical issues of homecoming always have fallen at the margins of the grand narratives in migration research, those of assimilation, multiculturalism/diaspora, and transnationalism/globalization.[3] A second possible reason is tied to the commonsense view dominated by the logic of sedentary thinking throughout much of the twentieth century (Gupta and Ferguson 1992, 1997; Malkki 1992) that homecoming is an act of unproblematic and natural reinsertion in the local or national community once left behind.

In the narrative of assimilation that dominated political and academic approaches to international migration until the late 1960s, and which certainly lingers in popular thinking, immigrants and refugees had come to stay in their new countries where they would cast off their homeland habits after a more or less painful process of assimilation (Gordon 1964). With few exceptions migration research treated migration as "a one-way process, with no return" (King 2000: 7) and was preoccupied with the effects of "uprootedness" and processes of "resocialization" in host societies (Brettell and Hollifield 2000: 15; Castles and Davidson 2000: 157–9; Eisenstadt 1954; Glick Schiller et al. 1995: 51). This bias was strengthened by the fact that many of the massive displacements that took place in this period became permanent. For example, the twelve million *Volksdeutsche*, or ethnic

Germans, who fled or were displaced from their homes in Central and Eastern Europe in the aftermath of World War II were not expected to return (Zolberg et al. 1989: 22). Likewise, for ideological reasons refugees who had escaped from the Communist East during the Cold War era were generally positively received in the West and not forced to return (Harrell-Bond 1986: 11; Markowitz 1993; Marrus 1985).

In the 1960s, prompted by the realization that many immigrants and refugees maintain elements of their home country culture and identity as well as symbolic, and to some extent also practical, links to their places of origin, academics and policymakers began to challenge the notion of assimilation and promoted policies of multiculturalism and integration (Glazer and Moynihan 1970). As this more dynamic approach to migration gained in adherents it was noted that many immigrants and refugees may arrive in their new domiciles with the intention of returning to the place of origin after a limited period of stay but in practice end up as permanent settlers.[4] In other words, while they evoke "next year in Jerusalem" or "next year in Havana" (Behar 1996: 145), with the passing of time the likelihood that the dream of return will be realized seems to diminish (Eastmond 1997; Malkki 1995a).[5] Much research in this vein revolved around the concept of "the myth of return" (Al-Rasheed 1994; Anwar 1979; Dahya 1973; Zetter 1994, 1999), "the return illusion" (Brettell 1979), or the "ideology of return" (Rubenstein 1979).

This image of migrants as "permanent transients" persists with a twist in the proliferating literature on diaspora (e.g., Clifford 1994; Cohen 1997; Hall 1990; Tölölyan 1996). While the emphasis on home and homeland as symbolic resources is an important corrective to earlier migration research, the possibility that some displaced people may in fact return to the homeland, thereby "demythologizing" the myth of return, remains strangely unexplored in these otherwise pathbreaking studies.

Yet recent "revisionist" scholarship has established that significant numbers of migrants returned to their countries of origin even during the heydays of assimilationism and the "melting pot" era (Foner 2000; Glick Schiller et al. 1995; Morawska 1991; Sarna 1985; Wyman 1993). Furthermore, over the years a scattered anthropologically informed literature on processes of return migration has developed (e.g., Gmelch 1980, 1995; King 1986, 2000; Stack 1996; Saloutos 1956; Thomas-Hope 1999, 2002; Useem and Useem 1955). Refugee repatriations also occurred during the Cold War, especially in the Third World, but without generating much political or scholarly attention (Rogge 1994). In the past decade the increasing scale of, and political emphasis on, refugee repatriation have prompted a proliferation of studies on this particular type of return (e.g., Allen 1996; Allen and Morsink 1994; Black and Koser 1999; Hammond 2004; Stefansson 2003, 2004).[6] In recent years studies of descendants of immigrants and exiles who embark upon what has been characterized variously as ancestral return, ethnic return migration, or post-colonial return have also become more frequent (e.g., Hirschon 1989; Lake 1995; Münz and Ohliger 2003; Ray 2000; Rock and Wolff 2002; Tsuda 2001, 2003; Uehling 2002, 2004; Voutira 1991).[7]

Many studies of return migration and repatriation, including several chapters in this volume, show that homecoming is a complex and contested experience even for people who return to countries where they lived prior to exodus (Black and Koser 1999; Gmelch 1995; Long and Oxfeld 2004; Stefansson 2003; Behar; Hammond; Huseby-Darvas; Stefansson, this volume). But the study of the ancestral return of those who lived centuries beyond the border of their homelands raises especially intriguing questions of the meaning of home and homecoming. When the diasporic peoples analyzed in the contributions by Anteby-Yemini, Holsey, Markowitz, Pattie, and Tsuda return to their historical homelands, they leave behind their places of birth and travel to countries in which they have never themselves set foot, thus critically blurring the heterofore sacrosanct emigration/immigration and home/host country dichotomies. In Levy's chapter this categorical confusion takes an ironic twist, as his Jewish informants, who in the 1950s return migrated from Morocco to their historical homeland of Israel, later revisit their natal homeland.[8]

This blurring of borders comes to the fore in studies of transnationalism that gathered momentum in the early 1990s. Here the stress on symbolic homelands as sources of diasporic identity has given way to a focus on the many concrete global ties that immigrants often maintain with their countries of origin, including remittances, construction of homes, participation in homeland politics and cultural activities, social relations, and periodical return visits (e.g., Al-Ali and Koser 2002; Basch et al. 1994; Glick Schiller et al. 1992, 1995; Levitt 2001; Levitt and Waters 2002). In contrast to conventional migration research which tended to regard emigration and return as permanent dislocations, studies of transnationalism refreshingly describe mobility as an integral and normal, indeed sometimes normative, part of migrants' lives. However, when "'emigration' and 'return' are seen less and less as discrete events and increasingly as part of wider ongoing processes of global mobility" (King 2000: 44) and when sending and receiving societies thus emerge as a single social field, paradoxically (permanent) return migration is also dissolved as a distinct category of interest (Brettell and Hollifield 2000: 16; Byron 1999: 296; Olwig 2001).

Although until a few decades ago return movements were barely noticed by migration scholars, today they are attracting attention, but now principally as merely brief intersections in a "transnational migration circuit" (Rouse 1991: 14). Ironically, because of the current power of the narrative of transnationalism it may be that the structural invisibility of homecoming within migration studies is in danger of coming full circle, and permanent, one-way return migration may be ignored. Several chapters in *Homecomings* demonstrate that return does not necessarily mark the end of the migratory cycle. It may be a temporary one-time journey (Holsey; Levy) or a part of more transnational movements between dwellings (Behar; Huseby-Darvas; Tsuda). For other of the groups of homecomers under study in this volume return has in fact taken on the character of finality. However, regardless of whether return is temporary or permanent *Homecomings* shows that homecoming is a meaningful concept and social practice for mobile people, and thus ought also to stay with researchers as a useful analytical category (see also Oxfeld and Long 2004: 3–4).

AMBIVALENT HOMECOMINGS: RETHINKING RETURN

One of the great merits of the literature on return lies in its deconstruction of the essentialized notion of the easy and "natural" homecoming that brings "uprooted" people back to their familiar sociocultural habitat, thus "healing the social body" (Eastmond 2001).[9] Yet it appears that in their effort to challenge static models of home and return, return migration scholars often provide rather one-sided, pessimistic pictures of homecoming, by privileging the "questions of unhappiness and dissatisfaction" (King 2000: 19) that plague the return over more encouraging elements of that experience. *Homecomings* presents more complex and balanced accounts of homecoming that capture what some researchers in this field recently have called the intrinsic "ambivalence" or "ambiguity" of return, including at the same time aspects of both disenchantment and satisfaction (Constable 1999, 2004; King 2000: 19–20; Stefansson 2003, 2004; Thomas-Hope 2002: 200; Uehling 2002).[10]

The chapters in this volume show the multiplicity and seriousness of the problems, challenges, and surprises of homecoming. Homecomings rarely turn out exactly as expected:

> The homecomer . . . expects to return to an environment of which he always had and—so he thinks—still has intimate knowledge and which he has just to take for granted in order to find his bearings within it. The approaching stranger has to anticipate in a more or less empty way what he will find; the homecomer has just to recur to the memories of his past. So he feels; and because he feels so, he will suffer the typical shock described by Homer [in *Odyssey*]." (Schutz 1976: 106–7)[11]

Because of the mismatch between the imagined and experienced homecoming, coming home can be more difficult and emotionally destabilizing than leaving home and settling in a new part of the world.

Zetter (1999: 6) suggests substituting for the myth of return as "the myth of 'home'" so as to stress that "what is mythologized is not return per se, but home." This indicates that when diasporic people return they often discover that the place of return bears little resemblance to the "imaginary homelands" (Rushdie 1991) constructed in the course of protracted exile, which can leave returnees disappointed and disillusioned, and sometimes alienated from the homeland. In this volume, the Ethiopian Jews explored by Anteby-Yemini believed that Israel would be "a land of milk and honey" or "the garden of Eden" but instead found themselves spatially segregated and socially marginalized in their homeland, where they were also dismayed to learn that a large part of Israel's Jewish population is not religiously observant. In a similar vein, Pattie's chapter describes how Syrian Armenians who repatriated to Soviet Armenia thought they were traveling to a promised land but after their return had to fight for survival in conditions of severe material hardship. Other chapters explore the substantial material and practical problems faced by returnees. Behar and Levy discuss the difficulties of gaining access to the homeland in the first place. Once they get there, returnees may be confronted by lack of legal recognition and unclear religious status (Markowitz), or occupation of their houses and unemployment (Stefansson).

Studies of return migration suggest that one of the most unexpected and disillusioning aspects of homecoming is the cool welcome, if not downright hostility, that the homecomers often receive from the population that stayed behind in the homeland (Eastmond and Öjendal 1999; Gmelch 1995; Hirschon 1989; Kibreab 2002; Stefansson 2003: Chapter 9; Tsuda 2003). Stayees, including close kin, may envy and nurture exaggerated images of the living conditions and the "easy" life that the returnees are supposed to have enjoyed abroad (Gmelch 1980: 143, 2004: 214). There can also be material conflicts and political animosity between the two groups.

The theme of social distance between returnees and stayees is central to most of the chapters in *Homecomings*. Holsey's essay describes the image among local Ghanaians of African American visitors as well-off people who want to reconnect to their past without feeling obliged to assist their African kin. My own chapter analyzes the ways in which the construction of different discourses of suffering, related to wartime hardships and refugee life, produced tension, envy, and social distance between Bosnian repatriates and stayees in postwar Sarajevo. In a similar vein, Huseby-Darvas writes about "an abyss of mutual misunderstandings" between Hungarian émigrés and their compatriots in the homeland, echoing Kundera's novel *Ignorance* (2002). In Levy's chapter the desire of Moroccan-born Israelis "to regain their authenticity as Moroccans" through visits to Morocco were doubly disputed by Moroccan Muslims who saw the Israelis as nothing but tourists and by the small group of Casablanca Jews who revealed the visitors' show of newly acquired wealth as betraying their "authentic" poor backgrounds.

Margold (2004: 49) argues that diasporic communities "see themselves refracted in their host's eyes," which leads to a redefinition of self and home.

But it is often only when confronted with the homeland, and in particular with the stayee population in this place, that they fully realize such changes and the extent to which they have been influenced by new social systems and cultural norms, in terms of work ethic, gender roles, urban living, and independence (Bascom 1998: 158; Constable 1999; Huseby-Darvas; Pattie; Stefansson; Tsuda, this volume). The new skills learned and outlooks adopted abroad can make the home appear "narrow and old-fashioned" (Oxfeld and Long 2004: 10), characterized as it apparently is by lack of development, inefficiency, authoritarian mentality, or the legacies of war and tyranny (Gmelch 1995: 290–5; Useem and Useem 1955: 42–57). But also in cases where the place of return is more industrially advanced than the host country, homecoming can lead to perplexing encounters with, as Anteby-Yemini writes, "a consumer society where one needs money for everything," and in which returnees' agricultural and pastoral skills are not really sought after in the labor market.

Often experiences of cultural difference and social distance lay the ground for the development of a separate "returnee identity" (Cornish et al. 1999: 275) and the creation of returnee "enclaves" (Byron 1999: 299; Eastmond 2001; Wyman 1993: 197; Anteby-Yemini; Levy; Markowitz; Stefansson, this volume). Tsuda's chapter describes how Japanese Brazilians, who "are ethnically excluded and socially marginalized as foreigners in their ethnic homeland," nonetheless gradually start to feel at home in Japan, albeit in their "Little Brazils" where they continue to speak Portuguese, eat Brazilian food, and follow mass media from their natal homeland. As this case suggests, return can result in a heightened sense of attachment to the place of diaspora, and indeed to the construction of new diasporas in the ethnic homeland.

On the basis of such disappointments and ruptured returns many return migration researchers draw the conclusion that return is experienced as a "culture shock," a trauma or a new displacement, whereby returnees become alienated from their homeland (Cornish et al. 1999; Davidson 1968; Graham and Khosravi 1997: 126; Majodina 1995: 210; Pilkington and Flynn 1999: 190–91). It is also noted how many returnees reemigrate to the country of initial immigration or engage in circular or transnational migration (Bovenkerk 1974: 29; Thomas-Hope 2002: 200; Zarzosa 1998). In such bleak circumstances it has been argued that homecoming is an "illusion" or "impossibility" (Chambers 1994: 5; Habib 1996: 101; Jansen 1998: 85; Warner 1994).[12]

Through the volume's wide range of ethnographic studies, *Homecomings* tempers the disappointments of return with encouraging experiences. In the final, self-reflexive chapter on the making of her film *Adio Kerida*, Behar writes that although Cuba will always in some sense remain an imaginary homeland for her and other Cuban exiles, she did in fact make several successful return visits. Holsey's chapter shows how African Americans' visits to slave dungeons in Ghana are a "positive experience from which they return home to the diaspora strengthened with the knowledge that their ancestors' courage continues to dwell in them." Pattie argues that in spite of economic hardships suffered by Armenian returnees, they were able to construct narratives that rendered meaning to their experience of homecoming, in particular by depicting themselves as people who "saved" backward Armenia through their sacrifices and industrious nature.

The contributions by Hammond, Markowitz, Pattie, and Stefansson demonstrate as well how "patriotism" and a sense of spiritual belonging act both as motivating forces in the decision to return and as factors that to some extent mitigate difficulties and disappointments confronted in the homeland (see also Uehling 2002). Furthermore, a number of chapters indicate that while first-generation returnees may remain on the margins of the homeland society there are signs that later generations will become more equal members of the home country community (Anteby-Yemini; Levy; Tsuda).

In a paradoxical way the experience of living away from home can lead to a "discovery" of and new sense of attachment to home (Tuan 2001). Exile life is often less "aesthetic" (Malkki 1995b: 514) than what is suggested by postmodern writers (Said 1992). It is frequently characterized more by poverty, marginalization, racism, and loss (Kaplan 1996; Mahler 1995; Tsuda 2003; Holsey; Markowitz; Stefansson; Tsuda, this volume) than by a privileged cosmopolitan consciousness. *Homecomings* thus argues that in some situations it may actually be the possibility of homecoming that holds the empowering, "liberating," or "progressive" potential (cf. Kibreab 1999), not the diasporic life of dislocated, hybrid "postnationals" (Appadurai 1996; Chambers 1994).

In this way, *Homecomings* challenges the notion of the "impossible homecoming." If mobility and transformation are inherent features of contemporary social life, as the newer theoretical agenda posits (Appadurai 1996; Gupta and Ferguson 1992, 1997; Olwig and Hastrup 1997; Rapport and Dawson 1998), then there is no a priori contradiction between sociocultural change and a sense of being at home or coming home (Casey 1993: 294; Stefansson 2003: 38). Much diasporic literature, however, persists in portraying homecoming in terms of a nostalgic longing for the past, or in Stratton's words a dream of "a return to a place of origin as it *was*, not as it is now" (1997: 317). Such returns to the predisplacement past are doomed to fail. But do diasporic people embarking upon return really believe themselves able to recapture the past, to travel in time, so to speak, and would they be interested in doing so at all? Several chapters reply "no" to this question. Hammond's chapter, for instance, describes how Ethiopian repatriates made a deliberate decision *not* to return to their former villages where they had lost their land rights. They settled instead in "an empty field" elsewhere in the country where they were allocated land by the state, which made their general livelihood opportunities better than in their original highland homes.

Hammond characterizes this process as "homemaking" (see also Hammond 1999, 2004). She argues in favor of a more "proactive" approach to return migration, one that regards return not as directed against a revival of the past but as a creative effort oriented toward constructing better and more satisfying futures. In this more pragmatic and future-oriented sense, homecomings are not impossible projects. As one African American internal migrant in the United States explained to anthropologist Carol Stack: "You can go home. But you can't start from where you left. To fit in, you have to create another place in that place you left behind" (1996: 199, emphasis removed). *Homecomings* shows that creating a new/old home at home is a complicated task, involving challenges, sufferings, and continual diasporic sentiments that may last for years, even for generations. The book's ultimate goal is to point out that the blessings of homecoming can make it well worth the struggle.

NOTES

I am grateful for the constructive comments from Fran Markowitz that have helped strengthen the argument presented in this chapter.

1. The exception to this structural logic is the volume's last chapter by Behar, which is placed at the end of the book due to its self-reflexive character. It should be stressed that the length of separation of diasporic people from their homeland does not necessarily entail a correlating degree of psychological or emotional distancing from home.

2. Fran Markowitz examines other important facets of homecomings in a separate part of the introduction.

3. Obviously, this three-fold temporal division, which will be further explored below, is extremely schematic, as it leaves out many important overlaps, nuances, and exceptions. Nonetheless, given limitations of space it does provide a meaningful overview of the role that the issue of homecoming has played in the history of migration research.

4. For example, a large proportion of the so-called *guest*workers that entered Western European countries in the 1960s and 1970s still live there, even though many are now retired.

5. An ironic take on the discrepancy between the passing of time and the likelihood of return: "A cartoon appeared in *Le Monde* several years ago, showing an old man who says: 'I have never lost hope in returning to my homeland some day. However, I no longer remember where I came from'" (Safran 1991: 91).

6. Only one work to date straddles the otherwise rather tight boundaries between return migration and repatriation research (Long and Oxfeld 2004).

7. As this brief overview indicates, there is a growing academic interest in the phenomena of return migration and repatriation. However, it is fair to argue that they remain relatively marginal issues in migration research. For example, a search on Amazon.com carried out in February 2004 revealed that while 7,575 books were

listed under the entry of "immigration/emigration," only 157 titles were found under "return migration."

8. See Lomsky-Feder and Rapoport 2003 for a similar discussion of the dual homecomings of Russian Jews in Israel who visit their preemigration places of living in Russia.

9. This is a line of thinking especially popular in contemporary repatriation discourse (Harrell-Bond 1989; Koser and Black 1999; Sepulveda 1995; Warner 1994).

10. Uehling (2002), for example, convincingly analyzes Crimean Tatars' ambivalent or "dialogic" attitudes toward homecoming, both prior to repatriation from Uzbekistan and upon their return, torn as they are between the greater sense of material security in their "historical" host country and their strong feelings of national belonging to Crimea.

11. Although this book is restricted to the homecomings of people in "diaspora," it is worthwhile to keep in mind that these are by no means the only groups of travelers who experience the destabilizing effects of homecoming, and that this issue is treated not only by academics. Ever since Odysseus managed to overcome his strong sense of homesickness by returning to Ithaca and his beloved Penelope, only painfully to learn that in his absence treason had been committed at home, homecoming has been a popular theme in works of fiction, for example, Erich Maria Remarque's *All Quiet on the Western Front*, Thomas Wolfe's short story "The Return of the Prodigal" and Milan Kundera's recent *Ignorance*. The difficulties many soldiers and prisoners of war face in coming to terms with the "peaceful" life at home after returning from warfare have been described in numerous novels, movies and academic studies (e.g., Elliott 1982; Figley and Leventman 1990; O'Nell 2000; Ross 1969). Less dramatically perhaps, a body of literature has started to appear on "the art of coming home" (Storti 2001) among long-term expatriates whose problems of adjustment to the home society apparently may turn them into "strangers at home" (Smith 1996; see also Black and Gregersen 1999; White 1988).

12. Only on rare occasions do dissenting voices interrupt the lithany of hardship and alienation, perhaps because more positive aspects of homecoming appear to run against the antiessentialist paradigm that influences many writings on return migration and repatriation. From a more macro-oriented perspective returnees are occasionally described as "innovators" (Cerase 1970; Saloutos 1956), as a "catalyst for development" (Hogg 1996: 162; see also Kibreab 2002; Thomas-Hope 1999), and as playing a role in peace and reconstruction processes in war-torn societies (Juergensen 2000; Koser 2000; Stepputat 1999). Other researchers have noted—but usually only in passing—that some returnees bring back with them economic and social capital that can raise their living standards and social status in the home communities (Gmelch 1995: 306–307; Wyman 1993: 195–97).

REFERENCES

Al-Ali, Nadje, and Khalid Koser, eds. *New Approaches to Migration? Transnational Communities and the Transformation of Home.* London and New York: Routledge, 2002.

Allen, Tim, ed. *In Search of Cool Ground: War, Flight and Homecoming in Northeast Africa*. London: James Currey, 1996.

Allen, Tim, and Hubert Morsink, eds. *When Refugees Go Home: African Experiences*. London: James Currey, 1994.

Al-Rasheed, Madawi. "The Myth of Return: Iraqi Arab and Assyrian Refugees in London." *Journal of Refugee Studies* 7, no. 2/3 (1994): 199–219.

Anwar, Muhammad. *The Myth of Return: Pakistanis in Britain*. London: Heinemann, 1979.

Appadurai, Arjun. *Modernity at Large: Cultural Dimensions of Globalization*. Minneapolis and London: University of Minnesota Press, 1996.

Basch, Linda, Nina Glick Schiller, and Christina S. Blanc. *Nations Unbound: Transnational Projects, Postcolonial Predicaments, and Deterritorialized Nation-States*. New York: Gordon and Breach, 1994.

Bascom, Jonathan. *Losing Place: Refugee Populations and Rural Transformations in East Africa*. New York and London: Berghahn Books, 1998.

Behar, Ruth. *The Vulnerable Observer: Anthropology That Breaks Your Heart*. Boston: Beacon Press, 1996.

Black, Richard, and Khalid Koser, eds. *The End of the Refugee Cycle? Refugee Repatriation and Reconstruction*. New York and Oxford: Berghahn Books, 1999.

Black, J. Stewart, and Hall B. Gregersen. *So You're Coming Home*. Global Business Publisher, 1999.

Borneman, John, and Jeffrey M. Peck. *Sojourners: The Return of German Jews and the Question of Identity*. Lincoln: University of Nebraska Press, 1995.

Bovenkerk, Frank. *The Sociology of Return Migration: A Bibliographic Essay*. The Hague: Martinus Nijhoff, 1974.

Brah, Avtar. *Cartograhies of Diaspora: Contesting Identities*. London: Routledge, 1996.

Brettell, Caroline B. "Emigrar para Voltar: A Portugese Ideology of Return Migration." *Papers in Anthropology* 20, no. 1 (1979): 1–20.

Brettell, Caroline B. and James F. Hollifield. "Migration Theory: Talking across Disciplines." Pp. 1–26 in *Migration Theory: Talking across Disciplines*, edited by Caroline B. Brettell and James F. Hollifield. New York and London: Routledge, 2000.

Bruner, Edward M. "Ethnography as Narrative." Pp. 139–55 in *The Anthropology of Experience*, edited by Victor W. Turner and Edward M. Bruner. Urbana and Chicago: University of Illinois Press, 1986.

Byron, Margaret. "The Caribbean-born Population in 1990s Britain: Who Will Return?" *Journal of Ethnic and Migration Studies* 25, no. 2 (1999): 285–301.

Casey, Edward S. *Getting Back into Place: Toward a Renewed Understanding of the Place-World*. Bloomington and Indianapolis: Indiana University Press, 1993.

Castles, Stephen, and Alastair Davidson. *Citizenship and Migration: Globalization and the Politics of Belonging*. London: Macmillan, 2000.

Cerase, Francesco. "Nostalgia or Disenchantment: Considerations on Return Migration." Pp. 217–39 in *The Italian Experience in the United States*, edited by Silvano M. Tomasi and Madeline H. Engel. New York: Center for Migration Studies of New York, 1970.

Chambers, Iain. *Migrancy, Culture, Identity*. London: Routledge, 1994.

Chimni, B. S. "Globalisation, Humanitarianism, and the Erosion of Refugee Protection." RSC Working Paper no. 3. Oxford: Refugee Studies Centre, University of Oxford, 2000.

Clifford, James. "Diasporas." *Cultural Anthropology* 9, no. 3 (1994): 302–38.
Cohen, Robin. *Global Diasporas: An Introduction*. London: UCL Press, 1997.
Constable, Nicole. "At Home but Not at Home: Filipina Narratives of Ambivalent Returns. *Cultural Anthropology* 14, no. 2 (1999): 203–28.
———. "Changing Filipina Identities and Ambivalent Returns." Pp. 104–24 in *Coming Home? Refugees, Migrants, and Those Who Stayed Behind*, edited by Lynellyn D. Long and Ellen Oxfeld. Philadelphia: University of Pennsylvania Press, 2004.
Cornish, Flora, Karl Peltzer, and Malcolm MacLachlan. "Returning Strangers: The Children of Malawian Refugees Come 'Home'?" *Journal of Refugee Studies* 12, no. 3 (1999): 264–83.
Dahya, B. "Pakistanis in Britain: Transients or Settlers?" *Race* 14, no. 3 (1973): 241–77.
Davison, Betty. "No Place Back Home: A Study of Jamaicans Returning to Kingston, Jamaica." *Race* 9, no. 4 (1968): 499–509.
Eastmond, Marita. *The Dilemmas of Exile: Chilean Refugees in the U.S.A*. Acta Universitatis Gothoburgensis. Gothenburg Studies in Social Anthropology No. 13, 1997.
———. "Repatriation and Notions of Home-coming: The Case of Cambodian Returnees." Paper presented at the annual meeting of the American Anthropological Association, Washington, DC, December 2001.
Eastmond, Marita, and Joakim Öjendal. "Revisiting a 'Repatriation' Success: The Case of Cambodia." Pp. 38–55 in *The End of the Refugee Cycle: Refugee Repatriation and Reconstruction*, edited by Richard Black and Khalid Koser. New York and Oxford: Berghahn Books, 1999.
Eisenstadt, Shmuel N. *The Absorption of Immigrants: A Comparative Study Based Mainly on the Jewish Community in Palestine and the State of Israel*. London: Routledge and Kegan Paul, 1954.
Elliott, Mark R. *Pawns of Yalta: Soviet Refugees and America's Role in Their Repatriation*. Urbana: University of Illinois Press, 1982.
Evans-Pritchard, E. E. *The Nuer*. Oxford: Clarendon Press, 1940.
Figley, Charles R., and Seymour Leventman, eds. *Strangers at Home: Vietnam Veterans Since the War*. New York: Bruner/Mazel Publishers, 1990.
Foner, Nancy. *From Ellis Island to JFK: New York's Two Great Waves of Immigration*. New Haven: Yale University Press, 2000.
Geertz, Clifford. "Distinguished Lecture: Anti Anti-Relativism." *American Anthropologist* 86, no. 2 (1984): 263–78.
Glazer, Nathan, and Patrick Moynihan. *Beyond the Melting Pot: The Negroes, Puerto Ricans, Jews, Italians, and Irish of New York City*. Cambridge, MA: MIT Press, 1970 [1963].
Glick Schiller, Nina, Linda Basch, and Christina S. Blanc, eds. *Towards a Transnational Perspective on Migration: Race, Class, Ethnicity, and Nationalism Reconsidered*. New York: New York Academy of Sciences, 1992.
Glick Schiller, Nina, Linda Basch, and Christina S. Blanc. "From Immigrant to Transmigrant: Theorizing Transnational Migration." *Anthropological Quarterly* 68, no. 1 (1995): 48–63.
Gmelch, George. "Return Migration." *Annual Review of Anthropology* 9 (1980): 135–59.
———. *Double Passage: The Lives of Caribbean Migrants Abroad and Back Home*. Ann Arbor: University of Michigan Press, 1995 [1992].

———. "West Indian Migrants and Their Rediscovery of Barbados." Pp. 206–23 in *Coming Home? Refugees, Migrants, and Those Who Stayed Behind*, edited by Lynellyn D. Long and Ellen Oxfeld. Philadelphia: University of Pennsylvania Press, 2004.

Gordon, Milton M. *Assimilation in American Life: The Role of Race, Religion, and National Origins*. New York: Oxford University Press, 1964.

Graham, Mark, and Shahram Khosravi. "Home is Where You Make It: Repatriation and Diaspora Culture among Iranians in Sweden." *Journal of Refugee Studies* 10, no. 2 (1997): 115–33.

Gupta, Akhil, and James Ferguson. "Beyond 'Culture': Space, Identity, and the Politics of Difference." *Cultural Anthropology* 7, no. 1 (1992): 6–23.

———. "Culture, Power, Place: Ethnography at the End of an Era." Pp. 1–29 in *Culture, Power, Place: Explorations in Critical Anthropology*, edited by Akhil Gupta and James Ferguson. Durham and London: Duke University Press, 1997.

Habib, Laila. "The Search for Home." *Journal of Refugee Studies* 9, no. 1 (1996): 96–102.

Hall, Stuart. "Cultural Identity and Diaspora." Pp. 222–37 in *Identity: Community, Culture, Difference*, edited by Jonathan Rutherford. London: Lawrence and Wishart, 1990.

Hammond, Laura. "Examining the Discourse of Repatriation: Towards a More Proactive Theory of Return Migration." Pp. 227–44 in *The End of the Refugee Cycle: Refugee Repatriation and Reconstruction*, edited by Richard Black and Khalid Koser. New York and Oxford: Berghahn Books, 1999.

———. *This Place Will Become Home: Refugee Repatriation to Ethiopia*. Ithaca: Cornell University Press, 2004.

Hannerz, Ulf. *Transnational Connections: Culture, People, Places*. London and New York: Routledge, 1996.

Harrell-Bond, Barbara E. *Imposing Aid: Emergency Assistance to Refugees*. Oxford: Oxford University Press, 1986.

———. "Repatriation: Under What Conditions Is It the Most Desirable Solution?" *African Studies Review* 32, no. 1 (1989): 41–69.

Hirschon, Renée. *Heirs of the Greek Catastrophe: The Social Life of Asia Minor Refugees in Piraeus*. New York and Oxford: Berghahn Books, 1998.

Hogg, Richard. "Changing Mandates in the Ethiopian Ogaden: The Impact of Somali 'Refugees and Returnees' on the UNHCR." Pp. 153–63 in *In Search of Cool Ground: War, Flight and Homecoming in Northeast Africa*, edited by Tim Allen. London: James Currey, 1996.

Jansen, Stef. "Homeless at Home: Narrations of Post-Yugoslav Identities." Pp. 85–109 in *Migrants of Identity: Perceptions of Home in a World of Movement*, edited by Nigel Rapport and Andrew Dawson. Oxford and New York: Berg, 1998.

Juergensen, Olaf T. "Repatriation as Peacebuilding and Reconstruction: The Case of Northern Mozambique, 1992–1995." New Issues in Refugee Research, No. 31. UNHCR, Evaluation and Policy Analysis Unit, 2000.

Kaplan, Caren. *Questions of Travel: Postmodern Discourses of Displacement*. Durham and London: Duke University Press, 1996.

Kearney, Michael. "The Local and the Global: The Anthropology of Globalization and Transnationalism." *Annual Review of Anthropology* 24 (1995): 547–65.

Kibreab, Gaim. "Revisiting the Debate on People, Place, Identity, and Displacement." *Journal of Refugee Studies* 12, no. 4 (1999): 384–410.

———. "When Refugees Come Home: The Relationship Between Stayees and Returnees in Post-Conflict Eritrea." *Journal of Contemporary African Studies* 20, no. 1 (2002): 53–80.

King, Russell, ed. *Return Migration and Regional Economic Problems*. London: Croom Helm, 1986.

———. "Generalizations from the History of Return Migration." Pp. 7–55 in *Return Migration: Journey of Hope or Despair?*, edited by Bimal Ghosh. Geneva: UN and IOM, 2000.

Koser, Khalid. "Return, Readmission, and Reintegration: Changing Agendas, Policy Frameworks, and Operational Programmes." Pp. 57–99 in *Return Migration: Journey of Hope or Despair?* edited by Bimal Ghosh. Geneva: UN and IOM, 2000.

Koser, Khalid, and Richard Black. "The End of the Refugee Cycle?" Pp. 2–17 in *The End of the Refugee Cycle? Refugee Repatriation and Reconstruction*, edited by Richard Black and Khalid Koser. New York and Oxford: Berghahn Books, 1999.

Kundera, Milan. *Ignorance*. New York: HarperCollins, 2002.

Lake, Obiagele. "Toward a Pan-African Identity: Diaspora African Repatriates in Ghana." *Anthropological Quarterly* 68, no. 1 (1995): 21–36.

Levitt, Peggy. *The Transnational Villagers*. Berkeley and Los Angeles: University of California Press, 2001.

Levitt, Peggy, and Mary C. Waters, eds. *The Changing Face of Home: The Transnational Lives of the Second Generation*. New York: Russell Sage, 2002.

Lomsky-Feder, Edna, and Tamar Rapoport. "Seeking a Place to Rest: Representation of Bounded Movement among Russian-Jewish Homecomers." *Ethos* 30, no. 3 (2003): 227–48.

Long, Lynellyn D., and Ellen Oxfeld, eds. *Coming Home? Refugees, Migrants, and Those Who Stayed Behind*. Philadelphia: University of Pennsylvania Press, 2004.

Mahler, Sarah J. *American Dreaming: Immigrant Life on the Margins*. Princeton: Princeton University Press, 1995.

Majodina, Zonke. "Dealing with Difficulties of Return to South Africa: The Role of Social Support and Coping." *Journal of Refugee Studies* 8, no. 2 (1995): 210–27.

Malkki, Liisa H. "National Geographic: The Rooting of Peoples and the Deterritorialization of National Identity Among Scholars and Refugees." *Cultural Anthropology* 7, no. 1 (1992): 24–39.

———. *Purity and Exile: Violence, Memory, and National Cosmology Among Hutu Refugees in Tanzania*. Chicago: University of Chicago Press, 1995a.

———. "Refugees and Exile: From 'Refugee Studies' to the National Order of Things." *Annual Review of Anthropology* 24 (1995b): 495–523.

Margold, Jane A. "Filipina Depictions of Migrant Life for Their Kin at Home." Pp. 49–62 in *Coming Home? Refugees, Migrants, and Those Who Stayed Behind*, edited by Lynellyn D. Long and Ellen Oxfeld. Philadelphia: University of Pennsylvania Press, 2004.

Markowitz, Fran. *A Community in Spite of Itself: Soviet Jewish Émigrés in New York*. Washington, DC: Smithsonian Institution Press, 1993.

Marrus, Michael R. *The Unwanted: European Refugees in the Twentieth Century*. New York and Oxford: Oxford University Press, 1985.

Morawska, Ewa. "Return Migrations: Theoretical and Research Agenda." Pp. 277–92 in *A Century of European Migrations, 1830–1930*, edited by Rudolph J. Vecoli and Suzanne M. Sinke. Urbana and Chicago: University of Illinois Press, 1991.

Münz, Rainer, and Rainer Ohliger. *Diasporas and Ethnic Migrants: Germany, Israel, and Post-Soviet Successor States in Comparative Perspective*. London: Frank Cass, 2003.

Olwig, Karen F. "Contested Homes: Home-making and the Making of Anthropology." Pp. 225–36 in *Migrants of Identity: Perceptions of Home in a World of Movement*, edited by Nigel Rapport and Andrew Dawson. Oxford and New York: Berg, 1998.

———. "Notions of Home and Return in Global Family Networks of Caribbean Background." Paper presented at the annual meeting of the American Anthropological Association, Washington, DC, December 2001.

———. "Narrating Deglobalization: Danish Perceptions of a Lost Empire." *Global Networks* 3, no. 3 (2003): 207–22.

O'Nell, Theresa D. "'Coming Home' among North Plains Vietnam Veterans: Psychological Transformations in Pragmatic Perspective." *Ethos* 27, no. 4 (2000): 441–65.

Oxfeld, Ellen, and Lynellyn D. Long. "Introduction: An Ethnography of Return." Pp. 1–15 in *Coming Home? Refugees, Migrants, and Those Who Stayed Behind*, edited by Lynellyn D. Long and Ellen Oxfeld. Philadelphia: University of Pennsylvania Press, 2004.

Pilkington, Hilary, and Moya Flynn. "From 'Refugee' to 'Repatriate': Russian Repatriation Discourse in the Making." Pp. 171–96 in *The End of the Refugee Cycle: Refugee Repatriation and Reconstruction*, edited by Richard Black and Khalid Koser. New York and Oxford: Berghahn Books, 1999.

Rapport, Nigel, and Andrew Dawson. "Home and Movement: A Polemic." Pp. 19–38 in *Migrants of Identity: Perceptions of Home in a World of Movement*, edited by Nigel Rapport and Andrew Dawson. Oxford and New York: Berg, 1998.

Ray, Kakoli. "Repatriation and De-territorialization: Meskhetian Turks' Conception of Home." *Journal of Refugee Studies* 13, no. 4 (2000): 391–414.

Rock, David, and Stefan Wolff, eds. *Coming Home to Germany? The Integration of Ethnic Germans from Central and Eastern Europe in the Federal Republic*. New York: Berghahn, 2002.

Rogge, John R. "Repatriation of Refugees: A Not So Simple 'Optimum' Solution." Pp. 14–49 in *When Refugees Go Home: African Experiences*, edited by Tim Allen and Hubert Morsink. London: James Currey, 1994.

Ross, David R. B. *Preparing for Ulysses: Politics and Veterans During World War II*. New York and London: Columbia University Press, 1969.

Rouse, Roger. "Mexican Migration and the Social Space of Postmodernism." *Diaspora* 1, no. 1 (1991): 8–23.

Rubenstein, Hymie. "The Return Ideology in West Indian Migration." *Papers in Anthropology* 20, no. 1 (1979): 21–38.

Rushdie, Salman. *Imaginary Homelands: Essays and Criticism, 1981–1991*. London: Granta Books, 1001.

Safran, William. "Diasporas in Modern Societies: Myths of Homeland and Return." *Diaspora* 1, no. 1 (1991): 83–99.

Said, Edward. "Reflections on Exile." Pp. 357–66 in *Out There: Marginalization and Contemporary Cultures*, edited by Russell Ferguson, Martha Gever, Trinh T. Minh-ha, and Cornel West. London: MIT Press, 1992.

Saloutos, Theodore. *They Remember America: The Story of the Repatriated Greek-Americans*. Berkeley and Los Angeles: University of California Press, 1956.

Sarna, Jonathan D. "The Myth of No Return: Jewish Return Migration to Eastern Europe, 1881–1914." Pp. 423–34 in *Labor Migration in the Atlantic Economies: The European and North American Working Classes During the Period of Industrialization*, edited by Dirk Hoerder. Westport and London: Greenwood Press, 1985.

Schutz, Alfred. "The Homecomer." Pp. 106–19 in *Collected Papers II: Studies in Social Theory*, edited by Arvid Brodersen. The Hague: Martinus Nijhoff, 1976 [1945].

Sepulveda, Danielle C. "Challenging the Assumptions of Repatriation." *The Courier* 150 (1995): 83–85.

Smith, Carolyn D., ed. *Strangers at Home: Essays on the Effects of Living Overseas and Coming "Home" to a Strange Land*. Bayside, NY: Aletheia Publications, 1996.

Stack, Carol. *Call to Home: African Americans Reclaim the Rural South*. New York: Basic Books, 1996.

Stefansson, Anders H. "Under My Own Sky? The Cultural Dynamics of Refugee Return and (Re)integration in Post-War Sarajevo." PhD diss. University of Copenhagen, 2003.

———. "Refugee Returns to Sarajevo and Their Challenge to Contemporary Narratives of Mobility." Pp. 170–86 in *Coming Home? Refugees, Migrants, and Those Who Stayed Behind*, edited by Lynellyn D. Long and Ellen Oxfeld. Philadelphia: University of Pennsylvania Press, 2004.

Stepputat, Finn. "Repatriation and Everyday Forms of State Formation in Guatemala." Pp. 210–26 in *The End of the Refugee Cycle: Refugee Repatriation and Reconstruction*, edited by Richard Black and Khalid Koser. New York and Oxford: Berghahn Books, 1999.

Storti, Craig. *The Art of Coming Home*. Intercultural Press, 2001.

Stratton, Jon. "(Dis)placing the Jews: Historicizing the Idea of Diaspora." *Diaspora* 6, no. 3 (1997): 301–29.

Thomas-Hope, Elizabeth. "Return Migration to Jamaica and Its Development Potential." *International Migration* 37, no. 1 (1999): 183–208.

———. "Transnational Livelihoods and Identities in Return Migration to the Caribbean: The Case of Skilled Returnees to Jamaica." Pp. 187–201 in *Work and Migration: Life and Livelihoods in a Globalizing World*, edited by Ninna N. Sørensen and Karen F. Olwig. London and New York: Routledge, 2002.

Tölölyan, Khachig. "Rethinking Diaspora(s): Stateless Power in the Transnational Moment." *Diaspora* 5, no. 1 (1996): 3–36.

Tsuda, Takeyuki. "From Ethnic Affinity to Alienation in the Global Ecumene: The Encounter between the Japanese and Japanese-Brazilian Return Migrants." *Diaspora* 10, no. 1 (2001): 53–91.

———. *Strangers in the Ethnic Homeland: Japanese Brazilian Return Migration in Transnational Perspective*. New York: Columbia University Press, 2003.

Tuan, Yi-Fu. *Space and Place: The Perspective of Experience*. Minneapolis and London: University of Minnesota Press, 2001 [1977].

Uehling, Greta. "Sitting on Suitcases: Ambivalence and Ambiguity in the Migration Intentions of Crimean Tatar Women." *Journal of Refugee Studies* 15, no. 4 (2002): 388–408.

———. *Beyond Memory: The Crimean Tatars' Deportation and Return*. New York: Palgrave Macmillan, 2004.

Useem, John, and Ruth H. Useem. *The Western-Educated Man in India: A Study of His Social Roles and Influence*. New York: Dryden Press, 1955.

Van Hear, Nicholas. *New Diasporas: The Mass Exodus, Dispersal and Regrouping of Migrant Communities*. London: UCL Press, 1998.

Voutira, Effie. "Pontic Greeks Today: Migrants or Refugees?" *Journal of Refugee Studies* 4, no. 4 (1991): 400–20.

Warner, Daniel. "Voluntary Repatriation and the Meaning of Return to Home: A Critique of Liberal Mathematics." *Journal of Refugee Studies* 7, no. 2/3 (1994): 160–74.

White, Merry. *The Japanese Overseas: Can They Go Home Again?* New York: Free Press, 1988.

Wyman, Mark. *Round-Trip to America: The Immigrants Return to Europe, 1880–1930*. Ithaca and London: Cornell University Press, 1993.

Zarzosa, Helia Lopez. "Internal Exile, Exile and Return: A Gendered View." *Journal of Refugee Studies* 11, no. 2 (1998): 189–98.

Zetter, Roger. "The Greek-Cypriot Refugees: Perceptions of Return under Conditions of Protracted Exile." *International Migration Review* 28, no. 2 (1994): 307–22.

———. "Reconceptualizing the Myth of Return: Continuity and Transition Amongst the Greek-Cypriot Refugees of 1974." *Journal of Refugee Studies* 12, no. 1 (1999): 1–22.

Zolberg, Aristide, Astri Suhrke, and Sergio Aguayo. *Escape From Violence: Conflict and the Refugee Crisis in the Developing World*. New York and Oxford: Oxford University Press, 1989.

2

The Home(s) of Homecomings

Fran Markowitz

> Migration and imagination are historically linked processes that produce memorable moments in the pasts of peoples, nations, communities, and individuals. Each sustains the other, expanding circumscribed experiences and elaborating localized meanings.
>
> —Sateny Shami (2001: 222)

The 1990s have been called the Age of Migration (Castles and Miller 1998)—a time of unprecedented movement within and beyond national borders. Accompanying mobile images, sounds, monies, and industries, contemporary migrants travel around the globe with unparalleled ease and at ever-increasing speeds (Appadurai 1996). Mixing languages and blending cultures, all this movement challenges what once seemed an intrinsic connection between a people and its place; it blurs boundaries of every sort, especially those that divide "us" from "them," terra firma from terra incognita, and "here" from "there" (Gupta and Ferguson 1992).

On the ground, globalized non-places—airport lounges, hotel chains and shopping malls that offer commodities and comfort to one and all regardless of where they've been or where they are going (Augé 1998)—and hybridized borderlands (Rosaldo 1989) are spreading everywhere to challenge state-based cartographies of bound nations (Basch et al. 1994; Malkki 1992; Sassen 1999; Soysal 1994). Nonetheless people the world over remain dependent on states and their institutions for services, shelter, and nourishment. Demands of family, livelihood, and heritage remain salient as well, as the cherished stuff of history and motivators of life goals. These dependencies and demands, however, often manifest in traveling cultures and as social patterns that look more like border-crossing circuitry or transnational networks than fixed ties to localities of neighborhood, workplace, ethnic group, and nation-state (Clifford 1988; Glick Schiller et al. 1995; Rouse 1991). And so too, it seems, do people's notions and practices of home.

It may well be that no one place, language, or tradition in the contemporary world can satiate the multifaceted, hyphenated identities of people-in-motion and their contradictory (desires for) belongings (Probyn 1996). When neither imagined nor practiced as a unique and fixed space, home demands reconfiguring. For some, it becomes tantamount to deterritorialization; home is a mobile habitat that can be carried on one's back and set up anywhere (Anzaldua 1987). Indeed, it may simply amount to "being in the world" (Chambers 1994: 4). Yet with the pronouncement of these ideas comes their converse: "The correlate of the migratory character . . . might be called a metaphysical loss of 'home'" (Berger et al. 1974: 82). If no one place can provide intimate familiarity and all the comforts of home, no matter where they go multiply constituted postmodern people are never quite at home (Rapport and Dawson 1998: 6). And so they move on.

What motivates the desire to pin down such an ever-changing and slippery concept as home? Even as postmodern theorists articulate—and often celebrate—the kaleidoscopic possibilities of multiple-partial identities and multiple-partial homes, many recognize as well that home persists as one of the few remaining utopian ideals, "a pastoral stability, free of the dissonance between place and desire" (Mufti and Shohat 1997: 1). The loss of permanent, stable, sanctified homeplaces piques cultural imaginaries of better elsewheres (Appadurai 1996; Bhabha 1997; Lotman 1990) and propels political action aimed at resolving the intersecting, even if often contradictory, claims for personal home spaces with the sovereign territory of nation-states (Anderson 1983, 1992; Van Hear 1998). The possibility of *a* home, the ultimate peaceful retreat, a this-worldly alternative to social fragmentation and tumultuous traveling (Hollander 1991; Rybczynski 1986), continues to resonate, and the call to home—a desire for reterritorialization in the homestead or homeland of past generations—still beckons as an antidote to partial belongings and unfulfilled dreams (Radhakrishnan 1996; Stack 1996). Indeed, as the essays that comprise this volume demonstrate, a home, a homeland, and a home in the homeland remain salient cultural imperatives that often grate against the ideational boundaries that confine "myths of return" to "imagined communities" and then burst into overt political action (cf. Gupta and Ferguson 1992: 10; Safran 1991).

In our aim to move migration studies out of the restricting binaries of emigration/immigration and place of departure/point of destination, our analyses reject the messages implicit in return migration, myth of return, and repatriation, to focus instead on homecomings. These homecomings are understood and treated as messy points of convergence between personal desires for authentic and satisfying lives bolstered by various cultural imaginaries, nourished in social groups and implemented through the practical action of moving. Moving, however, does not result solely from freewheeling individuals seeking a more fruitful home base. Despite images of global flow and easy travel that pervade the "age of migration," places the world over are encased in and represented by nation-states, and nation-state boundaries can obstruct these flows. While they encourage access for some, policed border crossings also make entry and exit, if not travel itself, difficult for others. Some nation-states demand a "uniqueness of belonging" (Levy, this volume), and cultural hybridity or diasporic multiplicity notwithstanding, preclude the homecomings of those deemed beyond the pale (see Behar; Markowitz, this volume).

As a whole, this volume responds to the subjective dimensions of belonging and citizenship that inspire diasporic peoples to leave the places where they are in order to (re)forge links to another, one that they deem as their ancestors'—and consequently their own—original home. Yet as many of the volume's chapters show, due to the very practices of nation-states that lead their diasporas to imagine and act on the conflation of their sovereign territory with the mythico-historic homeland, the imagined home and reality of life in the state-qua-homeland often clash. Those who come home in anticipation of an Edenic resolution of their worldly woes often find that their travails fail to cease (Anteby-Yemini; Levy; Pattie; Stefansson, this volume). *Homecomings* thereby interrogates, even disrupts, the increasingly accepted idea that the current postmodern moment has broken connections between peoples, territories, and cultures, even if, as several chapters show, homecomings may spur reappraisal of the diasporic homes left behind and spark investigations of the myriad possibilities inherent in multiple-partial homes.

Our focus on homecomings therefore highlights how people navigate, make meaningful, and attempt to reconfigure the vexing intersections of three overlapping yet often contradictory phenomena: homes, diasporas, and nation-states. First we consider the highly emotional and politically provocative problematics encoded in the symbol of home. Drawing attention to the similar role of defense played both by home-households and contemporary nation-states, Peter Taylor (1999: 100) notes that "they have become geographical havens within modernity, intimate places which provide important elements of identity to modern human beings." Home(land) is a highly packed signifier that encapsulates a concept and a place and encompasses a feeling born of desire, laced with nostalgia. It brings together memories and longings, spatialities and temporalities, immediate family and ancestors long-gone, the local and the global, and physical sensations with the intangible and that which cannot be spoken (Rapport and Dawson 1998: 8).

Home, then, is a social space but in a curiously private way as it keeps the world at bay while nurturing those who constitute its homeliness (Rybczynski

1986: 107–108). Home, as someone once said, is the place—and its people—that you come from and the place—and its people—that you return to (Hollander 1991: 32). In this sense, home is the healing response to all other places and peoples, the starting point and endpoint that provide a reprieve to all phases of in-betweenness—travel and adventure, newness and strangeness, alienation and confusion, and unpredictability. It is the opposite of all the other places out there rolled into one. Home is security, comfort, certainty, the people who "have to take you in" while understanding that the "have to" is not a matter of externally imposed law but an automatic response to similitude. It is Radcliffe-Brown's equivalence of siblings, Isaacs' idols of the tribe, Shils' primordiality, and the "natural rights" of citizens in modern nation-states (Herzfeld 1997).[1]

The very package of social, cultural, and political meanings delineating and animating "home" necessarily assumes a rupture, for if home is the place you return to, then you have to leave it first to know what it is. Such is the message of the immensely popular 1939 film *The Wizard of Oz*. Dorothy's black-and-white Kansas was a boring, lonely place with no particular warmth or homeliness until she found herself in the midst of a dizzyingly colorful adventure that she never, at least consciously, wished for. Ditto for Alice and her adventures in wonderland. Be it ever so humble, home-sweet-home gains its sweetness only in contrast to the piquancy of other places and the other people who live there. Yet take note that despite the romantic sentiments often attached to quaint, fixed places that defy the global age of migration, these are not necessarily warm and cozy homes. They may well be familiar, but they are not always comfortable. Fixed, unchanging places can be experienced as dull and lacking, as a restrictive "politics of exclusion" (Thompson and Tyagi 1996: ix–x), or as sites of inescapable violence (see Goldsack 1999; Holsey; Markowitz, this volume). Home is not an ontological given; it is always emergent.

The ruptures between (a) people and home(land), the original events and existential conditions of diaspora, provide *Homecomings* with its second point of departure. Simultaneously representing what now is *not* and what once was, these ruptures generate a further contradiction: nostalgic yearnings for the place of origin (Hobsbawm 1991: 65–67; Ray 2000: 401; Safran 1991) coupled with an unsettled and unsettling diasporic consciousness (Boyarin and Boyarin 1995; Chambers 1994). "The *concept* of diaspora," as Avtar Brah (1996: 192–93) explains, "places the discourse of 'home' and 'dispersion' in creative tension, inscribing a homing desire while simultaneously critiquing discourses of fixed origins."

Diaspora, however, is not only a theoretical concept, it is also a lived reality, and diasporic peoples do not hang suspended in space. They are located in particular places, and these often take on the features of home. Refugee camps, for example, are by definition anything but homey, for along with housing victims of disasters they serve symbolically and physically to separate those wanting in from residents holding rights in the homeland (Huseby-Darvas 2000). Yet lacking other abodes, these not very hospitable places may with time become the only home (Long 1993; Malkki 1995; Peteet 1995; Hammond, this volume).

By the same token, the ghettos and shtetls of Europe and the melahs of North Africa housed Jews for generations while segregating them from their Christian and Muslim "hosts" and demanding of them tribute, political subordination, and social humiliation (look at the gold embossed statue of Jesus Christ, King of the Jews, on Prague's Charles Bridge and at Shakespeare's *Merchant of Venice* for blatant European examples; see Levy, this volume for an example from the Maghreb). Even those most diasporic of all diasporean peoples, the Roma (Gypsies), who have no homeland myth (cf. Safran 1991) and sing of their singular fate as the homeless orphans of the world, have made homes throughout the harshly inhospitable space of Europe (Stewart 1997).

Sometimes, however, such diasporic homes turn out to be the homeliest of all, and reminiscences of a bygone golden age in the homeland function more to maintain diasporic community solidarity than to inspire movement homeward (Graham and Khosravi 1997; Pattie 1997). The vast and rich Greek Orthodox diasporic borderlands of Asia Minor were destroyed in the early part of the 20th century by implementation of what was supposed to be an emancipatory doctrine, the self-determination of nations. In 1923 the internationally negotiated Treaty of Lausanne resulted in the first compulsory exchange of minority populations, and the Greek Orthodox communities of the new nation-state of Turkey were repatriated to mainland Greece while Greece's Muslims were sent "back" to Turkey. Peoples who had for centuries been at home in diaspora overnight became refugees in the homeland (Hirschon 1998). As Koser and Black (1999: 6–7) cogently note, "For many . . . repatriation does not represent a homecoming; nor is there agreement in the literature on what 'going home' actually means." The power of states to draw and protect their borders, exclude some populations, and welcome (back) others complicates the dilemmas of diaspora and the vexing politics of homecomings (Rock and Wolff 2002; see Behar, this volume).

Which leads to the third facet of our focus: the concerted political action of homecomings. Despite the naysayers who warn that "the pursuit of . . . authenticity today hardly seems feasible [for] it is impossible to 'go home' again" (Chambers 1994: 74), postcolonials, ethnic minorities, and racially marked peoples the world over have been actively delineating, seeking and then reaching the "real home." While this search for home emerges from individual yearnings born in the dialectical alternation of feeling at home and homelessness, nursed by collective memories, and commoditized and celebrated from within the global cultural supermarket (Mathews 2000), it is pushed into practical action by the discourses and policies of nation-states.

These state policies legitimize narratives of nostalgia; they spatialize mythico-historic homelands within their sovereign territory and offer incentives to return (Huseby-Darvas, this volume), if not the ships (Pattie, this volume) or airplanes to do so (Anteby-Yemini, this volume). Saskia Sassen (1999: 84) has noted that "state-building processes contribute to mass flight and mass expulsions." But they also tap into their diasporas' hearts and pockets, rally their political consciousness, and entice them homeward.

State spatialization practices offer a radical simplification of what are often baffling narratives of group memory and conflicting interpretations of history. Such simplification nullifies regional rivalries, ignores the range of dialects and variegated cultural practices that disrupt the homogeneity of a nation, and change what was once an amorphously imagined homeland into a specifically bound nation-state (cf. Ferguson and Gupta 2002; Scott 1998). "In a world where intellectuals talk about transnationalism and diasporic subjects perhaps do it, the nation-state still holds a monopoly on representing political and economic interests and geographic claims of sovereignty" (Radhakrishnan 1996: 161; see also Malkki 1992). States' offers of home in the homeland can be convincingly compelling to ethnic, religious, and racial minorities the world over who seek a way out of the present ill of discrimination and subordination.

Ironically, however, homecoming to nation-states or places within them may not necessarily reunite people with their familial homesteads. In this volume, the chapters by Hammond and Stefansson demonstrate that changed social arrangements coupled with state policies often compel repatriating war refugees to forego their prewar home sites and settle elsewhere in the homeland. Similarly, the Japanese Brazilians whose return labor migration is examined in Tsuda's chapter come home to work in Japan's industrial centers, not to dwell in the rural areas from which their parents or grandparents emigrated decades ago. The conflation of a nation-state's territory with an imagined homeland is poignantly displayed in Holsey's analysis of the choice of Ghana as the destination of many African Americans' heritage tours. Pattie's investigation of how the state of Armenia, once a rocky backwater of historic Armenian lands, has gained central place as the contemporary homeland, is a most cogent example of the success of states in conjoining the nation with their sovereign territory.

Certainly the discourses and institutions of nation-states enable, even push, diasporic people(s) to transform their yearnings for the homeland into homecomings, but, as all the chapters show, their hegemony is far from absolute. My own chapter provides a striking example of self-defined Black Hebrews who defied the state of Israel's denial of their claims to a home in the homeland, remained steady in pressing those claims, and after thirty years of illegal residence gained rights and recognition. Radhakrishnan (1996: 166) notes that, "The return is a matter of political choice by a people on behalf of their own authenticity, and there is nothing regressive or atavistic about people revisiting the past with the intention of reclaiming it." Problems arise, however, when people in confrontation with the apparatus of the state fail to find the past they wish to reclaim (Anteby-Yemini; Hammond; Levy, this volume), when groups backed by state power deny others the right to return to the homeland (Beal 2002; Bisharat 1997; Behar; Markowitz, this volume), or when the state/place of origin reveals itself as the least attractive of less than homely alternatives (Holsey; Huseby-Darvas; Pattie; Stefansson; Tsuda, this volume).

Homecomings, in its entirety, presents a complex and unsettling struggle with the meanings and motivations of home through the practical actions of immigrants, refugees, exiles, diasporic groups, and individuals who confront the homes that they long for through their multiply refracted experiences of historical nostalgia, personal memory, discriminatory social practices, and the discourses and citizenship laws of nation-states. These homecomings are sensual, physical and visceral; they are mediated by rules and regulations and by imprecise mandates; and are often hard to achieve (Levy; Pattie; Tsuda, this volume). What at the start of a journey is conceived of as a homecoming might turn out to be the beginning of a new diaspora (see Markowitz 1995; Anteby-Yemini; Huseby-Darvas, this volume) or provoke a reconsideration of home disconnected from origins (Hammond; Holsey; Stefansson, this volume).

The variously articulated analyses of the curious set of historical contingencies that frame the homecomings described in this book have jolted me, a "diasporic self seek[ing] to reterritorialize itself and thereby acquire a name" (Radhakrishnan 1996: 173) to consider my own attempts to transcend the confusion of crisscrossing transnational, gender, and ethnic identities by coming home.

When I come home these days to my pretty house in the foothills of Israel's Negev, my little brown dog jumps into my arms and licks my face while my fluffy black cat rubs up against my legs. I kick off my shoes and come into the kitchen. I feed my pets. I prepare my dinner. And then we hunker down for the night. Stretching out on the sofa I thumb through a magazine, listen to music, catch up on the news, or watch a sitcom on TV. Maybe I curl up with yet another book. I am at home, feeling cozily safe and secure.

My home wasn't always like that. When I was a child I lived with my Mom, Dad, and brother in a three-room apartment in lower Manhattan. I liked school. I loved the library. It was hard to come home. I'd hesitate, preparing myself for what was behind the door. Would my Dad be in a good mood, or would he be angry? Would my Mom have a tasty dinner prepared, or something watery and overcooked? Would it be fun to talk with my brother, or would he tease me to tears? More times than I care to remember I was nervous coming home, afraid to believe that comforts awaited and sad to think that they would not. But I had nowhere else to come home to.

When I come home to the United States these days, the immigration officer at Newark airport looks at my passport, then looks at me and offers a warm smile. "You've been gone a while," he says. "Welcome home sweetheart!" My heart soars. I still belong, even though I no longer have a home in that homeland.

When I leave Israel these days, the security officer at Ben-Gurion Airport looks at my passport, gazes at me, and frowns. "How many years have you been in the land?" she asks. It's all there in my passport, but I answer anyway. She looks at me again, "Do you have family here?" I tell her that I have a house, a dog, and a cat. She frowns again and repeats her question. I repeat my response. Finally she goes through the list of categories that officially constitute family in Israel. Do I have, "A husband? Children? Parents? Siblings?" I answer, "No" to each of her questions. She grudgingly slaps stickers-of-approval on my luggage and hands back my passport with the reminder, "You have no family." Right, I got the message. I have no family in the Israeli homeland, and although I've lived (t)here for eleven years I remain suspended in an incongruous category. I have a house, a dog, a cat, a university professorship, and citizenship. But somehow, this border controller reminds me, I am really not at home.

Is my home in another land? Or am I homeless both in the United States and in Israel? Why did I leave my home in America? Like millions of worker migrants the world over, I left for a job.[2] I had applied for a dozen jobs in the United States and for one job in Israel. I got the one job in Israel, the ancient land of my ancestors' yearnings and the modern nation-state.

When I accepted my appointment at Ben-Gurion University, many of my Russian Jewish immigrant friends, entrenched for years as American citizens in New York and Chicago, greeted my news by declaring that now I would be returning to our historical homeland. Some said this with ironic sarcasm, aware that they had rejected the opportunity of linking their lives with that historical homeland to make their homes in the United States (see Markowitz 1993). The only links they had had with America were those imagined on the basis of promise—for human rights, dignity, and economic prosperity. Hoping, if not convinced, that life in America would offer them, or at least their children, more fulfillment than either the Russian *rodina* or the Jewish *moledet*, they "came home" to a place where they had no ties of blood, soil, or history.[3]

When the Soviet Union underwent perestroika and then fell apart, several of these friends "went back there" to have a look. Avoiding mention of homecoming from the start, this look at "there" confirmed what many had already told me years before, "*ia rodilsa amerikantsom*" [I was born an American]. In naturalizing their fates and characters to be part of the United States they confirmed the rectitude of emigration "from there" and the feeling that America had always beckoned, awaiting to be their true home.

My story does not end so elegantly. I made a home there—here in Israel. Like my friends and family in the United States I watch with horror the reports of suicide bombings on CNN, but unlike them, these murderous explosions are happening close to my cozy home. At the university, I remain alert to my partial belongings. I teach in a language that feels like sand in my mouth and encounter behaviors that defy much of what I cherish. And so I yearn for the homeland left behind—to walk and talk like everyone else; to be closer to my brothers, to my friends, to my Mom and to my father's grave. Then when I'm here—there, back in the United States, it doesn't take much for me to get fed up with all the materialism gone awry. Although the grass really *is* greener, I return once again to my house in the Negev, until the next time that I board a jet westward-homeward bound.

Continuing the trend of moving migration studies out of the restricting binary of emigration/immigration (Brettell and Hollifield 2000; Hammar et al. 1997; Glick Schiller et al. 1995), this *Homecomings* volume picks away at the often contentious congealing of home with homeland, homeland with nation-state, and the lingering idea that people's ultimate homes are sites of certainty that correspond to the place of their origin. Its three sections, "Homecomings of Immigrants and Refugees," "Blurred Diaspora-Homeland Boundaries," and "Contentious Homecomings," offer a takeoff point of comparison, but the book in its entirety suggests that the imaginings, practices, and politics of home and homeland cannot be reduced to one or another historical contingency, political moment, or geographic space. In its variety of returns home from a broad range of groups, families, and individuals, *Homecomings* destabilizes the key oppositions that have vexed the study of migration while offering, to paraphrase Geertz (1984), an anti-antiessentialism critique to postmodernist claims of deterritorialization and the decreasing importance of nation-states. In its proactively critical approach to the creative social projects that transform diasporic longings into homecomings, this volume opens up new space for understanding the myriad interactions between migrations, homes, historical narratives, state practices, and the people who make it all happen. Taking nothing for granted, *Homecomings* forges ahead toward our disruptive collective goals, each essay on its own unsettling path.

NOTES

Many thanks to Tania Forte and André Levy for their close and critical readings of an earlier draft.

1. See Radcliffe-Brown 1952; Isaacs 1974, and Shils 1957.
2. I recognize, of course, that I am part of the privileged international workforce. Like Mathews (2000) in Hong Kong and Chambers (1994) in Italy, my experiences are radically different from those of agricultural laborers, construction and factory workers, and people in domestic service (Kearney 1995). Moreover, I appreciate the privilege of holding not one, but two citizenships. My situation stands in stark contrast to that of my great grandparents who, as Jews confined to the Pale of Settlement in the tsarist Russian Empire, were precluded from citizenship. After the 1917 revolution they became citizens of the Soviet Union but brutally lost that citizenship—and their lives—with the Nazi occupation.
3. "Birth" is at the root of *rodina* in Russian and *moledet* in Hebrew. Although both could be glossed as birthplace, *rodina* usually translates as motherland, and *moledet* as homeland.

REFERENCES

Anderson, Benedict. *Imagined Communities*. London: Verso, 1983.
———. "Long-Distance Nationalism: World Capitalism and the Rise of Identity Politics." *New Left Review* 193 (1992): 3–13.
Anzaldua, Gloria. *Borderlands/La Frontera: The New Mestiza*. San Francisco: Spinsters/Aunt Lute, 1987.
Appadurai, Arjun. *Modernity at Large*. Minneapolis: University of Minnesota Press, 1996.
Augé, Marc. *Non-Places: Introduction to an Anthropology of Supermodernity*. London: Verso, 1998.
Basch, Linda, Nina Glick Schiller, and Cristina Szanton Blanc. *Nations Unbound: Transnational Projects, Postcolonial Predicaments, and Deterrritorialized Nation-States*. Langhorne: Gordon and Breach, 1994.
Beal, E. Ann. "The Hermeneutics of Uninvited Homecomings: Palestinian Returnees to Amman in the Wake of the Gulf War." Paper presented at the annual meetings of the American Anthropological Association, New Orleans, November 2002.
Berger, Peter, Brigitte Berger, and Hansfried Kellner. *The Homeless Mind: Modernization and Consciousness*. New York: Vintage Books, 1974.
Bhabha, Homi. "The World and the Home." Pp. 445–55 in *Dangerous Liaisons: Gender, Nation and Post Colonial Perspectives*, edited by Anne McClintock, Aamir Mufti, and Ella Shohat. Minneapolis: University of Minnesota Press, 1997.
Bisharat, George E. "Exile to Compatriot: Transformations in the Social Identity of Palestinian Refugees in the West Bank." Pp. 203–33 in *Culture, Power, Place: Explorations in Critical Anthropology*, edited by Akhil Gupta and James Ferguson. Durham: Duke University Press, 1997.

Boyarin, Daniel, and Jonathan Boyarin. "Diaspora, Generation and the Ground of Jewish Identity." Pp 305–37 in *Identities*, edited by Kwame Anthony Appiah and Henry Louis Gates, J. Chicago: University of Chicago Press, 1995.
Brah, Avtar. 1996. *Cartographies of Diaspora*. London: Routledge, 1996.
Brettell, Caroline B. "Theorizing Migration in Anthropology: The Social Construction of Networks, Identities, Communities, and Globalscapes." Pp. 97–135 in *Migration Theory: Talking across Disciplines*, edited by Caroline B. Brettell and James F. Hollifield. New York: Routledge, 2000.
Brettell, Caroline B., and James F. Hollifield, ed. *Migration Theory: Talking across Disciplines*. New York: Routledge, 2000.
Castles, Stephen, and Mark J. Miller. *The Age of Migration: International Population Movements in the Modern World*. Basingstoke: Macmillan, 2nd edition, 1998.
Chambers, Iain. *Migrancy, Culture, Identity*. London: Routledge, 1994.
Clifford, James. *The Predicament of Culture: Twentieth-Century Ethnography, Literature, and Art*. Cambridge: Harvard University Press, 1988.
———. "Diasporas." *Cultural Anthropology* 9, no. 3 (1994): 302–38.
Ferguson, James, and Akhil Gupta. "Spatializing States: Toward an Ethnography of Neoliberal Governmentality." *American Ethnologist* 29, no. 4 (2002): 981–1,002.
Geertz, Clifford. "Distinguished Lecture: Anti Anti-Relativism." *American Anthropologist* 86, no. 2 (1984): 263–78.
Glick Schiller, Nina, Linda Basch, and Cristina Szanton Blanc. "From Immigrant to Transmigrant: Theorizing Transnational Migration." *Anthropological Quarterly* 68, no. 2 (1995): 48–63.
Goldsack, Laura. "A Haven in a Heartless World? Women and Domestic Violence." Pp. 121–32 in *Ideal Homes? Social Change and Domestic Life*, edited by Tony Chapman and Jenny Hockey. London: Routledge, 1999.
Graham, Mark, and Shahram Khosravi. "Home Is Where You Make It: Repatriation and Diaspora among Iranians in Sweden." *Journal of Refugee Studies* 10, no. 2, (1997): 115–33.
Gupta, Akhil, and James Ferguson. "Beyond 'Culture': Space, Identity, and the Politics of Difference." *Cultural Anthropology* 7, no. 1 (1992): 6–23.
Hammar, Tomer, Grete Brahmann, Kristof Tamas, and Thomas Faist, eds. *International Migration, Immobility and Development: Multidisciplinary Perspectives*. Oxford: Berg, 1997.
Herzfeld, Michael. *Cultural Intimacy: Social Poetics in the Nation-State*. New York: Routledge.
Hirschon, Renée. *Heirs of the Greek Catastrophe: The Social Life of Asia Minor Refugees in Piraeus*. New York: Berghahn Books, 1998.
Hobsbawm, Eric. "Introduction." *Social Research* [Special Issue: *Home: A Place in the World*] 58, no. 1 (1991): 65–68.
Hollander, John. "It All Depends." *Social Research* [Special Issue: *Home: A Place in the World*] 58, no. 1 (1991): 31–49.
Huseby-Darvas, Éva V. "Refugee Women from Former Yugoslavia in the Camps of Rural Hungary." Pp. 339–56 in *Neighbors at War: Anthropological Perspectives on Yugoslav Ethnicity, Culture, and History*, edited by Joel M. Halpern and David A. Kideckel. University Park: Pennsylvania State University Press, 2000.

Isaacs, Harold. "Basic Group Identity: The Idols of the Tribe." *Ethnicity* 1 (1974): 15–42.

Kearney, Michael. "The Local and the Global: The Anthropology of Globalization and Transnationalism." *Annual Review of Anthropology* 24 (1995): 547–65.

Koser, Khalid, and Richard Black. "The End of the Refugee Cycle?" Pp. 2–17 in *The End of the Refugee Cycle? Refugee Repatriation and Reconstruction*, edited by Richard Black and Khalid Koser. New York: Berghahn Books, 1999.

Long, Lynellyn. *Ban Vinai: The Refugee Camp.* New York: Columbia University Press, 1993.

Lotman, Yuri. *Universe of the Mind: A Semiotic Theory of Culture*, translated by Ann Shukman. Bloomington: Indiana University Press, 1990.

Malkki, Liisa. "National Geographic: The Rooting of Peoples and the Territorialization of National Identity Among Scholars and Refugees." *Cultural Anthropology* 7, no. 1 (1992): 24–62.

———. *Purity and Exile: Violence, Memory and National Cosmology among Hutu Refugees in Tanzania.* Chicago: University of Chicago Press, 1995.

Markowitz, Fran. *A Community in Spite of Itself: Soviet Jewish Emigrés in New York.* Washington, DC: Smithsonian Institution Press, 1993.

———. "Criss-Crossing Identities: The Russian Jewish Diaspora and the Jewish Diaspora in Russia." *Diaspora* 4, no. 2, (1995): 201–10.

Mathews, Gordon. *Global Culture/Individual Identity: Searching for Home in the Cultural Supermarket.* London: Routledge, 2000.

Mufti, Aamir, and Ella Shohat. "Introduction." Pp. 1–12 in *Dangerous Liaisons: Gender, Nation and Post Colonial Perspectives*, edited by Anne McClintock, Aamir Mufti and Ella Shohat. Minneapolis: University of Minnesota Press, 1997.

Pattie, Susan P. *Faith in History: Armenians Re-Building Community.* Washington, DC: Smithsonian Institution Press, 1997.

Peteet, Julie M. "Transforming Trust: Dispossession and Empowerment among Palestinian Refugees". Pp. 168–86 in *Mistrusting Refugees*, edited by E. Valentine Daniel and John C. Knudsen. Berkeley: University of California Press, 1995.

Probyn, Elspeth. *Outside Belongings.* New York: Routledge, 1996.

Radcliffe-Brown, A. R. *Structure and Function in Primitive Society.* New York: Free Press, 1952.

Radhakrishnan, R. *Diasporic Mediations: Between Home and Location.* University of Minnesota Press, 1996.

Rapport, Nigel, and Andrew Dawson, eds. *Migrants of Identity: Perceptions of Home in a World of Movement.* Oxford: Berg, 1998.

Ray, Kakoli. "Repatriation and De-territorialization: Meskhetian Turks' Conception of Home." *Journal of Refugee Studies* 13, no. 4 (2000): 391–414.

Rock, David, and Stefan Wolff, eds. *Coming Home to Germany? The Integration of Ethnic Germans from Central and Eastern Europe in the Federal Republic.* New York: Berghahn, 2002.

Rosaldo, Renato. *Culture and Truth: The Remaking of Social Analysis.* Boston: Beacon Press, 1989.

Rybczynski, Witold. *Home: A Short History of an Idea.* New York: Penguin Books, 1986.

Rouse, Roger. "Mexican Migration and the Social Space of Postmodernism. *Diaspora* 1, no. 1 (1991): 8–23.

Safran, William. "Diasporas in Modern Societies: Myths of Homeland and Return." *Diaspora* 1, no. 1 (1991): 83–99.
Sassen, Saskia. *Guests and Aliens*. New York: The New Press, 1999.
Scott, James C. *Seeing Like a State*. New Haven: Yale University Press, 1998.
Shami, Seteny. "Prehistories of Globalization: Circassian Identity in Motion." Pp. 220–50 in *Globalization*, edited by Arjun Appadurai. Durham: Duke University Press, 2001.
Shils, Edward. "Primordial, Personal, Sacred, and Civil Ties." *British Journal of Sociology* 8, no. 2 (1957): 130–45.
Soysal, Yasemin N. *Limits of Citizenship: Migrants and Postnational Membership in Europe*. Chicago: University of Chicago Press, 1994.
Stack, Carol. *Call to Home: African Americans Reclaim the Rural South*. New York: Basic Books, 1996.
Stewart, Michael. *The Time of the Gypsies*. Boulder: Westview, 1997.
Taylor, Peter J. *Modernities: A Geohistorical Interpretation*. Cambridge: Polity Press, 1999.
Thompson, Becky and Sangeeta Tyagi. "Storytelling as Social Conscience." Pp. ix–xvii in *Names We Call Home: Autobiography on Racial Identity*, edited by Becky Thompson and Sangeeta Tyagi. New York: Routledge, 1996.
Van Hear, Nicholas. *New Diasporas: The Mass Exodus, Dispersal and Regrouping of Migrant Communities*. London: UCL Press, 1998.

II

HOMECOMINGS OF IMMIGRANTS AND REFUGEES

3

Tigrayan Returnees' Notions of Home: Five Variations on a Theme

Laura Hammond

"We lived in Sudan so long that that became like our home [*addina*]. Now we are here and this will become like home. Aside from the heat, this is a good place for a farmer."

With these words, my neighbor Mebrat, who had lived for nearly a decade in a refugee camp in Sudan before establishing her family in a settlement in northwestern Ethiopia, discounted my question about whether she would try to return to the Tigrayan highlands where she had been born and raised. She rejected this suggestion, saying that there was no farmland there. But what, I asked, if there was farmland? "Well, then we have no ox. No, this place is better."

My neighbor's response revealed an important aspect of the experience of homecoming for Tigrayan returnees. Whereas much of the academic and policy-oriented discourses on repatriation imply either that return is synonymous with homecoming, or that true homecoming is not possible (and thus that a person might remain forever homeless), Mebrat's perspective showed that her experience of repatriation was more a process of pragmatic homemaking than of return to something familiar.

"HOME" AS A PROBLEMATIC CONCEPT IN REPATRIATION STUDIES

In repatriation discourse, the term "home" has been given remarkably little critical analysis. Scholars argue about the conditions under which a person or group may feel "at home" (Warner 1994), whether it is possible to be or feel at home while in exile (Malkki 1995a and 1992), whether repatriation implies homecoming (Black and Koser 1999; Allen 1996), or whether it is possible for people to imagine, invent, or otherwise create a sense of home (Warner 1994; Hammond 1999). In all of these analyses, however, the term is used as a unit of measure to evaluate the quality of return or exile and is generally assumed to be commonly accepted and commonly applicable to all migrants from all cultures in all situations of dislocation, relocation, or return. Thus, the perennial research question asked about repatriating refugees remains, "Are they home yet?" without asking "How is home understood, and can it be created anew if it cannot be recaptured or fully returned to?"

That the term home should escape scrutiny seems strange, since the word has so many different meanings in English.[1] The unabridged Oxford English Dictionary (2003) has at least two dozen different definitions of home that could be used in an analysis of the relationship between person (in this case, a migrant or a community of migrants) and place. These definitions include locations of various levels of scale, including an individual dwelling, a village, a territory, region, or nation-state. Most usages of the term refer to an affective and somewhat abstract connection between person and place, though the nature of that association may vary widely. In this chapter, I consider how Tigrayan notions of home, embodied in distinct words none of which coincides completely with the English-language term, reveal a multifaceted way of viewing home, and, more importantly, the relationship between person and place. My initial lack of awareness of how these terms differed impeded my study of "homecoming"—that is, refugee repatriation in northwestern Ethiopia since 1993. I argue here that home, as used in most scholarly research involving migration and return, is bounded by Western notions that may not be easily applicable to certain non-Western contexts, and that the discourse on homecoming gives priority to the idea of a single home as occupying a seat of preference over all others.

DECISIONS TO RETURN AND THE QUESTION OF THE AVAILABILITY OF LAND

Refugees repatriating from Sudan to Ethiopia in the early and mid-1990s were returning to their country and region of origin, but most were not able to return to the highland villages they had left a decade earlier, for they had lost their land claims. Thus, the relationship between return and homecoming was perhaps more problematic than it would have been if they had been able to return to the villages and towns where they had ancestral and kinship ties. Settled in an empty field close to the Ethiopia/Sudan/Eritrea borders, their new "home" resembled the climatic/ecological environment of the camps more than it did the places that they had originated from. Return thus involved a process of "home-making" or emplacement, whereby new relationships between person/community and place were forged that gradually took on characteristics that in English are labeled "home-like."

For the last decade I have been conducting ethnographic research with a community of approximately eight thousand Tigrayan returnees who repatriated to Ethiopia that year after having lived in exile for nearly a decade. They had been among the two hundred thousand who fled civil war and famine in Ethiopia's northern Amhara and Tigray regions during 1984 and 1985. Approximately fifty thousand refugees returned to Tigray after living for only one year in the camps, despite the continuation of the war, so that they could resume their farming activities on their land (Hendrie 1996). Yet at least sixty thousand Ethiopian refugees remained in Sudan until the Ethiopian civil war ended in May 1991 and the Derg Government was replaced by the Ethiopian Peoples Revolutionary Democratic Front (EPRDF). The EPRDF was (and still is) dominated by the Tigrayan People's Liberation Front (TPLF), which as a rebel army had fought for seventeen years (1975 to 1991) for the liberation of Tigray region from Derg's domination. The TPLF had assisted people on their journey out of the highlands and into the relative safety of Sudan. Assisted by the TPLF's humanitarian wing, the Relief Society of Tigray (REST), the refugees had trekked on foot for four to six weeks to reach the Sudan, traveling mostly at night to avoid aerial bombardment from Ethiopian government planes. Refugees credited the TPLF and REST with having protected and cared for them during the years of "The Struggle," as they referred to the war, and felt a great deal of loyalty to the movement. After years of living in exile, and excited at the prospect of living in peace with the TPLF in power (regional politics have been almost exclusively led by the TPLF in post-war Ethiopia) the refugees were eager to return to Ethiopia when the EPRDF came to power. Thus, for many refugees who registered to return, repatriation signified the reestablishment of their national and political identity. They had little idea of the degree to which this understanding of homecoming would become overshadowed by social and economic considerations.

The first refugees to repatriate were assisted almost entirely by the new Ethiopian government, which considered that a highly visible mass return of refugees would validate its claims to legitimacy and popular support. Assistance from the United Nations High Commissioner for Refugees (UNHCR) was very basic during the first year (US$4 million for approximately fifteen thousand returnees), as no comprehensive tripartite agreement with Sudan and Ethiopia for assisting the repatriation operation had been signed by the time the operation began. Each returnee household received a nine-month food ration for each person, a box of cooking utensils, and a plastic sheet. Free health services were provided for the first year at small clinics established in the settlements by the Ethiopian government. Water and educational services were established by the end of the first year following return.

While the refugees and the new government were eager for the repatriation operation to Ethiopia to begin, both were concerned about the availability of land in areas of return. The central and eastern highlands from which the refugees had originally migrated suffered from extreme overcrowding, soil degradation, and erosion. Farm plots averaged 0.5 hectares (1.25 acres) in size, too small to produce enough food to cover a typical household's needs. Since the refugees had left the highlands in the mid-1980s, the land that they had left vacant had been reallocated by local government councils to land-poor and landless households who had remained behind, including an entire generation who had come of age during the decade that the refugees had been away.[2] Thus, prior to repatriation, potential returnees were informed by the Ethiopian government that while they were free to settle where they wished when they came back to Ethiopia, they would not receive land if they returned to their villages of origin. Instead, land would be allocated only to those who settled in the more sparsely populated lowlands of the western Tigray region, close to the Sudan and Eritrea borders near the town of Humera.

The offer of relatively large and fertile plots of land (at least two hectares) in the Humera area was attractive to most potential returnees, so decisions about where to repatriate were immediately conditioned by pragmatic economic considerations. Humera was agro-ecologically similar to the area around the refugee camps, and was known for being a fertile area in which to grow sesame, sorghum, and cotton as cash crops. Since the 1960s, Humera had been a commercial agriculture center, yet most large farms (including state farms that the Derg had established following the seizure of private farms in the late 1970s and early 1980s) had been abandoned during the war (McCann 1990; Clapham 1988: 165). With so much fertile land available, returnees saw the option of settling there and receiving land, with the possibility that more land could be rented from large landowners and that household income could be supplemented by wage labor on the commercial farms that were gradually restarting their operations, as important economic opportunities.

From the government's perspective, settling people in the western lowlands had distinct political advantages. For generations, the area had been inhabited by a mix of ethnic Amharas and Tigrayans. However, it had been administered from the Amhara city of Gondar. Following the EPRDF's rise to power, regional boundaries were redrawn so that the area was incorporated into the Tigray region. Increasing the proportion of Tigrayans resident in the Humera area helped to secure Tigray's claim over it. Redistricting also helped to stimulate surplus agricultural production which could be supplied to the central and eastern Tigrayan highlands to help relieve food insecurity and prevent famine. Thus, repatriation of ethnic Tigrayans to this new part of Tigray was a deliberate attempt on the part of the Ethiopian government to reclassify new areas as "home" to Tigrayans, and to try to encourage people to think of home in national and regional, rather than local, terms.

REPATRIATION IN NORTHWEST ETHIOPIA, 1993 TO 1995

Returnees were settled in three places: Mai Kadra (on the grounds of an old state farm), Rawayan (situated close to Humera on a major trade and access road to Ethiopian cities to the south), and Ada Bai (on the grounds of a former private commercial farm). Ada Bai was the largest of the settlements, with approximately seven thousand people. I have been conducting field research there since November 1993. Prior to arrival of the returnees, Ada Bai—which in Tigrinya means Big Land—was virtually an empty field. Approximately twenty agro-pastoralist households originally from Eritrea had settled there prior to the repatriation, but the place had virtually no social service infrastructure, no reliable source of water, and was accessible only by a rough tractor track, which became impassable in the rainy season. For returnees the process of "homecoming" therefore involved not so much a negotiation of relations with local hosts, as is seen in many refugee return contexts, but rather a process of establishing themselves in a new, and largely empty, place.[3]

I call this process one of "emplacement," whereby space that previously had no particular significance to an individual or group was rendered meaningful. This investment of physical space with meaning came through everyday practice: interaction with the environment, recoding of social relationships, and gradual familiarization of a person or group with their surroundings. This process could be understood not only by watching what people did in their daily lives, but also by considering the words that they used to refer to the same place over time.

Since November 1993, when I began my research in Ada Bai, I have been able to refine my understanding of Tigrayan returnees' notions of home, to see how emerging relations between people and places generated affective connections which were akin to different elements of the English-language notion of homecoming, but could not be referred to by a single term. Tigrayans did not have a single term that could neatly correspond to "homecoming." Instead, they used several different terms to describe their relationships to place, family, and identity, which, taken together, provided a hybrid picture of Tigrayan homecoming and notions of home. I suggest that considering these terms may challenge social scientists' own theoretical constructs and understandings of home.

TIGRAYAN NOTIONS OF HOME, PLACE, AND IDENTITY: METHODOLOGICAL CONSIDERATIONS

Rather than having a single word in Tigrinya that can be translated as "home," people in Ada Bai used at least five different terms to refer to the places that, in one context or another, might mean "home" to an English speaker. Some terms referred to the house that the person lived in (*geza, tukul*), others referred to his or her birthplace or family's place (*addi, hagere seb*), and another referred to the country or region from which the person originated and which gave him or her a sense of personal and collective identity (*hager*).

While asking people about the process of homecoming, and about the nature of their relationships with various meaningful places, I had to choose between these terms. This often determined the frame of reference for the answers that I received. While asking people about their sentimental or emotional connections to places, I could not ask "What place do you most associate with home?" Instead, I had to pick the nearest equivalent, which might be "Where do you think of as your *addi?*" or "What place (*hager*) do you come from?" People's responses, or at least the parameters of possible responses to such questions, were already somewhat circumscribed by my choice of words in framing the questions, and at first my informants responded merely by identifying themselves as living in that house, belonging to that family, originating from that village, or being a citizen of that country or region. I had a difficult time unpacking the English-language concept of home in order to discuss the quality of their relationships to specific places. This also hampered my ability to be able to judge when, in fact, people felt that they had "come home," were "at home," or were involved in "making a home" in the English-language sense, and made the task of understanding the processes of homecoming and homemaking very difficult to elucidate.

ONE HOME OR MANY?

Common English-language usage of the term "home" implies a relationship between person and place that gives the individual (or community) his primary sense of identity, or to which a degree of primacy in other terms is attributed. Home may be one's birthplace, the place in which a person or group feels most comfortable, and/or to which he/she/they feel the greatest sense of belonging. The same word can be used in English to refer to several different places, such as in returning home at the end of the day, going home for the holidays, or moving home after a period of exile. What is common to these uses is the sense that home is not only a place, but a state of being which conveys a sense of personal or collective identity (OED

2003). Home's quality of being both a place and a state of being, which dates from Old English, is what gives the researcher the most difficulty, for the particular meaning to which the word is being applied is evident only in its application. In trying to find a Tigrayan equivalent to one element of home's meaning, I found myself presupposing or predetermining the answer I was investigating.

Until the mid-1990s, migration researchers and policy makers assumed that refugees had only one notion of home, and that repatriation was equal to homecoming. This equation justified promotion of repatriation as the best possible solution, or as then-UNHCR Commissioner Sadako Ogata called it, "the least worst option in a no-win situation" (Ogata 1997). Scholars such as Malkki (1995b) and others (Warner 1994; Allen 1996; Black and Koser 1999; Hammond 1999; Appadurai 2003 [1996]; Clifford 1997) have challenged this paradigm by suggesting that refugees and other migrants could construct a new "sense of home" in the place of exile, or in a completely different place. While this emphasis on cultural creativity and improvisation was a much-needed corrective to thinking about homecoming, there was an underlying sense that among the many different relationships between person and place, one would take primacy, and thus would define the migrants' experience of "homecoming" or "homemaking." Thus, if you were a refugee who could not return to your place of origin, you might be able to create a new home in exile, which could replace the original home. Little scholarly attention, however, has yet been given to the possibility that one might be able to feel equally "at home" in two or more places simultaneously, or that one's sense of being "at home" could be derived from several different types of attachment to different places.

The idea that refugees could not construct new homes in new places has recently been used as justification for the granting of less-than-full rights of asylum, including temporary protection and exceptional leave to remain; the assumption being that forced migrants would never be able to—or, more xenophobically, should never be able to—feel "at home" in their country of asylum and thus should return to their country of origin as soon as possible. Where return to one's actual locality of origin is not possible, a next-best option is seen by European governments as "returning" the migrant to another part of their country of origin, in an arrangement known as exercising the internal flight option. Deportations from European countries of asylum seekers who are considered to have internal flight options often result in the person's being settled into an area in which he has never lived or even visited, has no ethnic or family ties, does not speak the language, and may in fact have reason to fear persecution of a different sort than that from which he originally fled in his locality of origin. The underlying logic to such "solutions" is that the closer a person is to his or her area of origin, the more "at home" he or she will be.

More current debates about relationships between persons and places have been less insistent on sedentarism and have considered the issue of whether it is possible to construct a new sense of home when return to one's place of origin is not possible. Such debates suggest that such home-building is possible, yet still imply that the goal of such emplacement is the generation of a new primary place-state relationship that may supplant the relationship that has been severed or rendered inaccessible through migration or displacement. The idea that a person can only have one true home is left unquestioned even as the potential to forge meaningful associations between a person and multiple places is acknowledged.[4]

Anthropologists' and other social scientists' analyses on migrants having a primary notion of home is a result of the fact that the English definitions of home consider person-place relationships in ways that some cultures may not share. To give an example of this, I return to the case of Tigrayan returnees in Ada Bai, and to the linguistic references to relationships between person and place contained in the Tigrinya language that reflect a pluralistic understanding of home concepts. These references are framed in relation to everyday practices that serve to strengthen ties between persons and places.

PLACE NAMES IN TIGRINYA

Bota

The Tigrinya language has many different words that refer to senses of place. *Bota* refers to a generic place to which a person does not have an explicit or meaningful relationship. Leslau (1976) defines *bota* as space, a geographic referent which carries no particular meaning for the subject, or with which the subject does not have a relationship. A person might refer to a town they had never visited before as a *bota*, or when asking the name of a place—for example, *Izzih bota intay iyu?*—What is this place? Or *Izzih bota intay zibehal?*—What is this place called? *Bota* is thus un-emplaced space, physical space which is unknown or uncoded with social significance. When returnees first came to Ada Bai, they often spoke of it as a *bota*. They complained about not knowing the place, and attributed this lack of local knowledge as being the main reason that their lives were so difficult. They did not know where to find building materials for their houses, did not know which local plants could be used for medicines, and did not have a strong enough farming practice to be able to support their families solely from their agricultural production. At a public meeting held to discuss the need to engage in malaria control activities, i.e., to refrain from planting vegetables near houses during the rainy season, one man said, "We do not know this place (*bota*); that is why we and our children are dying."

Hager

Ada Bai residents, like all Tigrinya speakers, identified some types of place by referring to their relationships to it. A person's country—either the nation from which he came or the general area in which he was born—was referred to as *hager*. Patriotic songs sung in the refugee camps and in Ethiopia during national holidays referred to Ethiopia and to Tigray Region as *hager*. Villages were often named "Place of _____," such as Hager Selam (Place of Peace) and Hager Mariam (St. Mary's Place), to imbue them with spiritual significance.

In redrawing the regional lines to include Humera, and then settling ethnic Tigrayan returnees on that land, the Ethiopian government was making a deliberate attempt to define repatriation, in the strict sense of returning a person to his or her nation or returning to a *hager*, as homecoming. Efforts were made soon after repatriation to register people for constitutional and local elections, and regular meetings were hosted by local political leaders to familiarize people with their rights and obligations as resident citizens of Ethiopia. As indicated earlier, people were at first eager to return, but when they found that the conditions and services made available to them were decidedly worse than what they had known in Sudan, disillusionment quickly set in.

Attachments to their *hager* were strongest for those who had had close relatives who had fought in the war. Their patriotism played a much larger role in their lives than it did for those who were more removed from the war. Families of veterans or of men and women who had been killed in the war regularly held tributes to their relatives. The discourse of patriotism, freedom, and the sense that repatriation signified an end to their wartime sacrifices, played a major role in their lives; thus homecoming was partly the realization of the goals that their loved ones had sacrificed for. Those who did not have relatives who had been involved in the war tended to be more focused on their attempts to make ends meet in their new homes; political rights and citizenship were more abstract concepts that did not play major roles in their everyday lives.

Addi, Hagere Seb

Addi, meaning land, usually referred to one's own farmland or to the general area (village, *tabia*, *woreda*, or *awraja*)[5] in which one's farmland was located. Farmland in general (not necessarily belonging to anyone) was also known as *hirsha* or *mareyt*. Despite the fact that land ownership in Ethiopia was nationalized, people referred to the land that they had been allocated to use in proprietary terms as their *addi*. They also referred to land that belonged to their families prior to nationalization of land as "theirs" even if they no longer had legal use rights over it. The fact that they referred to it in such terms did not necessarily mean that they felt that their tenures were secure, and in fact there did appear to be truth to the claims that national ownership of land had at least in some cases acted as a disincentive to investment in conservation, environmental protection, and fallowing activities in parts of the highlands.

To speak of one's *addi* was to refer to a place that carried a great deal of meaning, that had been fully emplaced. *Addi* tied an individual to a larger communal and familial unit, and was constitutive of important elements of one's identity. People often referred to the villages in the highlands from which they had migrated as *addina* (our places). When people in Ada Bai spoke of wanting to be buried in their birthplaces, they used the terms *hagere seb* and *addi*. These were considered more personalized terms than *woreda* or *tabia*, which were seen as administrative terms used by political leaders to refer to physical locations and areas. Suffixes indicating possession were not commonly attached to the terms *woreda* or *tabia*.

In highland Tigray, men often lived in the same villages for their entire lives, and women lived in the villages of their parents until marriage, when they would go to live with their husbands in their villages (often quite close to their own birthplaces). In highland Tigray, marriages were often arranged between families from the same *addi*; the bride and groom's characters were judged largely on the basis of what was known about their family, and a families who was from a nearby area was usually better known than one from further away.

In Ada Bai, the rules of marriage selection were less strict, but most people agreed that if possible, it was desirable to marry a person whose family came from the same place that he/she had. Informants told me that it was better to "know the people" of the person you were about to marry, and that coming from the same place was a basic guarantee of the person's essential good character.

Neighborhoods in Ada Bai were broken down according to the parts of Tigray from which people had come. Thus, while one might not have known one's neighbor prior to coming to Ada Bai, one said that one knew what sort of person he or she was by virtue of the fact that one had come from the same *addi*; this helped to build trust and cooperation between people as they set about forging a relationship with their new environment. Neighbors would help each other prepare feasts or funerals, share labor, and socialize most often with each other rather than with people from another neighborhood.

When used to refer to the specific place in which a person was born, the term *hagere seb*—meaning "place of my people"—was used. One's *hagere seb* could refer to the village that one had ancestral ties to or where one's parents or grandparents lived.[6]

While one's *hagere seb* or *addi* was clearly an extremely important place which helped to give a person his or her identity and clearly played a role in determining marriage patterns even while people were living in exile, many people had not actually lived in their *hagere seb* for many years. Many young adults who had been born in the Sudan had never even visited their *hagere seb*, nor did they personally know the relatives who lived there. They still, however, used it to define their identities, as an organizing principle to define themselves.

Geza

The physical house that one lived in was called a *geza*, and although people did refer to their houses in possessive terms (*gezana*—our house), the attachment to this place was not strictly the same as that which the English term "home" implies. Any house that a person or family lives in, even if temporarily, can be referred to as a *geza*, and while it might be important as a focus of domestic life, people did not become very sentimental about the actual structures. Houses in Ada Bai were made from straw and thatch, and were replaced every five to ten years. Even in highland Tigray where houses were commonly constructed of stone and mud and may last thirty years or more, they were not passed from one generation to another. A man demonstrated his worth as a husband and the head of his household by skillfully constructing a house for his new wife. Though he may have inherited use rights to the land that the house sat on from his father, he did not take up permanent residence in his father's house.

While the house structures themselves did not carry as much meaning for their residents, the process of constructing the houses brought both men and women into closer interactive relationships with their environment, and was a key element in the process of emplacement. During the first months after they arrived in Ada Bai, people had difficulty finding the right grasses, building poles, and mud to line the internal walls. They complained that they "did not know the place;" as they became better able to exploit the resources that their environment made available, their feelings of comfort increased and their sense of being "at home" deepened.

TOWARD A PRAGMATIC DEFINITION OF HOMECOMING

People in Ada Bai were involved in a continuous process of establishing themselves in their new environment. Most people fully expected to live in the village for the rest of their lives, to raise their children there, and eventually to die and be buried there. Thus, Ada Bai was the focus of their domestic lives, and as time went on, they developed a sense of belonging to the place that very closely resembled the attachment to place that in English might be defined as "home," or in Tigrinya, might be called *addina*. In Tigrinya, however, the relationship to this new place does not supplant people's attachments to their areas of origin; rather, the relationship embodied a different but also meaningful person-place relationship that is additional to the connection to area of origin. In this sense, returnees did not *come* home; rather, they made a new home that held meaning for them without negating the importance of the area of origin. New person-place associations were being forged at the same time that old associations were maintained; for many people, there was not a single primary place that could be thought of as home.

GENERATIONAL DIFFERENCES IN IDEAS ABOUT HOME

Person-place relationships differed generationally, and to a lesser extent by gender. Older people (particularly men) were more likely to think of their birthplaces or the ancestral homes of their families in an active sense, and expressed their desire to return to the highlands to be buried in the villages in which they had been born. They could create a new home in Ada Bai, but whatever affective ties they developed towards their new residence would not replace the strong attachment they felt for the place they had left. They said that their birthplaces were where people "know me best." Those who had spent most of their lives in the highlands as respected members of a community and church parish or mosque, were uncomfortable with the idea that they might be buried in a place with others whom they did not know well and who were not from the same place.[7] A man in his eighties told me:

> I look at my birthplace as my "eye". [That is, just as my eye can tell me whether things are bad or good, my birthplace shows me the same.] I am thinking about it all the time and want to go back. . . . Your birthplace is the place where you grew up and played with your friends, even where you quarreled. Whether it is bad or good the area itself never disappears from my eye. Even now. Everyone's birthplace is very nice if it is the same to others as it is to me. Here in Ac'a Bai we are saying that this is Tigray so it is our place. But it has a very great difference with my birth area and I will never see it as the same. I [think of] my birthplace all the time. Even as the sun rises and the sun sets, and the moon rises, they are different [here]. . . . Everyone [who has not left their birthplace] can see [the place] with his own eyes even if it is bad or good. [People don't know the suffering that I know because they have not left their birthplace.] So I like my country [birthplace]. I am very sad being far away from my area [of origin]. The people that repatriated in 1979 [1986 Gregorian calendar] from Sudan, they got farmland, oxen. . . . By now everything is OK for them. But for us still we are suffering and have a hard time. Here everything seems very bad to me and every day I am very sad. I have no helper, no land, everyone is in a problem too and I don't have any kind of chance to go home. I am old enough. I am nearly ready to die.

This man's desire to be close to his birthplace was directly related to the extent to which he felt tied to Ada Bai as a community. Elderly people spoke of wanting to return to their birthplaces to be buried properly, where those who had known them well, and who knew their families, would be able to hold public eulogy ceremonies known as *agobar* for them. The *agobar* would be held in a public space, usually a marketplace, and people would come from the surrounding villages to pay their respects to the family and to speak about the deceased's essential character, the good works that he had done, and their importance to the community at large. In Ada Bai, *agobar* were not held, as people had not been settled for long enough in the area to develop wide associative networks. Despite their expressed desire for returning to the highlands, most people could not afford the expense of the journey, or else were too weak to travel; thus, their wistful yearning to see their birthplaces again was in most cases never acted upon. Though they resigned themselves to their fates, they spoke often of their birthplaces. Thus, their newly created sense of home in Ada Bai was to a large degree a pragmatic compromise between wanting to return to their birthplaces and realizing that practical factors made such returns impossible.

Ada Bayans who were teenagers or young adults, who had come of age in the returnee settlement, were less concerned with returning to their birthplaces than they were with participating in the communities that they had helped to form in Ada Bai. Most had only vague memories of the highlands, if any, and did not feel such a strong desire to return. They felt that their economic prospects were better in the returnee settlement, and that in time Ada Bai would be as compelling a home as the highlands had been for their parents. Mikael explained the rationale for pragmatic homemaking to me when he said, "We see our life as two lives. The life before [1984, when we became refugees,] and the life after. The life before was better because we were in our homes [*addi*]. But this is a new life and we must try to make it as complete as possible."

Younger adults said that they had started their lives over so many times that the concept of "going back" to a life they had once known, or else had never known but had only heard about from their parents, was so unpractical as to be unthinkable. Belay said that he considered that he had lived three lives: one in the highlands, one in the Sudan, and one in Ada Bai. He said that he had no desire to go back to the highlands. Since leaving he had had numerous occupations, married a second time, had several more children, and made a complete break with his family in the highlands. These men were typical of the middle-aged group that had chosen to begin new lives in Ada Bai without apparent regret or longing for their birthplaces.

A key determinant of the success with which a person was able to make a new home in Ada Bai was his or her access to relatives living nearby. Some people had migrated to Sudan with their entire families, or had been reunited with relatives while they were living in Sudan. Many of those who did not have close kin living in the camps became involved in the invention of new kin ties and social networks. Distant relatives would be recast as "father," "uncle," or "sister." These newly defined kinship relationships could be relied upon for sharing resources and labor when needed. The more kin a person had, whether real or redefined, the easier it was for the person to feel "at home" in Ada Bai. Emplacement in this sense thus implied a recoding of relationships in a social landscape that gave the new place added meaning.

Despite such improvisation of kinship ties, relationships to the family or ancestral area of origin were actively maintained by people living in Ada Bai. As was the case in the refugee camps in Sudan, houses were clustered according to area of origin, so that one's neighbors tended to be people who were originally from one's same village, or at least the same general area. People believed that this made it easier to trust their neighbors, even if the individuals did not know each other before leaving Tigray, since the families were known to each other. Ties were also maintained by parents who taught their children their family histories from an early age. Mebrat, whose story I opened this chapter with, said that her children "know that they are from Abi Adi [a large town in central Tigray] by story [i.e., they have heard me talk about the place], but they do not know it [because they have never visited the place] so [instead] they can say 'Ada Bai is our home.'" Gidey, whose young daughter had just delivered her first baby, said "We are teaching our children now to be Ada Bai people. They should say they are from Ada Bai when someone asks them."

When I asked parents and grandparents how long it would take before their children thought of Ada Bai as their home, some told me that it would take three generations. At the point when a person could say that his father and paternal grandfather were both born in Ada Bai, they told me, he would be a true Ada Bai person. An individual's name is made up of his or her own name, the father's name, and the grandfather's name; thus these two generations are particularly important in giving an individual a sense of personal identity. Others saw the process as being even more prolonged. Children were taught to be able to name their paternal ancestors back through seven generations, so that they could show their eligibility for marriage. Parents said that when all relatives in the seven-generation lineage were Ada Bai residents, then the ties to the highland home would truly be broken.

In 2002, I asked several children to name their paternal ancestors; to my surprise, even six-year-old children could name their grandfathers five or six generations back. Though they did not know the details of these men's lives, they knew where many of them had lived in the highlands. Thus, while my earlier research suggested that the process of defining one's identity as belonging to a single place—that is, Ada Bai—might take place within a relatively short space of time, or at least within an individual's lifetime, further examination of this question has led me to the realization that several generations of people may maintain multiple senses of home simultaneously.

While the idea that Ada Bai was the best, or most practical, home for their children played an important role in parents' own ideas about Ada Bai as a home-like place, their children did not always adapt in the ways that their parents envisioned they would. On a visit to Ada Bai in June 2002, I asked several children, who had either been born in Sudan or in Ada Bai, which place they considered to be "home." I struggled with how to ask the question, and ultimately chose *addi*, so my question might have translated, "What place do your people come from?" A fourteen-year old girl, who had been born in the Sudan, said to me, "our home [*addina,* the place of our family] is in Axum" [the district in the central highlands from which her parents had come]—then she looked to her mother and asked, "What is it called?" "Adiet [meaning the name of the village]," she was told. Although she had never been to Adiet before, she said that she felt a strong connection to it because her family had originally come from that place and because she had heard about the relatives who were living there. Even without actually having ever seen the place, it had a formative influence in defining her personal identity, as it tied her to an ancestral home, to a family lineage, and to a community of people who shared certain cultural characteristics that people from other parts of Tigray did not have. Other children agreed that their *addi* was not Ada Bai.

I attempted to get at the question of whether the *addi* or Ada Bai occupied a place of primacy for the children by asking them which place was better or more important. A few children who had visited the family homes in the highlands since repatriating to Ada Bai said that they preferred Ada Bai, either because the school was closer to their houses, the water was closer, or, in the words of one seven-year-old girl, because the highlands were "full of stones . . . [and] you have to walk so far [to get from the village to the house]." Such pragmatic descriptions of the benefits of Ada Bai life were rooted in the sense that the place that one knows is better than the place that one does not know, but it does not necessarily mean that the preferred place provides a greater sense of definitional identity. Despite their preference for living in Ada Bai, the children's discussions of where their *addi* was revealed that they felt a strong identification with the place that the families had migrated from in the highlands. While Ada Bai was their "everyday home," the highlands was their "family home."[8] They had two important person-place relationships—one gave them a sense of their own personal and family history; the other helped to define them in the present, on a day-to-day basis. Neither was given priority over the other.

CONCLUSION

By 2002, Ada Bai had become the second-largest town in Western Tigray Zone with a population of approximately ten thousand. Young adults and children had developed a strong sense of being "at home" in Ada Bai, through going to school, herding animals, hauling water, and learning how to farm and collect wood. Many of those who had been young children when I first arrived in Ada Bai have since married others in the community. Through daily practice they have come to invest their environment with meaning, constructing a new home in a place that previously held no meaning for them, without relinquishing their attachment to their highland homes.

Taking as a central defining element the notion that home involves an abstract relationship between person and place, which involves a state of being that engenders comfort, security, and plays a role in the construction of personal identity, one can see that it is perfectly possible for a person to have two or more "homes" at any given time. Home need not be a single place of primary importance to the subject.

In Ada Bai, people identify both an everyday home and the ancestral or family home. They also, to a greater or lesser extent, consider both Ethiopia as a country and Tigray as a region, to be political homes. Yet to ask returnees when they expect to feel, or what they need in order to feel, that they are "at home" borders on the nonsensical. Insisting that a person choose one place to signify home is to deny the process of homebuilding that Tigrayan returnees have become involved in.

A more useful line of questioning might be to ask people whether the place that they inhabit is providing them the economic, social, and political resources that they need to feel that their lives (or livelihoods) are sustainable, and whether they are satisfied with their lives in the new place. A model that recognizes that there may be many different types of homes, and that people may be willing and able to adapt when necessary to create a new home to add to their repertoire of other home-like places, will produce analyses of migration and return that more closely and accurately define migrants' return experiences. Such an approach might also result in assistance policies that better target the real needs of returnees as they attempt to create new, viable, and sustainable homes.

NOTES

I would like to acknowledge the support of the UN Emergencies Unit for Ethiopia, the United Nations High Commissioner for Refugees, and the US Agency for International Development for support during research for this paper. Initial fieldwork was funded through a Fulbright grant and a fellowship from the John D. and Catherine T.

MacArthur Foundation. Thanks are, as always, due to the people of Ada Bai, for their continued collaboration and patience with my ongoing research.

1. And in some other European languages, though I restrict my analysis here to the English-language use of the term.
2. All land in Ethiopia was nationalized by the Derg in 1975. The EPRDF has maintained this policy, arguing that nationalized land ownership guarantees that poor farmers will never have to become disenfranchised from the land by having to sell it. This policy is the subject of lively debate, as many believe that without private land rights farmers will not invest adequately in protection and conservation measures and will not reap maximum benefit from the land that they occupy. Moreover, despite government ownership of land and regular (though infrequent) reallocations, many Tigrayan farmers remain landless or land-poor.
3. My research examines the social, cultural, political and economic aspects of return, and considers the processes by which returnees come to consider the anonymous space that they have been settled into as a meaningful place, and ultimately a home. I refer to this process of place-making as "emplacement." For full details of this research and a theoretical discussion of emplacement, see Hammond 2004.
4. An important exception to this argument is Anders Stefansson's Ph.D. dissertation (Stefansson 2003). Stefansson argues that it is possible for refugees and returnees to have multiple, sometimes contesting home-attachments. Other studies of transnationalism assert that migrants may have multiple homes in different places, though the tendency is to assume that the home in the place of origin has some sense of priority. See Ong 1999; Appadurai 2003 [1996].
5. *Tabia* refers to an area roughly equivalent to a parish in English; *woreda* is similar to a county, while *awraja* refers to a political unit equivalent to a district, subregion, or zone. Although the current government no longer refers to *awrajas*, local people continue to refer to places by their *awraja* names.
6. Typically, such lineage is traced through the father's line, since Tigrayan society is patrilineal and patrilocal, though a woman might refer to her own father's place as her *hagere seb* when speaking as an individual rather than as a member of her husband's household. A woman typically referred to her husband's patriline when speaking about her household's *hagere seb*.
7. Approximately 10 percent of all Tigrayans in the Tigray region are Muslim. In Ada Bai, approximately sixty households were Muslim. The settlement had one large church and two small mosques.
8. For a full examination of children's senses of place in Ada Bai, see Hammond 2003.

REFERENCES

Allen, Tim, ed. *In Search of Cool Ground: War, Flight and Homecoming in Northeast Africa*. Trenton, N.J.: Africa World Press, 1996.

Appadurai, Arjun. *Modernity at Large: Cultural Dimensions of Globalization*. Minneapolis: University of Minnesota Press, 2003 [1996].

Black, Richard, and Khalid Koser, eds. *The End of the Refugee Cycle? Refugee Repatriation and Reconstruction*. New York and Oxford: Berghahn Books, 1999.

Clapham, Christopher. *Transition and Continuity in Revolutionary Ethiopia*. Cambridge: Cambridge University Press, 1988.
Clifford, James. *Routes: Travel and Translation in the Late Twentieth Century*. Cambridge, Mass.: Harvard University Press, 1997.
Hammond, Laura. *This Place Will Become Home: Refugee Repatriation to Ethiopia*. Ithaca: Cornell University Press, Forthcoming 2004.
———. "How Will the Children Come Home? Emplacement and the Creation of the Social Body in an Ethiopian Returnee Settlement." Pp. 77–96 in *Children's Places: Cross-Cultural Perspectives*, edited by Karen Fog Olwig and Eva Gulløv. London: Routledge, 2003.
———. "Examining the Discourse of Repatriation: Towards a More Proactive Theory of Return Migration." Pp 227–246 in *The End of the Refugee Cycle: Refugee Repatriation and Reconstruction*, edited by Richard Black and Khalid Koser. Oxford: Berghahn Books, 1999.
Hendrie, Barbara. "Assisting Refugees in the Context of Warfare: Some Issues Arising from the Tigrayan Refugee Repatriation: Sudan to Ethiopia 1985–1987." Pp. 35–43 in *In Search of Cool Ground: War, Flight and Homecoming in Northeast Africa*, edited by Tim Allen. Trenton, N.J.: Africa World Press, 1996.
Kibreab, Gaim. "Revisiting the Debate on People, Place, Identity and Displacement." *Journal of Refugee Studies* 12, no. 4 (1999): 384–410.
Leslau, Wolf. *Concise Amharic Dictionary*. Berkeley: University of California Press, 1976.
Malkki, Liisa. "Refugees and Exile: From 'Refugee Studies' to the National Order of Things." *Annual Review of Anthropology* 24 (1995): 495–523.
———. "National Geographic: The Rooting of Peoples and the Territorialization of National Identity Among Scholars and Refugees." *Cultural Anthropology: Journal of the Society for Cultural Anthropology* 7, no. 1 (1992): 24–39.
McCann, James. "A Dura Revolution and Frontier Agriculture in Northwest Ethiopia, 1898–1920." *Journal of African History* 31 (1990): 121–34.
Ogata, Sadako. Statement to the Inter-Governmental Consultations on Asylum, Refugee and Migration Policies in Europe, North America and Australia (IGC), Washington, 6 May 1997.
Ong, Aihwa. *Flexible Citizenship: The Cultural Logics of Transnationality*. Durham, NC: Duke University Press, 1999.
Oxford English Dictionary. Oxford: Oxford University Press, 2003.
Stefansson, Anders. *Under My Own Sky? The Cultural Dynamics of Refugee Return and (Re)Integration in Post-War Sarajevo*. Ph.D. Diss., Institute of Anthropology, Copenhagen: University of Copenhagen, 2003.
Warner, Daniel. "Voluntary Repatriation and the Meaning of Return to Home: A Critique of Liberal Mathematics." *Journal of Refugee Studies* 7, no. 2/3 (1994): 160–74.

4

Sarajevo Suffering: Homecoming and the Hierarchy of Homeland Hardship

Anders H. Stefansson

> There was a popular joke at that time: If the siege [of Sarajevo] was to be lifted, everyone from the town would try to leave, and all the ones who fled would try to come back. When they met halfway, the people leaving and the people coming back would comment about each other: "Look at the idiot!"
>
> —Ivana Macek (2000: 111)

Ironically, while I was leaving home to carry out research on refugee return in Sarajevo, my Bosnian-born wife, Radana, who was accompanying me during fieldwork, was going home for the first time to the place where she lived prior to war and flight. Yet having stayed as a refugee in Denmark for seven years, she was afraid to return to the country that she for long had wished never to see again, and she insisted that her journey back was not really a "homecoming." First of all, Radana considered her homeland to be the *former* Yugoslavia—a country that was now a thing of the past—not the three radicalized "ethnic enclaves" making up the postwar state of Bosnia and Herzegovina (hereinafter Bosnia). Moreover, she feared that the people who had stayed behind in Bosnia would have changed beyond recognition during the years of violence and social decay.

In fact, during our stay in Sarajevo, Radana found, much to her surprise, that the cultural mentality of most ordinary Bosnians had not changed as radically as the political and social structures of the country. Nevertheless, she gradually realized that the significant structural transformations in the Bosnian society and the changes in her own situation made it very difficult for her to link up with remaining relatives and friends. As the initial joy of reunion subsided, she started to feel that the stayees, even those with whom she had once been so close, were envious of her economic security and foreign citizenship, and perceived her to be morally obliged to assist them financially in return for their homeland suffering. While the stayees complained endlessly of the hardships of life in Bosnia, Radana thought that they seemed unable to understand and uninterested in hearing about the legal, social, and psychological difficulties of refugee life in the West, clearly perceiving conditions in those countries as a "bed of roses." For example, at one point one of Radana's relatives stated that many refugees had returned to the area from Germany, with big cars and lots of money, which led her to conclude that "for many Bosnians the war has been of benefit." In the long run, such hurtful comments, different discourses of suffering, and other tensions caused by prolonged absence and unequal socioeconomic conditions of life made social interaction with her stayee relatives and friends too stressful for Radana. She therefore decided to keep contact with them at an absolute minimum for the remaining part of our stay in Bosnia.

While Radana could at least return to her new home in Denmark without being bothered too much in her everyday life by the changing nature of social relationships with the stayee population, for many refugees who had returned to stay in Bosnia this issue had much more immediate, practical consequences for their efforts to reintegrate into the homeland society. This chapter argues that although the challenges of homecoming in postwar Sarajevo were multiple and serious, such as internal displacement, bureaucratic obstacles, and strained living conditions, for repatriating refugees one of the most crucial and disillusioning aspects of return concerned the experience of being met by the local stayee population with envy, lack of empathy, resentment, and discrimination. The burgeoning academic literature on repatriation and return migration often hints at the importance of returnee-stayee social relations and collective cultural imaginations, but systematic, in-depth analyses of these issues have as yet been scant.[1] In an attempt to start filling this void, the first parts of the chapter explore the ways in which differing discourses of suffering, material interests, and transformations of identity caused conflict and social distance between returnees and stayees in Sarajevo, especially in the first years following mass repatriation. In contrast, the chapter's last section provides an account of those emerging strategies that, to some extent, bridged the social divide between stayees and returnees and paved the way for returnees' social reintegration.

The analysis presented in this chapter is based upon ethnographic fieldwork carried out in Sarajevo, the capital of Bosnia, in 1999 and 2001. Main informants during research in Sarajevo were repatriates who had returned from a variety of host countries in the West as well as from other parts of the former Yugoslavia, and who represented different ethnonational groups, geographical origins, and social class backgrounds. I also interacted with stayees, internally displaced persons (IDPs),[2] and visiting, "transnational" refugees.

My fieldwork conversations with returnee informants invariably touched on highly emotional aspects of their lives during the dramatic decade of the 1990s—that is, disintegration of the former Yugoslavia, war, flight, and exile, as well as the hardships of homecoming to troubled "postconflict" Bosnia. Unexpectedly, however, the issue of the returnees' relationships with those who had stayed behind in Sarajevo during the war years often produced the strongest outbursts of frustration and anger, not their memories of violence or the stigma of refugee life. For example, Alma, a forty-five-year-old woman who had repatriated from Germany, started to cry when she told me about the humiliating and discriminatory treatment she had received from her compatriots upon return, in stark contrast to how well she had been treated in her host country, by unknown people belonging to a different nation. While certainly not all Bosnian repatriates nurtured as rosy memories of exile life as Alma did, this chapter shows that her complaints about the inhospitable reception from those who had stayed behind were widely shared among returnee informants.

REALIZING RETURN

Exile has been characterized infamously as "the unhealable rift forced between a human being and a native place" (Said 1992: 357), a condition of displacement permeated by nostalgia, social marginalization, and cultural estrangement. In such circumstances of loss and longing, the promise of a homecoming to a distanced and idealized homeland often becomes a central part of the political agenda and cultural identity of diasporic people(s) (Bisharat 1997; Malkki 1995; Safran 1991; Zetter 1994; see also Anteby-Yemini; Markowitz; Pattie, this volume). Ironically, such strongly articulated claims of attachment to territorial homelands among ethnic minority groups are easily conflated with essentialized notions of belonging and identity popular among, for example, xenophobic sections of host country populations and within contemporary political repatriation discourse (Chimni 1999; Hammond 1999; Koser and Black 1999; Warner 1994). Academic analyses of refugee repatriation and return migration suggest, however, that when diasporic dreaming of home(land) and return is replaced with the practice of homecoming, the sad result in many cases is a shattering of illusions or "reverse culture shock" (Graham and Khosravi 1997: 126), a new incarnation of social marginalization at "home" and a myriad of practical and psychological problems of (re)integration (Allen 1996; Allen and Morsink 1994; Black and Koser 1999; Gmelch 1995; King 2000; Long and Oxfeld 2004). Returnees painfully discover that in their period of absence the homeland communities and their own identities have undergone transformation, and these ruptures and changes have serious implications for their ability to reclaim a sense of home upon homecoming.

The refugees who returned to Bosnia after the signing of the Dayton Peace Agreement in late 1995 certainly faced their share of homecoming hardships. The war in Bosnia, which was intimately tied to the broader process of the political disintegration of Yugoslavia, lasted more than three years and left the country politically and ethnically divided, materially destroyed and impoverished, and demographically and socioculturally transformed. As the violence primarily targeted civilians—usually those regarded as belonging to demonized ethnonational minorities in different parts of the country—more than half of the country's inhabitants fled their homes in the course of war. Approximately one million people were displaced within Bosnia, while 1.3 million sought refuge abroad. The homes of displaced people that were not destroyed, frequently as a result of systematic dynamiting or setting fire to property belonging to ethnic minorities (de Andrade and Delaney 2001: 324), were often occupied by groups of IDPs from other parts of the country. In Sarajevo the exodus of an estimated 240,000 prewar inhabitants of different ethnonational orientation was parallelled by the arrival of some 100,000 to 150,000 displaced Bosniacs (Bosnian Muslims), thereby dramatically altering both the overall population figure and the ethnic structure of the population (International Crisis Group 1998a, 1998b).[3]

Even though a central aim of the Dayton Peace Agreement was to reverse the effects of ethnic cleansing by stressing displaced people's "right freely to return to their homes of origin" (General Framework Agreement for Peace in Bosnia and Herzegovina 1995: Annex 7, chap. 1, art. I.1), the continued dominance and obstructionism of nationalist regimes in combination with serious socioeconomic problems have kept return of ethnic minorities at a minimum. The majority of Bosnian refugees who have received permanent residence rights, and sometimes citizenship, in host countries have therefore decided so far not to return permanently, even though mainly summer visits to the homeland are frequent.[4] An estimated 255,000 refugees returned from Germany, which practiced a form of involuntary repatriation (U.S. Committee for Refugees 2001), while much more limited return has taken place from host countries where the principle of voluntary repatriation has applied. A large part of the repatriates have been unable, or unwilling, to return to their places of origin and have thus relocated to new parts of the country where they belong to the local ethnic majority group. For example, many Bosniac repatriates originating from places now controlled by Bosnian Serbs and Bosnian Croats have settled in Sarajevo. But also repatriates who before the war lived in Sarajevo faced continued displacement and homelessness upon return, as they found their homes destroyed or inhabited. These difficulties of return were further strained by widespread unemployment, low salaries for those who managed to get jobs, and experiences of discrimination and resentment from the stayee population.

While research shows that some returnees are able to benefit from the economic, social, and symbolic capital that they bring back home (e.g., Gmelch 2004; Kibreab 2002), far more frequently social distance between returnees and stayees arises due to different codes of social behavior and cultural values that have developed in the course of absence (e.g., Habib 1996; Saloutos 1956; Wyman 1993). For instance, Leila Habib, a female academic who returned to Lebanon from France, writes about her own experiences:

> Those who had remained saw me as an outsider. The "Parisian," as they called me, had not shared their lives and, they thought, had not suffered like them, if at all.... The transformative powers of war and exile had split the people along additional "demarcation lines," there now was the culture of the war and the culture of exile, and they did not recognize each other. (1996: 101)

Similarly, in his 2002 novel, *Ignorance*, the exiled Czech writer Milan Kundera shows two emigrants visiting the post-Communist Czech Republic after twenty years in the West. Repeating the lesson learned long ago by the legendary Odysseus, the returning Czech exiles come to feel like strangers among their relatives and friends, who display a complete lack of interest in or ability to understand the returnees' experiences of life abroad. Kundera shows that both exiles and stayees are so obsessed with having their hardships recognized *by* the "Other" that they fail to attend to the suffering *of* the "Other."

As I shall explore in what follows, conflicting discourses of moral behavior and suffering (Eastmond 2001) and different cultural identities often led to antagonism and social distance in the relationship between returnees and stayees in Sarajevo.

FIGHT OR FLIGHT

Due to the nature of war-related displacement in Bosnia, the stayee population hardly perceived the Bosnians who returned after the end of conflict as heroic figures. In Sarajevo repatriates were at best regarded as innocent victims who had been violently expelled from their homes, and at worst as traitors who had voluntarily fled instead of engaging in the defence of Sarajevo and its "Sarajevanness," the urban, "cosmopolitan" values and ways of life there (Cattaruzza 2001; Macek 2000: 145; Stefansson 2003: 246–69). Thus a common term for refugees was *pobjeglice*, meaning those who ran away scared for no reason, implying cowardice. *Pobjeglice* was a recent linguistic invention that played on the regular term for refugees, *izbjeglice*. The message here, of course, was that a decision to stay in besieged Sarajevo was courageous and patriotic, but a decision to flee was tantamount to succumbing to one's fears and individual needs while shirking off the demands of solidarity with one's fellow Sarajevans.

Resentment against those who left Sarajevo was also expressed in public culture. For example, several popular wartime songs contained heavily antireturnee lyrics. One, performed by the well-known pop group Merlin, was titled "Where Were You When It Was Worst of All?"

> Some day when everything has become yesterday
> When the day dawns
> Then you will no longer be tormented
> And feel pain because you were not here
> When it was worst of all.
>
> (in Kusterer and Dugalic 1998: 57,
> my translation from Danish)

Another hit song carried the moralizing title "Ostajte Ovdje" (Remain Here) (Macek 2000: 172). After the end of the war accusations of betrayal continued to flourish in the public domain. For example, some local Sarajevans went around wearing T-shirts with the slogan, "I was here from 1992–95— where were you?" Whereas the official attitude of the Bosnian government was that all refugees were welcome to return in order to assist in the postconflict reconstruction of the war-devastated country, in practice authorities and employers privileged IDPs, demobilized soldiers, and relatives of people who had been killed during the war when it came to housing and jobs.

Many returnees challenged the stayees' patriotic discourse and accusations of betrayal and cowardice. Repatriates originating from Sarajevo stressed that their leaving the city and the country was a political and moral act that supported their antinationalist, multiethnic position and demonstrated their refusal to take part in the primitiveness and brutality of war:

> I get really mad at those people who say that they stayed here in order to defend the country. Everybody says that they wanted to defend the country, but I think that the only thing they defended was their own existence. Your own friends were shooting at you, how is it possible to understand that? Where is the idea about the defence of the country? It is simply stupidity. (Ismet, repatriate from Norway)

Returnees also pointed out that many of them had been exposed to more or less prolonged stays in war zones, and that expulsion or flight involved physical, economic, and psychological risks and hardships, since they had to cross enemy territory and leave behind property and jobs in exchange for an uncertain destiny as refugees in foreign countries. In this sense, they described the act of fleeing as an expression of courage and initiative rather than cowardice. Pointing the finger in the other direction, the Sarajevan returnees dismissed the stayees' claims to patriotism and heroism, arguing instead that they had remained due to more pragmatic considerations, like the fear of losing jobs and homes, long-term career opportunities, or obligations toward elderly parents who could not flee.

There was a widespread assumption among repatriates that if people in Sarajevo had realized how long the war would be waged, almost everybody would have left at the start, thus giving credence to the returnees' claim that the stayees remained not because of patriotism but because of their naïveté and conservatism. In this regard, the experience of two of my informants, Rejhana and Senada, who returned to besieged and terrorized Sarajevo in the middle of war after prolonged and dangerous return journeys, are significant. They both remembered how stayees in Sarajevo reacted with disbelief and shock when they heard that they had returned, regarding the returnees as an anomaly: "It was incomprehensible to everybody that a woman with two children would return to the city. [People commented:] 'She ran over the runway [at the Sarajevo airport] to get to the city! Are you crazy?' I reported to my workplace, and they treated me as if I was insane. They didn't want me back in my job," said Rejhana. Senada's daughter wrote a sentimental song after their return, its message being that all refugees should return so that everything would become like before. Her schoolmates, however, ridiculed the song and asked who would be crazy enough to return to the terrible situation in Sarajevo.

These incidents suggest that the issues of betrayal and lack of patriotism during the war were less central than what repatriates usually thought in fostering the "anti-returnee atmosphere" (Macek 2000: 112) that prevailed in Sarajevo, in particular in the first postwar years. It was my impression that many returnees—understandably sensitive in relation to the moral aspects of flight—often reacted more to an imagined sense of stayee accusations than to actual social practices. At least in my presence stayee informants generally voiced great understanding of the decision to flee and often said that they regretted having stayed behind.[5] According to Macek (2000), during the war national models of explanation gradually lost their power of rationale among Sarajevo's population. As political cynicism set in, Sarajevans, she claims, became increasingly inclined to accept efforts to desert the army and flee the besieged city as their minds, to varying degrees, were occupied by thoughts of flight. What came to matter most to Sarajevo's stayees was where people found refuge and how they behaved during exile.

The patriotic discourse was in fact adopted to some extent by returnees themselves as a strategy to legitimize their own flight vis-a-vis other categories of refugees. Thus in some cases returnee informants who originally came from ethnically cleansed areas questioned the motives for flight of refugees from Sarajevo. Returning refugees from Sarajevo occasionally provided a moral defense for their flight by <u>emphasizing that they spent part of the war in Sarajevo before fleeing the country</u>: *social pressure* / *public*

> I believe the fact that we spent a large part of the war here in Sarajevo makes our action [flight to Israel in 1994] more <u>acceptable</u>. We knew that we had a duty toward our children [who early on in the war went to Israel], and our patriotism had been reduced by this time. We think that on both issues we have acted responsibly, toward our children and toward society. (Samra, repatriate from Israel)

The implications of this buying into, and construction of, the moralizing "stayee" discourse among sections of repatriates are discussed in more detail toward the end of this chapter.

THE MONOPOLY OF SUFFERING

Cross-cultural research indicates that stayees may envy and nurture exaggerated images of the living conditions and the "easy" life that the returnees are supposed to have enjoyed abroad (Gmelch 1980: 143; Margold 2004). Conflicts between returnees and stayees may also arise from disagreements over access to property, land rights, and jobs (Kibreab 2002: 54; Oxfeld and Long 2004). Indeed, resentment of Bosnian returnees in Sarajevo was more important than the moral question of the betrayal of flight caused by perceptions of economic inequality, clashes of material interests, and different levels of suffering in the period of separation.

Stayees in Sarajevo stressed the great physical and material hardships they suffered during the war, such as shelling, sniper fire, and shortages of food, water, gas, and electricity (cf. Macek 2000). Sarajevo was thus widely known during 1992 through 1995 as the most dangerous city on earth, exposed to the longest siege in modern history. In contrast, refugees were seen as having lived in the safe and materially privileged conditions of the West. From the stayees' point of view, they were now returning with new cars, furniture, all kinds of consumer goods, and impressive financial savings. Returnees were also economically privileged, the stayees felt, having received generous repatriation grants and reconstruction assistance from Western host country governments and international organizations.[6] These economic resources, stayees thought, allowed returnees to build impressive houses or to reconstruct existing ones to a much higher standard than before the war, as well as to start private companies, shops, restaurants, cafés, etc. And now, with all that wealth, they unfairly evicted impoverished stayees from apartments and jobs.[7]

It is difficult to overstate the importance of this perception of material differences in creating animosity against the repatriates. In postwar Bosnia, plagued by the problems of physical destruction, poverty, skyrocketing unemployment, and large numbers of IDPs, the mass repatriation of refugees represented a serious threat to the livelihoods of the stayee population. The Bosniac IDPs in Sarajevo, in particular, faced a sinister combination of homelessness and unemployment when the repatriates succeeded in reclaiming their properties and jobs. Because of these differing material interests IDPs were often those who nurtured the most antagonistic attitudes toward the return of the refugees. They often refused to leave the homes that they had made in apartments earlier abandoned by refugees and did not allow returnees to visit these homes.

According to one returnee informant, the perception of an uneven level of hardship during and after the war made the stayees regard themselves as "little gods" who had a "monopoly of suffering" that allowed them to hold forth with moralizing "preachings" or "lecturings" on the sufferings of war. The returnees, by contrast, were silenced or not believed if they claimed to have suffered during exile. In particular, stayees tended to brush aside returnees' stories of the psychological or emotional hardships of refugee life as irrelevant in comparison with their own physical privations. In line with Kundera's diagnosis of the difficulties of accepting other people's sufferings after prolonged separation, Nadja, a returnee from Germany, needed to light a cigarette before she, on the verge of tears, was capable of explaining that "nobody seems to care about my experiences in Germany; [the stayees] merely want sunshine stories about the beauty of life as refugees."

The returnees, at least in the intimacy of conversation with me, challenged the stayees' monopoly of suffering by, for example, countering the myth of the romantic life abroad. Instead, they emphasized their experiences of being placed in collective refugee centers for extended periods of time, social stigma and dependence, cultural isolation, and the psychological difficulties of separation from the homeland and relatives left behind. Moreover, returnees stressed the hardships they suffered in order to assist relatives and friends economically in Bosnia throughout and after the war. By claiming that they had not neglected the ethos of assisting kinsmen and compatriots in dire trouble, returnees countered the idea that refugees had lost their moral bearings and patriotic zeal abroad.

Returnees also described the various practical, economic, and bureaucratic difficulties they faced upon return, e.g., homelessness, unemployment, forced payment of illegal fees or "war taxes," and other discriminatory practices. Because of the deliberately slow-going process of reclaiming prewar property, most of the repatriate informants whom I met during fieldwork in Sarajevo in 1999 and again in 2001 had not been able to return to their homes of origin or at least had had to wait several years before doing so. Thus many Sarajevan repatriates whose homes were destroyed or occupied by Bosniac IDPs found themselves in the peculiar situation of being displaced themselves when returning to their own city. They lived in alternative accommodations while filing all the necessary documents and waiting to repossess or reconstruct their homes. When repatriates did manage to repossess their prewar homes they often discovered that the temporary occupants or other intruders had damaged and looted their homes. Ismet described with disgust the behavior of the IDP family living in his apartment, which they only left three years after Ismet's return from Norway: "What can I say? They took the toilet with them! In the kitchen everything, only the plug hole was left. Imagine people who have been eating with your spoon and sleeping in your bed behaving like that. They should be grateful." In this way, the returnees claimed, it was actually the stayees who had profited from the war, for which reason it was they who had become structurally advantaged and morally suspect. Zilka, a stayee whose two sons were living abroad, expressed this sentiment:

> People who have stayed behind say that those who return come back loaded with money, they haven't fought, and they're buying cafés and working premises all around, opening restaurants and living a good life. But you forget that some of those who have stayed behind have stolen so much that even their grandchildren's children have been secured!

Thus, faced with the stayee dismissal of returnees' stories about the hardships of refugee life as nothing more than *izbjeglicka prica*, refugee adventures, returnees retorted by depicting stayees' claims to wartime suffering as *ostalacka prica*, stayee adventures.[8]

RETURNEE IDENTITY IN THE MAKING

Apart from conflicting discourses of suffering and material interests, social distance between returnees and stayees can arise from different experiences and the development of different cultural identities in the course of absence (Gmelch 1995; Habib 1996; Winland 2002; Huseby-Darvas, this volume). Returnees carry with them new ideas and customs from their host countries, and sometimes dress and speak in ways that make them stand out in the home community (Saloutos 1956; Useem and Useem 1955; Wyman 1993). Stayees therefore often blame returnees for arrogant behavior (King 2000), or "putting on airs" (Wyman 1993: 195), and apply stigmatizing collective labels to them. For example, migrants returning from the U.S. to Europe in the late nineteenth and early twentieth centuries "discovered that, whereas in America they had been regarded as Poles (or Italians, or Magyars, or Irish), back home they were considered Americans" (Wyman 1993: 197).[9]

This characterization very much applies to the Bosnian case. Both returnees and stayees believed that the "Other" had changed their ways, usually for the worse, while they themselves had developed in a positive direction. While stayees generally saw themselves as morally superior because of their wartime suffering, they accused returnees of having adopted "Western" cultural values, like individualism and materialism, and of having lost their sense of kinship obligations. Stayees claimed as well that returnees stood out in public life because of their rather "non-Bosnian" ways of dressing, behaving, and speaking. Children seemed to be particular targets for such accusations, due to their sometimes limited knowledge of their mother tongue and homeland culture.[10] Refugees were frequently called *svabe*, literally, "people from Schwaben" (i.e., Germany), or *amerikanci*, Americans, who returned, permanently or on holiday, to show off their newly acquired Western wealth and habits.[11]

Returnees retorted to such criticism and "Othering" by describing stayees as negatively affected by their experiences of war, brutality, and social degradation, which tended to make them fatalistic, nationalistic, cold, primitive, greedy, and crazy. In contrast, returnees thought of themselves as having been positively influenced by their experiences of the social structures, cultural values, life-styles, gender roles, and education systems in the Western host countries:

> We have all changed. People who stayed behind used to say that they have become a little bit crazy, and we who went away have had other experiences. I believe we have become developed, in all ways, with respect to education, behavior and culture. We have seen that it's possible to live better and more beautifully. In this way, we have become like minus and plus. Many [stayees] in our neighborhood think that our children are too free, they put on too little clothing, listen to too loud music, we're crazy because we have a dog in the house, that's typically German, they say. To be honest I'm also tired of all their war stories. It was their own choice to stay here. I went away and thank God for that! All this make us very different. (Alma, repatriate from Germany)

Alma said that in Germany she had decided to bring up her children in a liberal fashion that did not fit well with what she described as the "authoritarian" mentality in Bosnia. Her attitude toward gender roles had also changed in a more egalitarian direction while being in Germany (cf. Al-Ali 2002). The stayees, however, had "returned to live by their instincts" and "react in brutish ways," she argued. Returnees were also influenced, for example, by Western ways of organizing the home and everyday lives. Because of their experiences in the West, the returnees often looked on the Bosnian society with new and more critical eyes than before and claimed to be less inclined to accept as givens the circumstances of life in Bosnia than those who stayed behind.

However, because of their structurally inferior moral and political position in Bosnia, returnees were careful about articulating criticism against stayees, and usually did so only when the latter were well out of sight. In order to avoid creating resentment, in general returnees adopted a "strategy of invisibility," trying to keep a low profile both as private persons and as a group. A young woman who had returned from the U.S. told me that initially on returning she talked openly about her former refugee status, but later she learned to keep silent about this aspect of her life in order not to create difficulties for herself. Ismet, who repatriated from Norway, explained what happened to his son when his classmates in high school discovered that he was a returnee:

> My son didn't immediately say in school that he had been a refugee. We told him that he shouldn't say it to other people. He was popular among his schoolmates. Then one day his teacher asked him where he had been during the war. And his "friends" were disappointed [and said]: "Aha, you have been listening to CDs and had all the best, enjoyed life abroad." The human psychology is strange: people love a person, but then they ask why he hasn't suffered with them.

Another sign of returnees' wish for invisibility was that despite their high numbers returnees did not have any official meeting places in Sarajevo, such as separate clubs, associations or institutions, unlike what has been reported in other returnee contexts (e.g., Byron 1999: 299; Eastmond 2001; Olwig 2001; Wyman 1993: 197). Repatriates were also surprisingly absent in the local media, although this might not have been a "choice" of their own, in stark contrast to the immense attention paid to the politicized question of minority return *within* Bosnia in the media.[12]

In a less formal sense, though, returnee communities were in fact emerging. Faced with antagonism and social exclusion, many returnees preferred to socialize privately with other returnees with whom they could exchange memories of life in exile and discuss common problems of (re)integration in Bosnia. According to Alma, a repatriate from Germany, because of the differences between returnees and stayees, the two groups had "few common themes to talk about," and it was thus better "to stay in your own world." Jasminka, having returned from Norway, explained that although she got on rather well with most of her prewar stayee friends, she felt closer to Bosnians with whom she shared the refugee experience:

> I have friends in Sarajevo whom I have known for twenty to thirty years, but it's something different with my friends from Norway, friends from the refugee life. We shared the same destiny up there. We had the same thoughts and worries: that our relatives [in Bosnia] should survive, that they should not become disabled. And that was the kind of thoughts that have tied us together, so much so that we still know each other, like a family.

Thus the combination of specific exile experiences and social antagonism from the stayee population upon return laid the ground for the development of feelings of solidarity and community with fellow repatriates in Sarajevo, and hence for a "returnee identity" in the making (Cornish et al. 1999: 275; see also Hirschon 1998; Skinner 1993: 30–31; Tsuda 2003, this volume), at least in the private social circles of some groups of repatriates.

NEGOTIATING HOMECOMING

The gap between returnees and stayees presented above, however, was not absolute, stable, or impossible to bridge. Without exactly providing a happy end to this chapter, in this section I discuss returnee-stayee relations as contested, contextually changing, and parts of broader negotiations of identity in postwar Sarajevo.

Competing discourses of suffering created extremely powerful cultural stereotypes that could, but did not necessarily, affect actual relations between returnees and stayees in everyday life in Sarajevo. Clearly, love and affection between relatives and close friends did not always die out during the period of separation, and many people across the barrier of separation found themselves rather happily reunited, although frequently with the character of interaction transformed and redefined. Neither repatriates nor stayees were homogeneous communities but contained their own internal rifts and conflicts, and not everyone accepted the dominant narratives on returnee-stayee moral behavior and wartime suffering. Instead some created social networks on the basis of other shared personal and social characteristics, such as level of education, geographical origin, economic resources, age, gender, political attitudes, religion, and cultural traditions.

Returnee informants also disagreed about the scale and significance of stayee resentment. While many perceived it as an extremely serious and sensitive issue, others interpreted the stayees' stories of suffering as nothing but understandable expressions of frustration that were not so difficult to bear:

> But it's only minor provocations [from stayees]. The discrimination isn't so serious that they say, "Get away, you didn't stay here." In those three years [after her return in 1998] people have after all understood that somebody needs to do specialised work and that it's less important whether or not you've stayed here. (Nadja, repatriate from Germany)

Nadja's statement indicates that returnee–stayee relations evolved and to some degree "normalized" over time. Thus many informants strongly articulated their disappointment with their reception by stayees during my first part of fieldwork in 1999, while in 2001, when the second part of my fieldwork took place, they expressed much less radical opinions on the matter. During fieldwork in 2001, Mihajlo, a stayee informant, quite frankly admitted that, in his capacity of being a high-ranking employee in an international organization, he had had the power, and desire, to discriminate against returnees with respect to access to the labor market. But then he noted that in the years after the war the situation gradually changed: "I used to be one of the discriminators. Today nobody thinks about who has been here and who has been abroad. We just hire the best candidate [for the job]." After 2001 returnee-stayee relations are likely to have further improved, or at least have receded in importance due to other challenges of postconflict reconstruction.

One common strategy of creating social (re)integration was for returnees to display a submissive attitude toward those who stayed behind throughout their exile and upon return by showing solidarity and agreement with, as well as modesty and generosity toward, stayees. Several informants stressed that during stays abroad they stayed in touch with and economically assisted as much as possible the relatives and friends they had left behind, partly as a deliberate postwar return strategy. Asked how she was received by stayee friends, Jasminka, who had repatriated from Norway, replied:

> Fine, but I have also stayed in contact with them all of the time. When the telephones started to work again, I called everyone. I sent them as much as I could afford to. I didn't live just for myself abroad, I also lived for the others down here. I wanted to help my country, also the [Government] army. Maybe that's the reason why I wasn't rejected [upon return].

Upon return many repatriates continued their humble behavior toward the stayees, at least in the presence of the latter, by acknowledging "the experiential gap" (Søfting 2002: 156) in terms of war experience; listening approvingly to stayee stories of suffering, danger, and heroic acts; desisting from criticizing conditions in Bosnia (leaving it to stayees to do so); and keeping silent about those aspects of refugee life that did not fit in well with the dominant stayee narrative of the West as a land of "milk and honey." An alternative way of avoiding tension between returnees and stayees was to stay clear of discussing the topic of moral behavior during the war. This "taboo" on sensitive political and moral issues also existed in interethnic relations and can be regarded as local people's strategy of recreating peaceful coexistence between different groups.

Returnees also strived for social acceptance by showing generosity toward stayees, for example by assisting stayees economically or, more symbolically, buying rounds of coffee or *rakija* (brandy) to stayee friends. Partly helped by financial resources brought with them, returnees from the West were a major group of contractors in Bosnia, and in this capacity had the opportunity to employ stayee workers. While these economic resources, as we have seen, on the one hand fueled stayee feelings of envy and images of luxury lives led by refugees abroad, on the other hand they could translate into an increase in social status and influence in local communities upon return. A returnee schoolgirl from Germany told me that "poor" people—in this case meaning those who had stayed behind in troubled Bosnia—liked to stick around with "rich" people (the returnees from Western countries). At least in some contexts, she believed, it could be socially advantageous to be a returnee.[13]

Another way to pay "the price of admission" (Søfting 2002: 152) into Sarajevo involved distancing oneself from other categories of refugees and returnees with less moral and cultural capital than one's own group, thus appropriating the hegemonic stayee discourse of suffering. With the purpose of negotiating a place for themselves back home, repatriates sometimes voiced criticism of refugees who continued to stay abroad, citing their strange ways and arrogance and their ignorance of conditions in Bosnia. Refugees who left late in the war in some cases considered themselves morally superior to those who had not experienced the war at all. Well-educated elite or middle-class returnees frequently ostracized low-class refugees for "performing" exile life and return like the stereotypes of stigmatized guestworkers. Repatriates from neighboring countries, primarily Croatia and the Federal Republic of Yugoslavia (today's Serbia and Montenegro), saw themselves as having remained within their "own" sociocultural sphere, and they often shared the stayee "monopoly of suffering" and envied those who had left for the West.

Perhaps the most valuable cultural capital of the part of returnees who lived in Sarajevo prior to the war in terms of mitigating antagonism from the stayee population was their "Sarajevanness." Local stayees often stated that only the return of the native, urban refugees could reverse the cultural deterioration of Sarajevo, which from this perspective had been transformed from a refined, "European" city into a provincial backwater, or "one big village," due to the "invasion" of rural, "primitive" newcomers from other parts of the country during and after the war.[14] Using this strongly articulated cultural dichotomy between natives and newcomers and between urban and rural people strategically to gain acceptance from the stayee population, repatriates originating from Sarajevo disassociated themselves quite decidedly from what they perceived as the less urban and cosmopolitan new inhabitants of Sarajevo. As many of those people who now lived as displaced persons in Sarajevo were repatriates who were unable or unwilling to return to their local places of origin, the cultural stereotyping of newcomers obviously placed this group of returnees in a doubly marginal position in their new domicile, despised both as morally inferior returnees and as culturally backward newcomers.[15] Such tensions between different subgroups of repatriates also explain why feelings of exclusion and difference did not channel into the development of an encompassing, homogeneous returnee community and (counter)identity.

CONCLUSION

In this chapter I have argued that returnee–stayee social relations constitute a central and multifacetted element in the experience of homecoming. The sociocultural cleavage between returnees and stayees in Sarajevo not only affected public discourses or impersonal relations, it also on many occasions increased social distance between relatives, friends, neighbors, and colleagues, sometimes putting an end to social interaction altogether. For many returnees, the hostile reception of the stayee population was experienced as one of the most disenchanting aspects, if not *the* most disenchanting, of their contested homecoming. Exactly because many returnees during exile longed for, and often motivated their return in terms of their desire to be reunited with, the homeland community, the experience of being treated like *pobjeglice*, unpatriotic cowards, and *svabe*, economically affluent and culturally alien "Germans," was immensely disappointing. Whereas returnees had to some extent expected the severe material and economic conditions in postwar Bosnia, which were, moreover, affecting the Bosnian population in general, they were less prepared for the severity of stayee antagonism.

Thus, in contrast to popular thinking among repatriation advocates and circles within refugee diasporas, homecoming is not merely the physical journey back to the familiar sociocultural habitat of the homeland, "the end of the refugee cycle" (Black and Koser 1999). At the same time the chapter has explored the dynamic, negotiated nature of homecoming that over time may rebuild social trust between returnees and stayees and in this way lead to a (partial) integration of the returnees into the homeland community. The majority of studies of return migration are geared toward the "problems of return" (Chimni 2000: 13), and it is generally neglected, or at least not considered as academically interesting, that "[i]n reality the migrants' return is often accompanied by considerable ambivalence" (King 2000: 19). In returnees' complex and ambigious meeting with a "new/old place" (Casey 1993: 294) aspects of rupture and alienation are parallelled by the comforts of homecoming and continuous attachment, albeit obviously to varying degrees in different settings and for different individuals (see also Constable 1999; Stefansson 2003, 2004; Uehling 2002).

Return is a prolonged and strenuous process of what has been termed *desexilio* (Benedetti 1985 cited in Myrvold 1992: 1), homemaking

(Hammond 2004, this volume) or postreturn (re)integration (Stefansson 2003). In what are as a rule fragile, scarce, and competitive postconflict settings, both returnees and stayees require time to come to terms with the presence of each other and with the fact that the very visible transformation of identity among the "Other" mirrors more unnoticed changes in one's own group. It is important to bear in mind, for national politicians as well as for international organizations, that in postconflict societies reconciliation is not only a matter of appeasing what are considered to be the "warring sides." Reconciliation also involves bridging other social barriers caused or intensified by warfare, flight, and, not to forget, homecoming.

NOTES

Research for this chapter is based on a Ph.D. grant from the Danish Research Council for the Humanities, for which I am grateful. I would also like to thank Fran Markowitz and Karen F. Olwig for helpful comments on various versions of the chapter, and my wife Radana for multilevel support throughout the entire research phase.

1. Notable exceptions within studies of refugee repatriation and return migration are Kibreab 2002; Long and Oxfeld 2004. In the broader fields of ancestral return migration and transnationalism the issue has been treated in some detail by, among others, Hirschon 1998; Levitt 2001; Tsuda 2001, 2003. See also other chapters in this volume, in particular those by Anteby-Yemini, Huseby-Darvas, Holsey, Levy, and Tsuda.

2. In this chapter IDPs are, unless otherwise specified, incorporated into the category of stayees, but it is important to keep in mind that, like refugees, IDPs have experienced flight, although not across internationally recognized borders.

3. During the war, Sarajevo was divided into areas controlled by the (Bosniac-dominated) government army and the Bosnian Serb army respectively. As part of the 1995 Dayton Peace Agreement, the city was reintegrated, except for some neighborhoods and surrounding villages that became part of Srpsko Sarajevo (Serb Sarajevo) within Republika Srpska (the Serb Republic).

4. By October 2003 an estimated 438,000 refugees had repatriated to Bosnia, and 430,000 ethnic minorities had returned to their homes of origin (UNHCR 2003). Before 2000 ethnic minority returns were negligible. It needs to be remembered that refugee statistics are often less than accurate (Crisp 1999). See International Crisis Group (1999: 68–9) for a discussion of the (un)reliability of official figures for returnees in Bosnia.

5. Undoubtedly, stayee expressions of sympathy toward refugees were to some extent due to informants' awareness that my own Yugoslav/Bosnian-born wife was living as a refugee in Denmark.

6. For this reason, it has been argued that in postconflict situations international assistance should be allocated to the communities of return rather than just to

repatriating refugees, so as not to create tension between the local population and the returnees (Kibreab 2002).

7. Accusations were common against Bosnian Serb refugees in particular for returning merely to reclaim, privatize, and sell their apartments before leaving once again for their new domiciles in Republika Srpska, Serbia, or Western countries, in the process evicting displaced Bosniacs, who often could not return to their own former homes.

8. For a further discussion of the returnees' problems with and strategies for reclaiming property and economic (re)integration see Stefansson 2003.

9. In a similar vein, "return Yanks" is a deprecating term used in Ireland for those emigrants who have returned from the U.S. but continue to behave as if they were still there (Gmelch 1986: 165). Repatriated Turks are mocked for being *Alamanyali*, "Germanlike," and returned Portuguese migrants are known as *brasileiros* or *franceses* (Mandel 1989 and Brettell 1979, 1986 cited in Brettell 2000: 101).

10. On the other hand, children to a much greater extent than adults had the ability to overcome the social distance between returnees and stayees, especially because of their flexibility, lower levels of awareness of political questions, and action-oriented types of social interaction.

11. In many cases both of the terms *svabe* and *amerikanci* were used as "deterritorialized" categorizations of refugees/returnees in general, taking little notice of whether or not people had actually lived in either Germany or North America. *Svabo* (pl. *svabe*) is a word that before the exodus of the Bosnian refugees was used as a derogatory label not only for Germans, but also for the many Yugoslav guestworkers, or *gastarbejteri*, in Germany.

12. Nor did the media pay more than occasional attention to the Bosnian diaspora, even though it still numbered more than a million refugees and emigrants. Although as a result of the mass war-related emigration Bosnia surely has become a "deterritorialized nation-state" (Basch et al. 1994), with many members of the diaspora sending back remittances, reclaiming property, and taking part in elections, there is as yet little formal official recognition of the importance of the large-scale diaspora for political, economic, and cultural developments in the homeland.

13. There were other contexts in which returnee identity could ease social interaction, for example, in terms of relations with people of different ethnic backgrounds. One day I accompanied two of my informants, Jasna and Haris, on a journey to a village in Republika Srpska, where they wanted to visit old Bosnian Serb acquaintances. Themselves being of Bosniac/Croatian origins and living in Sarajevo, when greeting the local Bosnian Serbs, some of whom were IDPs, they immediately stressed that during the war they had lived as refugees in Canada. This was a way to emphasize to the Bosnian Serbs that they had not taken a part in the war, that they were politically "neutral," to the extent that this was possible in Bosnia.

14. The fact that the returnees who returned to their prewar homes in Sarajevo in many cases belonged to the non-Bosniac minorities (most often Serbs) or to nationally "mixed" groups emphasizes the fallacy of arguments that reduce the extraordinary sociocultural complexity and "hybridity" of Bosnia to "the banalities of ethnic essentialism" (Campbell 1998: 56; cf. Bringa 1995; Donia and Fine 1994).

15. For more extensive analyses of the powerful distinctions in the territories of the former Yugoslavia between rural and urban people and between "cultured" and "uncultured" people, consult Bringa 1995; Simic 1983; Stefansson 2003: Chapter 10; van de Port 1998.

REFERENCES

Al-Ali, Nadje. "Gender Relations, Transnational Ties and Rituals among Bosnian Refugees." *Global Networks: A Journal of Transnational Affairs* 2, no. 3 (2002): 249–62.

Allen, Tim, ed. *In Search of Cool Ground: War, Flight, and Homecoming in Northeast Africa.* London: James Currey, 1996.

Allen, Tim, and Hubert Morsink, ed. *When Refugees Go Home: African Experiences.* London: James Currey, 1994.

Basch, Linda, Nina Glick Schiller, and Christina S. Blanc. *Nations Unbound: Transnational Projects, Postcolonial Predicaments and Deterritorialized Nation-States.* New York: Gordon and Breach, 1994.

Bisharat, George E. "Exile to Compatriot: Transformations in the Social Identity of Palestinian Refugees in the West Bank." Pp. 203–33 in *Culture, Power, Place: Explorations in Critical Anthropology*, edited by Akhil Gupta and James Ferguson. Durham and London: Duke University Press, 1997.

Black, Richard, and Khalid Koser, eds. *The End of the Refugee Cycle? Refugee Repatriation and Reconstruction.* New York and Oxford: Berghahn Books, 1999.

Brettell, Caroline B. "Theorizing Migration in Anthropology: The Social Construction of Networks, Identities, Communities, and Globalscapes." Pp. 97–135 in *Migration Theory: Talking across Disciplines*, edited by Caroline B. Brettell and James F. Hollifield. New York and London: Routledge, 2000.

Bringa, Tone. *Being Muslim the Bosnian Way: Identity in a Central Bosnian Village.* Princeton: Princeton University Press, 1995.

Byron, Margaret. "The Caribbean-born Population in 1990s Britain: Who Will Return?" *Journal of Ethnic and Migration Studies* 25, no. 2 (1999): 285–301.

Campbell, David. *National Deconstruction: Violence, Identity, and Justice in Bosnia.* Minneapolis and London: University of Minnesota Press, 1998.

Casey, Edward S. *Getting Back into Place: Toward a Renewed Understanding of the Place-World.* Bloomington and Indianapolis: Indiana University Press, 1993.

Cattaruzza, Amael. "Sarajevo, Capitale Incertaine." *Balkanologie* 5, no. 1/2 (2001): 67–75.

Chimni, B.S. "From Resettlement to Involuntary Repatriation: Towards a Critical History of Durable Solutions to Refugee Problems." UNHCR Working Paper no. 2. Geneva: Centre for Documentation and Research, 1999.

———. "Globalisation, Humanitarianism and the Erosion of Refugee Protection." RSC Working Paper no. 3. Oxford: Refugee Studies Centre, University of Oxford, 2000.

Constable, Nicole. "At Home but Not at Home: Filipina Narratives of Ambivalent Returns. *Cultural Anthropology* 14, no. 2 (1999): 203–28.

Cornish, Flora, Karl Peltzer, and Malcolm MacLachlan. "Returning Strangers: The Children of Malawian Refugees Come 'Home'?" *Journal of Refugee Studies* 12, no. 3 (1999): 264–83.

Crisp, Jeff. "Who Has Counted the Refugees? UNHCR and the Politics of Numbers." *New Issues in Refugee Research* no. 12. UNHCR, Evaluation and Policy Analysis Unit, 1999.

de Andrade, José H.F., and Nicole B. Delaney. "Minority Return to South-Eastern Bosnia and Herzegovina: A Review of the 2000 Return Season." *Journal of Refugee Studies* 14, no. 3 (2001): 315–30.

Donia, Robert J., and John V. A. Fine. *Bosnia and Hercegovina: A Tradition Betrayed*. New York: Columbia University Press, 1994.

Eastmond, Marita. "Repatriation and Notions of Home-coming: The Case of Cambodian Returnees." Paper presented at the annual meeting of the American Anthropological Association, Washington, DC, December 2001.

Gmelch, George. "Return Migration." *Annual Review of Anthropology* 9 (1980): 135–59.

———. "The Readjustment of Return Migrants in Western Ireland." Pp. 152–70 in *Return Migration and Regional Economic Problems*, edited by Russell King. London: Croom Helm, 1986.

———. *Double Passage: The Lives of Caribbean Migrants Abroad and Back Home*. Ann Arbor: University of Michigan Press, 1995.

———. "West Indian Migrants and Their Rediscovery of Barbados." Pp. 206–23 in *Coming Home? Refugees, Migrants, and Those Who Stayed Behind*, edited by Lynellyn D. Long and Ellen Oxfeld. Philadelphia: University of Pennsylvania Press, 2004.

Graham, Mark, and Shahram Khosravi. "Home is Where You Make It: Repatriation and Diaspora Culture among Iranians in Sweden." *Journal of Refugee Studies* 10, no. 2 (1997): 115–33.

Habib, Laila. "The Search for Home." *Journal of Refugee Studies* 9, no. 1 (1996): 96–102.

Hammond, Laura. "Examining the Discourse of Repatriation: Towards a More Proactive Theory of Return Migration." Pp. 227–44 in *The End of the Refugee Cycle: Refugee Repatriation and Reconstruction*, edited by Richard Black and Khalid Koser. New York and Oxford: Berghahn Books, 1999.

———. *This Place Will Become Home: Refugee Repatriation to Ethiopia*. Ithaca: Cornell University Press, 2004.

Hirschon, Renée. *Heirs of the Greek Catastrophe: The Social Life of Asia Minor Refugees in Piraeus*. New York and Oxford: Berghahn Books, 1998.

International Crisis Group. "Rebuilding a Multi-Ethnic Sarajevo: A Strategy for Promoting the Return of Minorities to the Bosnian Capital." International Crisis Group Balkans Report no. 30. Sarajevo/Brussels, 1998a.

———. "Too Little Too Late: Implementation of the Sarajevo Declaration." International Crisis Group Balkans Report no. 44. Sarajevo/Brussels, 1998b.

———. "Is Dayton Failing? Bosnia Four Years After the Peace Agreement." International Crisis Group Balkans Report no. 80. Sarajevo/Brussels, 1999.

Kibreab, Gaim. "When Refugees Come Home: The Relationship Between Stayees and Returnees in Post-Conflict Eritrea." *Journal of Contemporary African Studies* 20, no. 1 (2002): 53–80.

King, Russell. "Generalizations from the History of Return Migration." Pp. 7–55 in *Return Migration: Journey of Hope or Despair?* edited by Bimal Ghosh. Geneva: UN and IOM, 2000.

Koser, Khalid, and Richard Black. "The End of the Refugee Cycle?" Pp. 2–17 in *The End of the Refugee Cycle? Refugee Repatriation and Reconstruction*, edited by Richard Black and Khalid Koser. New York and Oxford: Berghahn Books, 1999.

Kundera, Milan. *Ignorance*. New York: HarperCollins, 2002.

Kusterer, Karin, and Edita Dugalic. *Tilbage til Bosnien: Edita vender hjem* [Back to Bosnia: Edita Returns Home]. Århus: CDR Forlag, 1998.

Levitt, Peggy. *The Transnational Villagers*. Berkeley and Los Angeles: University of California Press, 2001.

Long, Lynellyn D., and Ellen Oxfeld, eds. *Coming Home? Refugees, Migrants, and Those Who Stayed Behind*. Philadelphia: University of Pennsylvania Press, 2004.

Macek, Ivana. *War Within: Everyday Life in Sarajevo under Siege*. Acta Universitatis Upsaliensis, Uppsala Studies in Cultural Anthropology 29, 2000.

Malkki, Liisa H. *Purity and Exile: Violence, Memory, and National Cosmology Among Hutu Refugees in Tanzania*. Chicago: University of Chicago Press, 1995.

Margold, Jane A. "Filipina Depictions of Migrant Life for Their Kin at Home." Pp. 49–62 in *Coming Home? Refugees, Migrants, and Those Who Stayed Behind*, edited by Lynellyn D. Long and Ellen Oxfeld. Philadelphia: University of Pennsylvania Press, 2004.

Myrvold, Hanne M. "Chile, endelig! Repatriering av chilenske flyktninger fra Skandinavia" [Chile, at last! Repatriation of Chilean refugees from Scandinavia]. Master's thesis, University of Bergen, 1992.

Olwig, Karen F. "Notions of Home and Return in Global Family Networks of Caribbean Background." Paper presented at the annual meeting of the American Anthropological Association, Washington, DC, December 2001.

Oxfeld, Ellen, and Lynellyn D. Long. "Introduction: An Ethnography of Return." Pp. 1–15 in *Coming Home? Refugees, Migrants, and Those Who Stayed Behind*, edited by Lynellyn D. Long and Ellen Oxfeld. Philadelphia: University of Pennsylvania Press, 2004.

Safran, William. "Diasporas in Modern Societies: Myths of Homeland and Return." *Diaspora* 1, no. 1 (1991): 83–99.

Said, Edward. "Reflections on Exile." Pp. 357–66 in *Out There: Marginalization and Contemporary Cultures*, edited by Russell Ferguson, Martha Gever, Trinh T. Minh-ha and Cornel West. London: MIT Press, 1992.

Saloutos, Theodore. *They Remember America: The Story of the Repatriated Greek-Americans*. Berkeley and Los Angeles: University of California Press, 1956.

Simic, Andrei. "Urbanization and Modernization in Yugoslavia: Adaptive and Maladaptive Aspects of Traditional Culture." Pp. 203–24 in *Urban Life in Mediterranean Europe: Anthropological Perspectives*, edited by Michael Kenny and David I. Kertzer. Urbana: University of Illinois Press, 1983.

Skinner, Elliott P. "The Dialectic between Diasporas and Homelands." Pp. 11–40 in *Global Dimensions of the African Diaspora*, edited by Joseph E. Harris. Washington, DC: Howard University Press, 1993.

Stefansson, Anders H. "Under My Own Sky? The Cultural Dynamics of Refugee Return and (Re)integration in Post–War Sarajevo." PhD diss. University of Copenhagen, 2003.

———. "Refugee Returns to Sarajevo and Their Challenge to Contemporary Narratives of Mobility." Pp. 170–86 in *Coming Home? Refugees, Migrants, and Those Who Stayed Behind*, edited by Lynellyn D. Long and Ellen Oxfeld. Philadelphia: University of Pennsylvania Press, 2004.

Søfting, Gunn H. "Finding Home: Lifeworld, Place, and Identity among Refugees Returning to Sarajevo." Master's thesis, University of Bergen, 2002.

Tsuda, Takeyuki. "From Ethnic Affinity to Alienation in the Global Ecumene: The Encounter between the Japanese and Japanese-Brazilian Return Migrants." *Diaspora* 10, no. 1 (2001): 53–91.

———. *Strangers in the Ethnic Homeland: Japanese Brazilian Return Migration in Transnational Perspective*. New York: Columbia University Press, 2003.

Uehling, Greta. "Sitting on Suitcases: Ambivalence and Ambiguity in the Migration Intentions of Crimean Tatar Women." *Journal of Refugee Studies* 15, no. 4 (2002): 388–408.

UNHCR. "Return Statistics." www.unhcr.ba/return/index.htm (21 December 2003).

U.S. Committee for Refugees. "Country Report: Germany 2001." www.refugees.org/world/countryrpt/europe/2001/germany.htm (21 December 2003).

Useem, John, and Ruth H. Useem. *The Western-Educated Man in India: A Study of His Social Roles and Influence*. New York: Dryden Press, 1955.

van de Port, Mattijs. *Gypsies, Wars and Other Instances of the Wild: Civilisation and Its Discontents in a Serbian Town*. Amsterdam: Amsterdam University Press, 1998.

Warner, Daniel. "Voluntary Repatriation and the Meaning of Return to Home: A Critique of Liberal Mathematics." *Journal of Refugee Studies* 7, no. 2/3 (1994): 160–74.

Winland, Daphne. "The Politics of Desire and Disdain: Croatian Identity between 'Home' and 'Homeland.'" *American Ethnologist* 29, no. 3 (2002): 693–718.

Wyman, Mark. *Round-Trip to America: The Immigrants Return to Europe, 1880–1930*. Ithaca and London: Cornell University Press, 1993.

Zetter, Roger. "The Greek-Cypriot Refugees: Perceptions of Return under Conditions of Protracted Exile." *International Migration Review* 28, no. 2 (1994): 307–22.

5

Extra Hungariam Non Est Vita? The Relationships between Hungarian Immigrants and Their Homeland

Éva V. Huseby-Darvas

According to the often-quoted maxim, "*extra Hungariam non est vita*," or, outside of Hungary there is no life.[1] Ever since the late nineteenth century, however, many Hungarians indeed have lived outside of Hungary. About a million and half people emigrated from just the Hungarian part of the Austro-Hungarian monarchy between the 1880s and the outbreak of World War I, causing what contemporary observers called a "social and psychological upheaval in the country" (Frank 1999: 134). We do not know the exact number of those who returned permanently; the rough estimate is anywhere between 16 and 30 percent. A popular saying at the time was that rather than coming back with wealth, "the returnees from America brought home glaucoma and weird religious sects." Though several pragmatic students of contemporary Hungarian society called emigration a much-needed safety valve, it evoked immensely negative public and political opinion in the nation whose "solemn sustaining myths [included] . . . a stubborn isolation of a God-given separate identity . . . an irrepressible yearning for a return to the grandeur of ancient virtues, and a quixotic predilection to live in the alternative reality of a mythic past" (Fenyvesi 2003: 20).

Of course, neither such myths nor the accompanying ideology stopped emigration, though the motivations, the push factors to leave the country changed from one emigrant wave to the other. The immigration laws instituted in 1924 in the United States radically slowed down immigration but did not stop it. Instead, they changed the emigrants' destination to Canada, Australia, and South America. Emigration did not stop at the turn of the twentieth century, either, when a "million and a half of . . . people staggered out to America" (József 1937). Rather, it continued throughout much of the twentieth century. People left during and past the years of goulash communism, as the period between 1968 and 1989 was called in Hungary. Goulash communism contained less rigid central planning and offered more economical freedom and considerably more consumer goods than did other countries in the Soviet bloc.

Unlike the economically motivated, mostly rural emigrants who left Hungary during the late nineteenth and early twentieth centuries, later emigrants left mainly for political reasons. These include the people who left in between the two world wars, as well as the many Displaced Persons (DPs) who left after World War II and were mainly urban, professional, and educated. So too were the approximately two hundred thousand '56ers who fled their homeland after the revolution of 1956, although they hailed from both rural and urban Hungary. Tens of thousands of ethnic Hungarians who left their homeland after the 1970s usually offered political motivations as well.

Like many other immigrants and refugees (see Anderson 1983, 1992; Kearney 1986; Safran 1991; Said 1992; Trix 2001; Tsuda 2000), the majority of Hungarians also maintained ties with their homeland, though the nature and intensity of these ties depended on, among other things, the global politics of the times. For example, during the two world wars and in part of the period between 1948 and 1989 the relationship between immigrants and the homeland was limited at best, and almost nonexistent at worse.

Since push and pull factors were more or less similar within each distinct group, Hungarians tend to stratify according to when they left their homeland, what kinds of ideological baggage they carried with them, and when they arrived in North America. These factors seem to be critical in understanding the various groups' different images and notions about and relationships and attachments to their homeland and therefore directly relevant to the meanings of homecoming.

The end of communism following the *annus mirabilis* of 1989 inspired some Hungarian-Americans to remigrate, and many more to visit their homeland. There are perhaps as many different types of homecomings as there are remigrants and those who dream of returning to their natal land. My concern in the first part of this chapter is with the homecomings of political émigrés. Their homecomings are often virtual: they are yearned for, frequently discussed, but seldom physically carried out. In other words, I probe the question: Why did so few of those émigrés who declared for many decades and keep declaring that they left their "beloved homeland just to escape communism" move back there since 1989 when the regime changed?

When immigrants and refugees did return to Hungary, the country that they found bore little resemblance to the place of their dreams. Instead of the imagined homeland and the crucial roles that they would play in it, the returnees found poverty and troublesome shadows of past regimes. For their part, the "natives," those who had remained in Hungary, perceived the returnees as strangers who were unable to understand contemporary Hungarian ways and often rejected the western expertise that the returnees were so eager to offer. Thus, instead of the warm homecoming imagined by the émigrés, they often descended into an abyss of mutual misunderstanding with their Hungarian counterparts (see also Kundera 2001; Stefansson, this volume).

The chapter first contrasts an example of virtual homecoming by those who practice what Benedict Anderson (1992) calls long-distance nationalism and achieve a sense of return without actually moving from their adopted homes in North America to those who do return and import long-distance nationalism. The discussion then moves to less politically motivated returns, those connected to life cycle passages—retirement homecomings and the "return" of children and grandchildren of immigrants via academic and investment programs, heritage, and "roots" tours. I round out this discussion by describing what can be called the ultimate homecoming, the return of the dead to the sacred soil of the motherland. Then, on a critical note, I offer a brief presentation of the theme of homecomings as it appears in contemporary Hungarian and American-Hungarian performing arts. Finally, dusting off an old cliché, I suggest that in cases where the imagined place and expectations on the one hand, and the actual site and the realities of (un)welcome on the other clash so sharply in people's experience, one can never really go home again.

TYPES OF HOMECOMINGS

The Virtual Homecoming of Long Distance Nationalists

In what Viktor Frankl (2000) called "man's eternal search for meaning," the importance of long-distance nationalism or diaspora nationalism for many immigrants cannot be overstated. Since the late 1970s I have found this to be the case over and again. I was often surprised, however, to see that long-distance nationalism among Hungarian-Americans cuts across class lines but not gender divisions. Just as Benedict Anderson has noted, it appears to be entirely a male domain.

The following excerpts are from my field notes of March 1994:

> For the 1994 commemoration of the Hungarian Revolution of 1848, there were about 120 people in the Michigan church's social hall where these events are usually held. In the audience there were more men present than women; mostly middle aged or older folks and just a few young people and children. All participants were dressed in their Sunday best, and were wearing the traditional red-white-and-green cockade, the Hungarian colors and symbol, on the left side of their chest. . . . During this observance, a clergyman—a very popular indi-

vidual, who is greatly admired by members of his congregation—gave the main address. Among other things, he said,

> We, who gathered here, believe in a *szebb, jobb, magyarabb* (a lovelier, better, more Hungarian) future.... Our task is to remember and to remind! We should dare to be Hungarians! We, here, are deeply concerned about the fate of our beloved homeland. Thus we must teach those who are at home! For the sake of a happier Hungarian future of all Hungarians: at home, abroad, and on the dismembered territories [*az elszakított területeken*].... The fight today [the time reference was to the upcoming 1994 elections in Hungary] is a life and death struggle.... We protest while raising our voices against the internal and external enemies of our homeland! Hungary is for the Hungarians! "Each Hungarian," if I may quote István Csurka, "must be tested for their Hungarianness!" What does it mean to be a Hungarian today? It means to take our responsibility for our common destiny. We do not want to be different from our forefathers! Was there really a true change of regime in the past four years in Hungary? Can Hungarian mothers be proud, once again? Sadly, the answer is No! The internal and external enemies are still at work against our nation. ... It is our responsibility to help our people to find the way, the way of justice and truth.... A nation dies not when it is subjected to outside tyranny, but when it forgets its national calling and mission.... We are here to remember and remind." [All translation is mine.]

His concluding remarks reminded the audience that, "It is our responsibility [here] to write to our kin, friends, former neighbors and tell them to cast their votes for the [individual and Party that] will make . . . the Hungarian mothers once again proud."

This vignette represents, I believe, a classic case of long-distance nationalism. The clergyman's address legitimates not returning permanently to Hungary because the diaspora possesses a kind of insight and impact that is lacking among the natives in the homeland. It is a kind of virtual homecoming, one where actually moving from the United States is replaced by an ideological springboard for remaining abroad to actively shape Hungary's contemporary political events and the future of the homeland.

Actual Homecomings: Importing Long-Distance Nationalism

The following homecoming examples demonstrate the imported long-distance nationalism of émigrés who actually return to pursue a definite political agenda. These returnees are zealous, often fanatical, and do not ask if their beliefs, teachings, and actions are appropriate for contemporary Hungary.

The cases of Albert Szabó and István Porubszky show what happens when, after decades as immigrants, individuals inspired by atavistic ideology return to the homeland. Szabó, an immigrant in Australia, returned to Hungary in the early 1990s and organized a neo-Nazi party that was explicitly modeled after Ferenc Szálasi's fascist Arrow Cross Party. Szálasi, this Nazi German–aligned party's leader, was put in power in October 1944 at Hitler's order (Hockenos 1993: 155). After Szabó's neo-Nazi party was outlawed, he founded another one, this time innocently named the Hungarian People's Welfare Federation.

During the 1990s, Szabó was arrested several times for using Nazi emblems, and for "incitement against a community." In 1996 during a rally for the 1956 Hungarian Revolution he called for the resettlement of Hungary's Jews in Israel. A day later, the presidium of István Csurka's far-right Hungarian Justice and Life Party disassociated itself from Szabó and asked the police to keep both him and his associates away from its gathering. Later in the decade Albert Szabó left Hungary and rumor has it that he returned to Australia. According to members of his organization Szabó only left temporarily to get financial support for his party, and his plan is to return to the Hungarian homeland.

István Porubszky's actions can be seen in a similar vein, yet, since he has been organizing and "educating" teenage youth in Hungary, his actions may very likely yield more far-reaching results than those of Szabó. Porubszky fled Hungary after the Revolution of 1956 in which it is said that he fought and returned from Canada to his homeland in the early 1980s. Shortly thereafter he became the leader of the 1956 Anti-Fascist and Anti-Bolshevik Association, which, among other things, trains skinheads in right-wing philosophy and gathers teenage youth into a group called the National Conservative-Thinking Boys. These young men, who affectionately refer to Porubszky as *Potyka bácsi* or Uncle Potyka, listen to lectures on a particular version of Hungarian history, celebrate the mythical Turul bird, a symbol of national unity, and demand the overturn of the 1920 Trianon Treaty that dismembered the Hungarian motherland.

It is one of the many ironies of post-1989 Hungary that while Albert Szabó was officially criticized and arrested for some of his actions, Porubszky was given a hero's medal for his in 1998, much to the eventual embarrassment and explicit public apologies of members of the government. These government figures claimed that the medal and accolades were conferred because of Porubszky's heroism in the 1956 Revolution, and that they were unaware of his political activities in Hungary after his return from Canada.

Of course the majority of returnees or would-be-returnees to Hungary are far from the aforementioned extremes. Motivations to return home or to stay away rarely revolve around political factors. More frequently the dilemma of returning from or staying in the West is determined by personal or familial circumstances; in particular, children, grandchildren, and valued social relations with special friends and neighbors in current living places as well as the difficulties of travel and being away from comfort are mentioned from time to time as the key factors for not returning. Still, ambivalence lingers, especially in view of some attractive-sounding offers by the Hungarian state to those who return and resettle there.

Hazacsalogatók: Soliciting the Return of Retired and Other Immigrants

A clearly stated intent of the Hungarian government and private entrepreneurs alike is to attract more and more investors from among the various overseas Hungarians, especially North Americans. The number of visitors to Hungary from the United States annually was 220,000 in 1990, 358,000 in 1998, and 356,000 in 2000 (*MSZs* 2001: 269). A large portion of these visitors are immigrants and their children and grandchildren. The Hungarian state makes serious and often successful attempts to encourage immigrants to visit and consider resettling in the homeland. At the risk of sounding cynical, these attempts are designed to attract some Western capital, if not always the actual bodies, to come home. Particularly in the last decades various attempts have been made to reach out to immigrants in the West and make it increasingly appealing for them to set up a second residence and invest in Hungary. Just since January 2000 alone, $600 million was invested in hotels and hotel improvements, primarily by American and American Hungarian investors. The solicitations via various forms of media, websites, embassy programs, and by Hungarian delegations visiting larger immigrant communities are what some Hungarians in North America facetiously, and at times dismissively, call *hazacsalogatók*, which roughly translates as temptations to return.

Some programs attempt to awaken a general interest in Hungary. For example the program called "Routes to your Roots: Hungarian Heritage Tours" is clearly intended for immigrants of just about any age and their offspring. The organizers include in these tours individualized trips to the visitors' own or ancestral settlements where they may be encouraged to help the local churches or schools or invest outright in an economic venture. The travelers and investors are also led to various websites where they can do research on their families' "roots." Creating a concerned diaspora and potential homecomers via academic programs and heritage tours is also an aim of the Hungarian state. Several universities and other institutes, such as the recently founded Bálint Balassi School, organize youth and language programs that, judging from the curriculum, are aimed particularly at the offspring of immigrants. The curriculum does not deal as much with Hungarian culture and society as it focuses on Hungarian immigration through the ages. It poignantly concludes with a unit on "the future of immigrants and the responsibility of immigrant communities."

Numerous solicitations appeal to elderly immigrants, in particular a type of medical tourism. Dental, medical, and spa tours are offered, still fairly reasonably priced package deals for retired, aging immigrants. While the prices charged for them are higher than those for "natives," these are still much less expensive than similar medical services in the West. Another attempt is contacting elderly immigrants who are either retired or getting ready to retire and encourage them to return and resettle in Hungary. Many elderly folks often revert to the language of their formative years and forget all or parts of their adopted language (Nóra Arató, personal communication), and for these pensioners, returning to Hungary can be an economically sound step in addition to an emotionally rewarding one. Even though the cost of living has been continuously increasing as Hungary prepares to join the European Union (MSZs 2001: 189–209), most retired folks realize that their U.S. retirement pensions go much further in Hungary and can even provide them with elements of luxury.

One retirement home, the *Arany Alkony Otthon*, or the Golden Dusk Home, makes remarkable use of language in its advertisements that appeal to potential homecomers. These are carefully composed appeals that are nostalgia-evoking on the one hand, and pragmatic-sounding on the other. It promises elderly immigrants that heeding the beckoning of the *Nagy Visszatérés Periódusa*, or the "period of great return," will richly pay off (see also Kundera 2001: 6 for nearly the same phrase). They will, once again, feel the spirit of the beauty of their childhood and youth while, at the same time, they will live out the rest of their days comfortably and content, "on Hungarian soil, amid Hungarians [the ads refer to other actual and also potential owners in the Golden Dusk Home as "members of the Hungarian upper and upper-middle class"], surrounded by their own people and speak their own mother-tongue, the unique and beautiful Hungarian language." All this, and the promise of security, safety, luxury, privacy, independent living, as the advertisers state, will allow the returnees to enjoy the good life of a solid "Western life style."

However, for those immigrants who do not take advantage of these and similar tempting offers but go gently (or otherwise) into the night in the United States, there remain various opportunities for going home after they breathe their last breath.

Homecoming in Death?

A number of poignant works deal with explicitly politically motivated (re)burials of refugees, émigrés, and immigrants (in addition to Holsey, this volume, see also Gal 1991; Rév 1995; Verdery 1999; Zempléni 2003). The interment of immigrants in Hungarian soil (one way or another), is not only *the* definitive, final homecoming, but also a political statement of those family members who insist on it.

Shortly before his premature death Attila József (1937/b) wrote in a poem titled "Homeland":

> And so I've found my native country,
> That soil the gravedigger will frame,
> Where they who write the words above me
> Do not for once misspell my name.

These lines reverberated in my mind each time I attended the funeral of Hungarian-American acquaintances. After one such event I realized that the funeral portrayed a type of homecoming after death—without leaving the United States:

> We attended the open-casket visitation, . . . then the actual burial the day after. . . . [His older sister] Julia, hailing from rural Hungary, who could not get a flight out earlier, just arrived in Michigan on the morning of the ['56er's] funeral. At the grave she took a crumpled silver ribbon off a red-white-and-green box and, disregarding the "proper" order, went ahead of the [widow] and the kids . . . to the grave . . . , she reached into the box and slowly poured handfuls of what looked like brown dust on top of the lowered casket. . . . Later, back at the house during the wake while expressing my condolences to members of the family, I asked Julia [known for her fine embroidery work], to tell me about her trip and what she had brought with her at this sad time. After a while she said "Look, *Öcsi* [nickname, referring to or addressing a younger brother] would never be in peace in foreign soil. Just could not rest. He must have had a premonition a couple of weeks ago. He called and asked to bring him some earth from our [family] orchard. So now that is all I brought."

In a sense placing Hungarian soil, particularly from the family's homestead, in the grave that is in the United States legitimizes staying abroad while maintaining Hungarian ties. But shipping bodies or ashes back to be buried in Hungary is, I contend, the ultimate homecoming.

A retired Ford Motor Company assembly-line worker, a '56er, insisted that his wife's body be taken back to Hungary. This was a costly affair that required more money than he could easily afford. After battling with his children, who did not understand why he insisted on this overseas burial, and with bureaucracy on both sides of the ocean, he succeeded in having her buried in her natal small town beside their kin. For this Hungarian American it was of crucial importance that his wife be "reunited" with her family. I have often been given additional explanations, such as to rest in "sacred home soil," or "sleep his eternal sleep" next to long-dead family members, or simply to place "his bones where he belongs."

In several cases only the ashes of immigrants were returned to Hungary and buried in private rites of passage in family plots. In one particular instance, although cremation was against the religion of the family, a middle-aged '56-er university professor brought his mother's ashes back to Budapest. He took a small toy shovel to the cemetery and in a very private ceremony attended by only two people buried the ashes alongside his long-deceased father's grave. The reason he gave me was that "you know that she was left as a widow [forty-six years before]. Mother never remarried. It gives me a kind of peace of mind to reunite them once more." He hired one of the cemetery workers on the spot and had his mother's names engraved in gold letters on the black granite headstone of his father. Her long name, with all the correct diacritical marks in place, was, finally, not misspelled.

CRITIQUES OF HOMECOMINGS

Artists' Leer on Homecomings

From the considerable variety of critiques of homecoming to Hungary two stand out as culturally salient and politically provocative. The first is a group of artistic productions that cast the issue of homecoming in sharp relief as they ponder and reflect, ridicule and toy with the relationship between natives and immigrants. The second is the continuing social process of emigration from Hungary to North America, expressing the desire of individuals seeking more fruitful homes than the one offered by the homeland.

The reality of possible remigration with all its ambivalence, implications, and effects became a hot topic since the fall of the Iron Curtain in 1989. Besides exerting its presence in economic and political arenas, remigration has surfaced as a central theme in literature, the cinema and theater. A key example is György Spiró's 1996 play *Kvartett* ["Quartet"] which was made into a movie a year after its initial stage production. "Quartet" continues to be successful both in Hungarian theaters and in numerous immigrant cultural centers as it portrays an encounter between two worlds. After forty-some years an immigrant returns to Budapest from the United States just to reunite with the man who saved his life during the Revolution of 1956 and to shower his savior with everything that money can buy. The much-awaited and highly anticipated return results in misunderstanding; it is a total fiasco. Very different sets of values, worldviews, ideologies, and beliefs emerge, meet and clash. After both sides register disillusionment, the "native" is frustrated, angry, and accusatory, while the immigrant realizes that his homeland is no longer his home, and departs for the United States—finally, it can be presumed. The abyss between the returnee and those who stayed at home is portrayed as unbridgeable (cf. Kundera 2001).

The 2001 low-budget Hungarian comedy, *Valami Amerika* ["Some America"] unexpectedly became one of the most popular films of recent years in Hungary and was also shown in a number of immigrant communities in the West. It is about a returnee, who calls himself Alex Bruebaker, and as viewers are informed at the beginning of the film when he enters the country from Austria, driving a large, unusually luxurious car while puffing on a large, presumably expensive cigar, waited for many years to go back home, taste familiar foods, and see beloved sites. This scene implies that he is hoping for the warmth of home, though without giving himself away, without telling anyone that he is originally from Hungary, while three brothers in Budapest are eagerly waiting for him, plotting and scheming in expectation that that he will solve their financial difficulty.

Valami Amerika ends by revealing that Alex, the returnee, is a liar who hides his true identity from the brothers by pretending to be an American film producer with money to invest, and pretending not to understand any Hungarian. He is really a returning emigrant who is still fluent in the language and thus understands every word that the brothers say about him and their plans. Alex also turns out to be a thief who disappears with what little money the brothers have and takes away one of their girlfriends.

Both films are thought-provoking critiques of homecoming. In "Quartet" Spíró's main question is: how could one go home again, when an immigrant's expectations and hopes are so distorted by memories that they can not even be comprehended by the people in the homeland? The message in "Some America" is that both natives and homecomers scheme shamelessly to take advantage of the other.

An American Rhapsody is an autobiographical film written and directed by the Hungarian-American Éva Gárdos. It deals with identity crises, loss, disappointment, and cross-cultural and cross-generational miscommunication all embedded in a coming-of-age story. Gárdos' alter-ego, Zsuzsi, or Suzanne, has two sets of parents. One resides in a small, quaint Hungarian village where Zsuzsi was raised with much love and warmth until age six. The other set, her biological parents, are political refugees who fled Hungary in the early 1950s and lived during the late 1950s and early 1960s in urban Los Angeles where Zsuzsi, who then becomes Suzanne, is sent from Hungary by her maternal grandmother. Suzanne realizes her much-longed-for and dreamt about return to Hungary and reuniting with her dearly loved rural (surrogate) parents when she is fifteen. In Hungary she comes to understand that she is no longer really home in her homeland as she finally learns about the past, the reasons for her parents' forced emigration and their overprotectiveness in Los Angeles. She returns to the United States, presumably a calmer, wiser young woman who more or less knows where she belongs.

Disappointment in Homecoming:
Desires to Leave the Homeland

In Taylor, Michigan, a sixty-year-old man just after returning from spending six weeks in the homeland where he had considered resettling, reported, "[in

Hungary] the wife and I realized that it is easier to be a Hungarian here, from afar." It was not a joke: when some people smiled he got angry and went into great details about what they experienced during their long visit. Among other things, he said, the young tended to be too cynical; people no longer knew or seemed to care much for their own country's history; even in the countryside almost everything was too westernized. For example, there were too many signs and advertisements, and the people didn't even talk real Hungarian anymore: they used too many English words and often used them incorrectly.

Thus, the other critique of the homecoming issue responds to the claim extra Hungariam non est vita, that in fact there *is* life outside of Hungary. This critique comes from those who actually experience that homeland, who return from abroad and come face to face with that much dreamt about land and its people after decades of hoping to return. Many return to North America disappointed, and discuss what they experienced in Hungary, particularly the plight of many young people who cannot find jobs, the struggle of pensioners to make ends meet, and that of the former middle classes who lost their footing and a sense of social security as a result of the radical changes that followed 1989.

A parallel critique is the potential for and actual emigration from Hungary, or brain drain. It is a frequent topic in electronic communications where the frustration and ambivalence of white collar technical professionals and others are most evident. For example, in an early April 1995 electronic mail communication one young Hungarian engineer, working in the United States, wrote:

> Here it is possible to work, at home it is not! Here you can exist on your income, at home you cannot!
> Here there is tolerance, at home [it does not exist]!
> Here it counts what you accomplish, at home it does not!
> Here it counts what you have accomplished, at home it does not!
> Here they appreciate your work, at home they do not!
> Here they are not envious, at home they are! Here they use you, at home they exploit you!
> Still. Why is it that I only wish to come here for one or two years? Why is it that I want to live at home? I do not know! There is no rational answer. But if they destroy the country, they destroy my life and then I will not think for long [to emigrate permanently].

CONCLUSION: IS THERE A SAFE RETURN AMID AN ABYSS OF MISUNDERSTANDINGS?

Immigrants often voice how much they have sacrificed financially and morally for their homeland from afar without mentioning or perhaps even realizing that these actions, whether actual or imagined, gave them good reason for staying away from that home. In spite of mostly good intentions both among Hungarian-American immigrants and Hungarian visitors from the homeland, dialogues between these two groups often appear to be mutually incomprehensible. Neither party seems to listen to the other. There is little, if any, mutual understanding, but considerable aggregate, yet unshared, resentment. The Hungarian-Americans resent that visitors from Hungary refuse to acknowledge their professional and economic accomplishments in the West or their alleged sacrifice for their homeland. Rather, they believe that the Hungarian natives, either openly or furtively, make them feel as traitors who left their homeland and the people there in the lurch after World War II or after the revolution of 1956. The question "How could you?" is always implied, even when not articulated. For their part, the natives, either at home in Hungary or during visits from the homeland, resent what they perceive as the immigrants' condescension and what they often see as the immigrants' being out of touch with Hungarian reality, although they talk as if they know it all; moreover, many clearly state that they wish to interfere in and profit from Hungary's post-1989 polity and economy.

As this chapter has shown, for many Hungarian immigrants in North America time has stood still ever since they left Hungary. They look at their frozen-in-time natal country through an idealized, romanticized, nostalgic prism that not only distorts the already static image but also makes their image of Hungary more enduring and tantalizing from the distance. While occasional visits in Hungary may somewhat alter this image, the visits do not destroy it.

This chapter has reviewed several types of homecomings while glancing at the state's and entrepreneurs' motivations to encourage return migration and investments. Its major finding is that despite the variety of motivations and returns, and stated desires for one all-encompassing Hungarian identity and homeland, misunderstandings characterize most encounters between returning immigrants and those who stayed at home. Perhaps one reason for this gap lies in the decades-long practice by some immigrants of long-distance nationalism that achieves a sense of return without actually moving, or its parallel manifestation of imported long-distance nationalism by returnees.

Long before the dramatic events of 1989 Iván Sanders (1974: 91), with impressive insight, wrote that "My experiences led me to the regrettable conclusion that it is not always possible for those Hungarians who live outside of Hungary to get on the same wave length with those from home, even if they really want to get close to one another." Indeed, the relationship between immigrants and those in their homelands is a highly complex, ambivalent, and difficult one and, as I have shown, this adds to the problems and ambiguities of homecomings.

Is there a "safe return," a good homecoming? Can one indeed go home again? I venture to say that a modern-day version of the old, early twentieth century strategy of circular or pendular migration with binational residences and jobs and transnational networks and families would come close to a positive answer for the young, mobile generations as a sort of a homecoming. For those who return with a specific political agenda along with the moral and financial help of far-away immigrant communities, as did Szabó and Porubszky, going home gives a reason for being. However, I would suggest that their return is not really a homecoming; rather it continues the chase after the mythical dreams of long-distance nationalists. For the aging or aged immigrants with dreams about a glorious homecoming and a life of comfort and ease, I would say that the answer is to have enough money when they return to create and maintain an isolated bubble, removed from the contemporary reality of everyday Hungary. The Golden Dusk Home presents an excellent example of this strategy. So too do the handful of individuals I interviewed who bought luxury apartments in secure buildings in relatively quiet and calm provincial cities and live among, commiserate, and swagger along with fellow returnees.

Let me close with my favorite story of a homecoming dream. While collecting the life histories of elderly Hungarian Americans, one man kept insisting through three long, open-ended interviews that he would never go back to his homeland because, as he informed me coldly and with obvious conviction, "Hungary ceased to exist on the afternoon of December 24th 1944 [when he left the country]. It became a Soviet Dominion." Finally, when we got to the last interview I asked him where he would like to be buried. At this point the man, who was extremely polite, elegant, proud, stiff, and stoic throughout all our encounters, started to cry and said that he does not want to be buried. Rather, he wants to be cremated and have his ashes scattered here so the wind will take at least parts of him back to his beloved homeland. He died in 2000. I know that his sister had him cremated, but I cannot tell you if his wish came true.

NOTES

Discussions with friends and colleagues—Noémi Barabás, György Csepeli, Krisztina Fehérváry, Miklós Kontra, Zsolt Lavicza, and István Mikó—helped with many difficult issues in this paper. I am most thankful to Fran Markowitz and Anders Stefansson who painstakingly read several drafts of this effort and patiently made invaluable suggestions. The chapter is based on fieldwork among Hungarian immigrants and their offspring in North America that began in 1978 and has continued ever since. First I participated in an NEH-supported project led by Professor Béla Máday in which we collected 150 life histories as part of *Project ÁMEN* (Hungarian acronym for the Ethnography of American Hungarians). Then I worked in a binational project of the American Council of Learned Societies and the Hungarian Academy of Sciences that was led by Professors Linda Dégh and Tamás Hofer; and also did fieldwork that was supported by the University of Michigan Alcohol Research Center's grant No. P50-AA07378. The generous assistance of these institutions is most appreciated.

1. The complete maxim reads *"Extra Hungariam non est vita—Si est vita, non est ita"* [Outside of Hungary there is no life—And if there is [life], it is not the same]. The original source of it is not known. This couplet is in a collection of folk proverbs edited by Hans Walther (1965–1983). The only source there cited, however, is another collection, indicating that this is just a popular saying not traceable to a specific source.

REFERENCES

Anderson, Benedict. *Imagined Communities*. London: Verso, 1983.
———. "Long-Distance Nationalism: World Capitalism and the Rise of Identity Politics." *New Left Review* 193 (May–June 1992): 3–13.
———. "Exile." *Critical Inquiry* 20, no. 2 (1994): 314–327.
Allen, Tim, and Hubert Morsink, ed. *When Refugees Go Home: African Experiences*. London: James Currey, 1994.
Csepeli, György. *A Nagyvilágon E Kivül . . . Nemzeti Tudat és Érzésvilág Magyarországon 1970–2002*. [Beyond this (land) in the whole wide world . . . National awareness and feeling in Hungary 1970–2002]. Budapest: Jószöveg, 2002.
Csepeli, György, and Tibor Závecz. "Conflicting Bonds of Nationality in Hungary. National Identity, Minority Status and Ethnicity. *Innovation* 5, no. 2 (1992): 77–94.
Deák, István. Post-Communist Hungary. *New York Review of Books* 94 (August 11, 1994): 33–38.
Fenyvesi, Charles. *When Angels Fooled the World: Rescuers of Jews in Wartime Hungary*. Madison, WI: University of Wisconsin Press, 2003.
Frankl, Viktor E. *Men's Search for Meaning*. New York: Washington Square Press, 2000 [1946].
Gal, Susan. "Bartók's Funeral: Representation of Europe in Hungarian Political Rhetoric." *American Ethnologist* 18 (1991): 440–58.
Hockenos, Paul. *Free to Hate: The Rise of the Right in Post-Communist Eastern Europe*. New York and London: Routledge, 1993/a.
———. "Racism Unbound in the Land of the Magyars. *New Politics* IV, no. 2 (1993/b): .
Huseby, Éva V. *Community Cohesion and Identity Maintenance in a Hungarian Village*. Ph.D. Dissertation. Ann Arbor, MI: University of Michigan, 1984.
———. *Hungarians in Michigan*. East Lansing: Michigan State University Press, 2003.
Jackson, Michael. *At Home in the World*. Durham and London: Duke University Press, 1995.
József, Attila. *Hazám: Összegyüjtött Versek* [My Homeland: Collected Poems]. 1937/a.
———. "Íme, hát megleltem hazámat" [And I found my homeland]. *The Hungarian Quarterly* no. 148–49 (winter 1997—spring 1998 [1937/b]): (Poems translated by Anton Nyerges).

Kearney, Michael. "From the Invisible Hand to Visible Feet: Anthropological Studies of Migration and Development. *Annual Review of Anthropology* 15 (1986): 331–61.
Kundera, Milan. *Nemtudás* [Ignorance]. Budapest: Európa, 2001.
Lengyel, Emil. *Americans from Hungary*. Westport, CT: Greenwood Press, 1974 [1948].
Magyar Statisztikai Zsebkönyv (MSZs) 2000. *Hungarian Statistical Handbook 2000*. Budapest: Hungarian Statistical Office, 2001.
Malkki, Liisa H. "Refugees and Exile: From 'Refugee Studies' to the National Order of Things." *Annual Review of Anthropology* 24 (1995): 495–523.
Mendoza, Louis and S. Shankar, ed. *Crossing into America: The New Literature of Immigration*. New York: New Press, 2003.
Rév, István. "Parallel Autopsies." *Representations* 49 (1995): 15–39.
Safran, William. "Diasporas in Modern Societies: Myths of Homeland and Return." *Diaspora* 1, no. 1 (1991): 83–99.
Said, Edward. "Reflections on Exile." Pp. 357–66 in *Out There: Marginalization and Contemporary Cultures*, edited by Russell Ferguson, Martha Gever, Trinh T. Minh-ha, and Cornel West. London: MIT Press, 1992.
Sanders, Iván. "Két világ között: egy amerikai magyar vallomása." [Between two worlds: Confession of an American Hungarian]. *Valóság* 8 (1974): 84–94.
Teleky, Richard. *Hungarian Rhapsodies: Essays on Ethnicity, Identity and Culture*. Seattle: University of Washington Press, 1997.
Trix, Frances. *Albanians in Michigan*. East Lansing: Michigan State University Press, 2001.
Tsuda, Takeyuki. "Migration and Alienation: Japanese-Brazilian Return Migrants and the Search for Homeland Abroad." The Center for Comparative Immigration Studies, University of California, Working Paper no. 24, 2000.
Várdy, Steven Béla. *The Hungarian Americans*. Boston: Twayne, 1985.
Verdery, Katherine. *The Political Lives of Dead Bodies: Reburial and Postsocialist Change*. New York: Columbia University Press, 1999.
Walter, Hans, ed. *Sententiaeque Proverbia latinitatis Medii aevi. Lateinische Sprichwörter und Sentenzen of Mittelalters in alphabetischer Anordnung*. Göttingen: Utrecht, 1965–1983.

III
BLURRIED HOMES, BLURRED DIASPORA-HOMELAND BOUNDARIES

6

Homecoming to the Diaspora: Nation and State in Visits of Israelis to Morocco

André Levy

We had just escaped from the unbearable city heat of Marrakech as we headed south on one of the roads that crosses the High Atlas Mountains. The bus drove slowly, maneuvering its way through the narrow and beautiful Ourika Valley. The scenery was breathtaking. The streams flowed magnificently and the trees were a perfect deep green. The travelers, all Moroccan-born Israelis returning to Morocco for the first time after having emigrated decades ago, were captivated by the picturesque landscape. Their faces were glued to the bus windows.[1]

One middle-aged woman, Simi, captured my attention. Usually, she was quiet, demure. She hardly said a word during the six or seven days we had thus far spent in Morocco. At this particular moment, however, Simi looked nervous and jumpy and was extremely talkative. She asked me to sit beside her, and instantly launched into a monologue, speaking in a typical mélange of Hebrew, French and Maghrebi Arabic:

> Look how wonderful everything is! Look at these apple trees, the peaches. . . . Look how big the pears are. What a wonderful place! I can't control my emotions. . . . You know, we are approaching the grave of my *tsaddiq* [Heb.: pious man], Rabbi Shlomo Bel-Khens.[2] He is a marvelous tsaddiq. He saved me once, when I was young. I just got married . . . when I had this nervous breakdown. I couldn't control my body. . . . I was shivering and shaking all day long. . . . My husband took me to rabbis, who prescribed all kind of magical things, . . . but it didn't help. Then, one day, we came to the *hillulah* [annual celebration of the tsaddiq's death] of Rabbi Shlomo Bel-Khens. There were so many people. And I was taken to his grave. Many men carried me high, and then put me on his grave. I laid on his grave and instantly fainted. I can't remember anything. . . . I

woke up suddenly, and many men carried me high, in their arms. My illness never returned. . . . I couldn't overcome my emotions. Look—look how wonderful this place is! No wonder the tsaddiq chose to die here.

Simi suddenly stopped. All of a sudden her face contorted in pain. She sighed and continued, explaining the dramatic and unexpected shift:

You know André, this is strange. . . . I don't remember seeing the landscape when I made my yearly pilgrimage. When we were here in Morocco, when I was young . . . I never noticed the landscape.

Simi's insight was painful as she realized that the place is not taken for granted; commonplace has turned into a landscape. The unexpected emergence of a fissure between her memories and the most intimate spaces of her life was a shocking revelation. Her insight provoked my reflections on the failure of people's attempts to intimately and unreservedly come to their past home. While I tried to comprehend the travels to a Morocco that is practically emptied of Jews, I am, like other Moroccan Israelis, a cause of the contemporary void of Jews in Morocco. Therefore, I participated in this travel as a peculiar kind of native anthropologist, equipped with "a native's point of view," and biographically tied to the fieldwork scene. As such, I could not escape the mix between my personal longings and my intellectual curiosity. Indeed, Morocco's lingering presence in my everyday life in Israel deeply influenced my professional career as well as my personal development. Morocco captured my imagination and shaped my identity even before I had my first opportunity to visit it as an adult. My decision to study Moroccan Jews demonstrates my longings. Thus, I am thick in the evolving story of the Jews within and without Morocco in general, and of the traveling Moroccan Israelis in particular. As I pondered the failures to reconnect Morocco over time, it occurred to me that the disjuncture was not simply between individuals and the intimate spaces of their past but, as they crossed borders in traveling between homes, a hidden actor—the nation-state—also emerged to play a role in this rupture.

It is frequent that people aspire to go back to their pasts and poetically evoke them through the language of space. Through it people emplace their evasive and eluding pasts in concrete spaces (compare with Bahloul 1996; Nora 1989). Spaces are constructed as embodying uncontaminated, authentic memories since they are the material through which people supposedly can prove for themselves and for others the authenticity of their own past (Herzfeld 1997). The poetic acts of emplacement turn people's pasts into everlasting objects and grant them an ontological stature. These acts also underline the enduring and abiding aspects of spaces that carry the past safely through the corrosion of time. Yet, these efforts sometimes fail.

Simi's inability to retrieve the past in Morocco's memory-laden landscapes was the lot of every traveler. This destabilizing experience seems to support

Alfred Schutz's assertion regarding the impossibility of reconnecting with the past (Schutz 1945). By definition, says Schutz, such efforts are doomed to fail because social life, like water in the river, is in constant flux. Thus, one can never go back to the social reality of the past. A closer look at this truism reveals other and deeper layers of experience. Instead of focusing, like Schutz, on individuals as autonomous psychosociological units who are motivated, for whatever reasons, to reconnect with their pasts, I suggest including in the interpretation larger ideological, sociological, and political frameworks. These are crucial to the construction of the experience of rupture. I refer here mainly to nationalism and bureaucratic institutions within the constructed framework of nation-state (cf. Herzfeld 1992).

Through its discourses, rhetoric, and institutions, the nation-state constructs unambiguous dichotomies between, among others, us and them, sacred and profane, homeland and diaspora, and here and abroad. By these means the state emplaces its inhabitants on one side or the other of these dichotomies while fixating the relations between it and its people (see Ferguson and Gupta, 2002). As a result, the state's primordial ontology is reaffirmed so that its people may internalize a uniqueness of belonging (Levy 2000; Levy 2001). This chapter's focus is on the successes and failures of the discourses of nationalism and rhetoric in its name that motivate, generate, and mold attempts of citizens of one state to encounter past home places located in other nation-states. I am contending that the fissures revealed in these encounters unravel the constructed dichotomies related to the bonds between a nation-state and its people that grants it an ontological stature. Through vignettes and stories of Moroccan-born Israelis traveling in Morocco, I aim to clarify and refine my contention that attempts to reconnect to past home spaces reinforce state discourses, since failures and successes are framed and reframed within their logic. The chapter thereby illustrates how nation-state discourses work as a double-edged sword that feeds, generates, and underpins attempts to reconnect with past homes while contributing to the realization that achievement of these homecomings is impossible.

MOROCCO, ISRAEL, AND WHAT'S IN BETWEEN

Before delving into the homecoming visits of Moroccan-born Israelis, it is necessary to account for the circumstances that directed them to Israel in the first place. It would be safe to assert that competing state discourses of belonging (i.e., Morocco's, Israel's, and France's) generated existential fears that undermined the common sense of everyday life and impelled most Moroccan Jews to leave. And as a somewhat simplistic bottom line conclusion one could argue that Jews in the Moroccan diaspora returned to the Jewish homeland. Yet, have they become, in a way, Moroccans in the Israeli diaspora (e.g., Cohen 1984)? A sketchy historical account is presented below.

Jews have been part of Morocco's ethnoscape for at least two millennia (Hirschberg 1974), and any understanding of the history of Jews in Morocco necessitates contextualization within the broader political and socioeconomic developments of the region. Jews were part and parcel of these processes. They suffered when local regimes were feeble and flourished when times were politically calm. With the success of the spread of Islam into North Africa, Jews were symbolically and legally constituted as *dhimmi*, a tolerated minority allowed religious autonomy. In practical terms, dhimmi status involved protection by local patrons and the sultan in return for their submission and discrimination. For example, Jews were forbidden to ride horses (for these are noble beasts), to wear shoes in the vicinity of mosques, to wear colorful clothes, and to carry arms. Despite legal and sociocultural discrimination, most scholars agree that Morocco's precolonial era was characterized by intimate and close sociocultural interchange between Jews and Muslims (see, for example: Flamand, 1959; Goldberg, 1978; Hirschberg, 1974; Stillman, 1991).[3]

The French protectorate (1912–1952), to use the French euphemism for direct colonial rule, provoked deep changes in Morocco. One immediate consequence of it was annulment of the dhimmi status. Another was the destabilization of the Jews' feelings of natural bonds to their place. This was clearly manifested in their massive movement from remote small villages to Morocco's larger cities, so that they could enter the spaces that French colonialists constructed as cosmopolitan (see, for example: Adam, 1950; Flamand, 1959; Ossman, 1994). The Jews hoped thereby to benefit from the egalitarian promise of the discourse of *liberté, égalité, fraternité*. Jewish enthusiasm for the French modernist promise brought about tensions between Jews and Muslims, as the latter comprehended their identification with France as a betrayal of Morocco's nationalistic dreams.[4]

Morocco's independence in 1952 brought about more changes as the Maghrebi Kingdom gradually embraced the cultural and political idea of Arabization (Entelis 1989). At the same time as King Hassan II, along with Morocco's state institutions, acted to strengthen their citizens' identification with Islam (Combs-Shilling 1989; Suleiman 1989) Zionist activists encouraged Jews to immigrate to Israel (Segev 1984). These interrelated factors did not leave much room for Morocco's Jews to maneuver their position.[5] Emigration seemed almost an inevitable solution, with the new state of Israel becoming their main destination. Morocco's Jewish population rapidly dropped. While at its peak (in the 1940s) it numbered about 250,000, demographers nowadays estimate the number of the Jewish population in Morocco as at the most 3,500 persons. Although not all Moroccan Jews chose Israel as their destination, in the mid 1950s a large portion of them chose Israel as their migration target. For instance, between 1952 and 1956 some 77,500 Moroccan Jews came to Israel. As time passed and more options for migration became clear, Jews preferred migrating to France and Canada, gradually neglecting almost entirely the migration option of Israel.

Those Jews who migrated to Israel encountered a host of harsh circumstances. Lack of material resources in the new country that was flooded by migrants almost tripled its population in less than a decade and resulted in a large-scale housing shortage and unemployment. Many of the Moroccan newcomers were relegated to the bottom of the socioeconomic ladder (Horowitz and Lissak 1989). In carrying out the Zionist vision of population dispersal, making the desert bloom, and defending the borders, many of the new migrants were settled in hastily erected development towns and *moshavim* (semi-cooperative villages), located in the unattractive periphery, where economic opportunities were particularly bleak (Hasson 1981). These difficulties were augmented, and even exploited, by the ethnocentric and condescending attitudes of the absorbing mainstream, mostly secular Ashkenazim (Jews of European extraction). In the name of melting pot integration, strong pressures were exerted on the newcomers to divest themselves of their traditions and become Israelis (Eisenstadt 1954).[6] This policy corresponded with the formal Zionist vision of creating a new Israeli identity stripped of all diasporic scars (e.g., Almog 2000).[7] This process, based on "desocialization and resocialization" (Bar-Yosef 1966), produced much pain and a strong sense of acrimony on the part of the Moroccan newcomers. At the same time, it stigmatized them as hot-tempered, primitive, and more problematic than other immigrants. These processes crystallized feelings of alienation from hegemonic Israeli discourse.

One outcome of the dispersal policy was the gradual dissolving of past community-based networks that collapsed group identities from active social relations into past memories. Over the years, with the modest but systematic rise of some Moroccans to prominent positions in the sociopolitical structure, a sense of belonging to Israel was gradually acquired, even in the most peripheral development towns. At the same time, this identification was strongly informed by a seemingly contradictory nostalgic discourse that some politicians used to glorify what was coined as the Heritage of the Maghreb and to delineate a collective Moroccan experience in Israel.[8]

A series of social crises involving second-generation Moroccan Jewish youth crystallized in an emerging political identity. Suffice here to mention the short-lived Wadi Salib rebellion (in Haifa in 1959) and the high-profile rebellion of the Black Panthers in Israel in the early 1970s (concentrated in Jerusalem). Beyond the particularities of each of these revolts, or "violent protests," as they were called by the Israeli establishment, what connects them is the linkage between socioeconomic protest and the ethnic background of the protestors. Both Wadi Salib and Black Panthers were young, unemployed North African immigrants of low socioeconomic background who felt that discrimination was based on ethnic grounds. More than any other ethnic group in Israel, Moroccan Jews were responsible for the dramatic turnover that brought the right-wing Likud party to power in 1977 after three uninterrupted decades of rule by the founding socialist-labor party. The oppositional Likud party was perceived as an appropriate vehicle for a political turnover since, like North African immigrants, it suffered from suppression by the elite socialist hegemony.[9] Nonetheless, the traumatic past continues to exert its consequences; Israelis of Moroccan origin are overrepresented in the lower socioeconomic strata. It is from the sociopolitical and geographical margins that they raise their voice in Israel.

POLITICS AND PILGRIMAGE

By their very presence in the marginal towns of Israel, Moroccan, Jews both implemented the Zionist vision and took the opportunity to creatively express their unique cultural yearnings. A central cultural idiom of Jews in Morocco was the revitalized tradition of pilgrimage to the tombs of *tsaddiqim*. Tsaddiqim were charismatic persons, distinguished by their erudition and piety. They were believed to possess special spiritual forces similar to the Muslim *baraka* (Jamous 1981; Rabinow 1975), that usually revealed themselves after death. In the context of a low sociopolitical and cultural status as dhimmis, this belief had a reassuring role. Consequently, the tombs of tsaddiqim, scattered all over the country, became pilgrimage sites. The main event in the veneration of each tsaddiq was the collective pilgrimage to his tomb on the anniversary of his death and the *hillulah* there. The hillulah was a multivocal event that combined deep spirituality and ecstatic devotion with a picnic-like atmosphere.

The massive migration of Morocco's Jews during the 1950s put the continuity of hagiolatric practices under serious threat since the tsaddiqim's sanctuaries had been left behind and Israelis were forbidden entry to Morocco. Moreover, the Zionism prevailing in Israel of the 1950s and 1960s precluded all but a secular cosmology. But, as already noted above, this process of cultural attenuation reversed itself in the 1970s and 1980s (Ben-Ari and Bilu 1987). North African Israelis in general, and Moroccan Israelis in particular, have adopted old-time native sanctuaries as their own, created new traditions of hillulot around those sages who died in Israel, and imported the bones of holy tsadiqqim from Morocco and placed them in new tombs (Bilu 1987). Yet, the revitalization of hagiolatry should not be understood as a quaint practice restricted to Moroccan Jews in Israel. The grand hillulot are televised on national TV, are visited by the Prime Minister, cabinet ministers, and Knesset members, and are part of Israel's cultural scene. At a deeper level, the sanctification of space on Israel's peripheries resonates with the demands of secular Zionism to strengthen its claims to the land and to foster the identification of it with the nation (cf. Bilu 1998).

As much as these spectacles of cultural revitalization may compensate Moroccan Israelis for their missing tsaddiqim, none of them could fill the void created by politics of nostalgia. Returning to Simi's reminiscences, nothing but direct and unmediated contacts with the sites of Morocco can satisfy these longings.

MOROCCAN TRAVELS

From the mid-1980s until the second Intifada that began in October 2000, two to three thousand Moroccan-born Israelis visited Morocco yearly in organized tour groups. Many took the opportunity offered by King Hassan II, who, after meeting with the Israeli Prime Minister, Shimon Peres, in his Ifrane palace in July 1986, opened Morocco's borders to visits. This initiative marked a breakthrough for Moroccan Israelis who had been certain that they would never see Morocco again.

A characteristic organized tour lasted for three weeks and centered on the tourists' old homes, family graves, tombs of tsaddiqim, and major cities (such as Marrakech and Casablanca) and their *suqs* (bazaars). The participants ranged in age from their late thirties to the late sixties. Even if travelers had not known each other before the tour, they shared a crucial factor in their biographies: they all emigrated as youngsters or adults from Morocco to Israel. The tours were frequently composed of small familial groups and/or clusters of close friends. As typical of Moroccans in Israel, they were usually of the working class and resided in peripheral villages and development towns. Most travelers mentioned the same reasons for the tour: to visit family graves and old tsaddiqim sites, to meet relatives in Casablanca, to see the houses left behind, or to meet up with old Muslim friends. Yet, these and other reasons were not spelled out clearly by the travelers. Such a question seemed odd to them; they wanted to go because they wanted to go.

In April 1986 I traveled to Morocco with my mother and my older sister, along with a group of some forty people. Most of us were seeking evidence to confirm our memories of past times and places. Travelers were looking for the same sites, smells, sounds, people, and feelings that they remembered as emplaced in Morocco. After the trip, looking back, Michel, one of the youngest travelers in our group, said: "I wanted to be back where I grew up . . . to take a walk around the neighborhood, to feel young again. I wanted to see if I could do the same things again." For all the travelers, finding "the same" was confirmation of their experience as unmediated contact with the past.[10]

Michel was exceptional in planning his endeavors, and he made sure that no one would join him in his walk along the streets of his past:

> You know, I begun to ask myself if I can find my mother's tomb in the cemetery . . . with no help. On my own . . . I made it my main objective. I said to myself that if I'll fail in it, then it's no good. It would mean that I have been living with illusions all my life [ever since emigration]. As if . . . I don't know if you understand me, but I wished to get there alone, like I used to go there with my father [when I was a child]. Sometimes he used to take me with him there at 4 o'clock in the morning.
>
> "Remember this road," [I said to myself]. . . . I pretended that I am a kid again. I tried to be fifteen again [when his mother died]. To see myself walk alone, turn towards the grave. And really, when I got there I exploded. I remembered the graveyard, but I did not feel much until I got to my mother's grave. Then I saw my mother-in-law and I felt ashamed that I was busted up. I told her 'get out of my sight'. I wanted to be alone. I stayed there alone about forty-five minutes.

Michel's unremitting desire to find his mother's grave was his self-motivated test to confirm the authenticity of his memories. Because places carry an aura of stability, Michel and all the other tourists tested their memories mainly through their encounters with space that was supposedly known intimately. After all, this assumption of intimacy was at the heart of this tour. No wonder that upon arrival some travelers kissed the soil of Morocco as Jewish pilgrims to the Holy Land do. That assumption of intimacy with the space was frequently contested by their Moroccan hosts. One poignant example was that the travelers constantly haggled with Moroccans at the suq demanding the native price of merchandise that they remembered from the old days. This effort, however, always failed because after some thirty years in Israel they embodied otherness. On the rare occasions that they used Maghrebi-Arabic and gestures appropriately, they still did not succeed since the merchants recognized and treated them as tourists. The irony of travelers trying to obtain nontourist prices for supposedly authentic Moroccan souvenirs did not escape the eyes of their hosts.

These two examples that demonstrate the inaccessibility of past landscapes occurred in various forms to everyone over the course of the trip. In order to comprehend the plight of people wishing to meet up with their pasts, I suggest that inclusion of larger ideological, sociological, and political frameworks of nationalism and the nation-state is called for. Indeed, as I will show, nationalism with its varied executive apparatus profits by contributing to the construction of rupture from past landscapes and plays an active part in initiating the efforts that are doomed to fail. Let us return to Israel for a moment, to glimpse how nationalism plays a crucial role there and how this role is manifested during these Moroccan tours.

HOME, HOMELAND, AND FOREIGN SPACES: THE WORK OF NATIONALISM

As part of the regular curriculum all school pupils in Israel approaching the age of thirteen (their bar-mitzvah) are required to discover and research their families' roots. The Israeli state, so it appears, encourages youngsters to link up with the (personal) past at the same time as they learn in their history classes that the diasporic past has been superceded by the Israeli present. These efforts are not limited to elementary schools; they are even enhanced in high schools. For instance the Israeli Ministry of Education encourages and partially subsidizes high school students to join organized tours to the Nazi-era death camps in Poland. By exposing young travelers to the atrocities of the Holocaust and by witnessing the ruins of the Polish Jewish community, high school students acknowledge the finality of the Polish diasporic existence and by implication all diasporas. The necessity of maintaining and fortifying Israel, the nation-state that protects all Jews, is consequently fortified as well (Feldman 2002).

Despite the difference between these school-organized travels to Poland and the voluntary group tours to Morocco, an invisible key player undergirds them both: the Israeli nation-state and its rhetoric of nationalism. In both cases Israel could not operate alone; these tours were dependent on the consent of the Polish and Moroccan states.

From its establishment in 1948 none of the Arab countries of the Middle East and North Africa—including Morocco—had formal diplomatic relationships with Israel. When the Moroccan monarch, Hassan II, publicly invited his sons to return to their native land in the mid 1980s, virtually all Israeli Moroccans were exuberant. Hassan II explained that each and every son of Morocco is also his son. They were invited to return whenever they wish; sons can never leave their family. This appeal to every Moroccan in the diaspora was part of a change in Moroccan politics towards Israel. The king's announcement marked a new, out in the open, facet of his Mediterranean and global politics. For a long period of time the king played an important behind-the-scenes role in the peace process in the Middle East. For instance, he is credited with being a key influence in the signing of the 1979 peace treaty between Israel and Egypt.

The opening of the borders to Moroccan-born Israelis was the tip of the iceberg of his regional and global politics. The king's peace-oriented involvement, both open and secretive, was based on the hope that it would strengthen Morocco's political and economic liaisons with the United States through the good rapport Israel has with Washington administration. The king's long involvement in peace initiatives had other, deeper, layers and ramifications. As of May 1979 the king was elected president of the Al-Quds (Jerusalem) Committee, stemming from the Organization of Islamic Conference (see Tessler 1988). This role granted him involvement in the long crisis of the Middle East, even if he represented a state that was in the far west of the Muslim world.

But beyond these important international considerations, Morocco's specific national discourse was involved in the king's opening the borders for Moroccan-born Israelis. Like other national discourses, Morocco's national discourse evokes kin idioms to articulate the relationships between the people and their state (Herzfeld, 1997), but in this case the discourse is related not only to the land, but also to the king himself.[11] Thus, the king addressed Moroccan Israelis as his own lost sons; they were like sons who can never give up their links to their family. Thus, Moroccan Jews never lost their nationality. By evoking kinship terms the king did not clarify if he meant that Jews are welcomed merely to visit Morocco or perhaps to permanently return.

The king's blurred rhetoric avoided public acknowledgement or recognition of Israel's right to exist as a Jewish homeland. In fact, his blurred attitude rejected the Zionist discourse as it announced that the "natural" place for former Moroccan Jews was in Morocco. The king's blurred language also enabled him to defend his decision to open up Morocco's border from domestic and Islamic criticism.

High-level politics, then, enabled the seemingly personally motivated travels by Moroccan-born Israelis to take place. Yet, national discourse on this initiative was not uniform, nor unwavering. When the interview with Hassan II was broadcast on national TV, the Ashkenazi commentator expressed his astonishment when some Moroccan Israelis unreservedly manifested their enthusiasm: "Aren't you Israelis? How come you have such feelings towards the king? He is not your king, after all!"

The implications of the high-level politics surfaced recurrently during the voyage. For instance, the travelers were tightly supervised, and they felt it. The police were visible at every stop along the route, in hotels, and at pilgrimage sites. Even before entering Morocco, obtaining visas was a complex and highly sensitive procedure. In the first years all groups had to enter Morocco from Spain, where they met personally with the Moroccan consul in Malaga. In the group I joined, the consul who issued the visas congratulated each visitor and made a public speech echoing the king's invitation. He welcomed us, "sons of the Maghreb," and reminded all of the good Muslim-Jewish relationships of the past. When the consul began his speech in French a loud protest was made: "Speak in our language!" He smiled with satisfaction, changed to Maghrebi-Arabic and continued: "Anyone who wishes to stay in Morocco is welcomed to do so. Those who are not interested in staying—may God lead them back safely to their homes."

Clearly political tension was built into his speech, reflecting the granting of travel visas to citizens of a country not formally recognized by Morocco. The Israeli travelers were not happy about his attitude towards their country, manifested by his deliberate omission of its name. "We entered Morocco like thieves in the dark!" remarked Joe retrospectively with a bitter tone. Joe's remark reveals dissatisfaction about the high, yet overtly concealed, politics that was involved in the travel. His words demonstrate an understanding that most travelers shared that there are mysterious behind-the-scenes moves that affect the travel, but that cannot be known.[12] Joe's remark was indicative of things to come. Travelers were instructed not to reveal their nationality in all documents and to omit it at every hotel registration. For example, the laissez-passer left the rubric "current nationality" blank while place of birth was always designated as Morocco. In addition, the tour guides instructed the travelers to refrain from speaking Hebrew in public, and men who ordinarily wore a kippah (skullcap) removed it and put on French berets instead.

A number of national elements unique to the Jewish Maghrebi experience in Israel were invoked during the course of travel. The itinerary itself was interpreted as encapsulating their Jewish historiography: exile from Israel to Spain, the 1492 expulsion from Spain to Morocco, their centuries-long sojourn in Morocco, followed by their return to the land of Israel. For example, when the lights of Malaga airport first came into view people shouted "There's Haifa! There's Haifa!" and "When we came on *aliya* [immigration to Israel], we clapped our hands and said, 'There's Haifa! There's Haifa!'" Someone else said in Arabic, "N'amlu kif 'amlu jadudna di harzu mil'Maser" ("Let us do as our forefathers did when they left Egypt").[13] Although travelers were on their way to Morocco, the immediate association was with their immigration to Israel several decades ago. The clearest expression of the reliving of their Jewish experience was enunciated by the Israeli Moroccan tour guide who, while we were moving along the southeastern coast of Spain, stated that this was the route taken by our forefathers when they were expelled from that country. Like pilgrims who follow the footsteps of their forefathers, the travelers were fully aware of the religious and historical meaning of their travels. The salience of the structure of their trip was most conspicuous during their pilgrimage to holy sites.

The presence of Maghrebi royalty and the state was apparent everywhere—in the Jewish cemeteries and at the shrines of tsaddiqim. The portraits of the king and his heir stared out from every wall. Morocco's red flag with its green star waved high and proudly in the wind over the sites of each hillulah. As if the king's symbols were not enough, he sent his own men, official emissaries of the state, to bless the pilgrims. The state's symbols of protection were clearly visible in the armed soldiers and policemen who were positioned to guard the sites.

In sum, national narratives and practices were at the heart of the tour and interplayed between Israel and Morocco. Both state officials and travelers used and provoked symbols and metaphors of their state(s), which framed, if not prevented, an unmediated connection with the travelers' past. National narratives played a key role in the construction of a partitioning wall between past and present, between here and there, and between homeland and diaspora.

THE PERPLEXING PLACE OF DIASPORA AND HOMELAND

In the very encounters between Israeli Jewish travelers and the remaining Jews in Morocco the relations between the concepts of homelands and diasporas surfaced. This dynamic, in turn, reproduced the schism between the travelers and their past. If Moroccan Muslims' rejection of the travelers' ability to regain their authenticity as Moroccans was harsh, this paled in comparison to their encounter with Jews, fixed in the Moroccan homeland. In anticipation of the reunion with their kin, the travelers had imagined Moroccan Jews as extensions of themselves. The schism that developed out of this encounter assumed crisis-like proportions. These encounters started only a couple of days into the trip, as the travelers confronted the Jews who tended to the cemeteries and oversaw the shrines of tsaddiqim. But the dramatic manifestation of the encounters only occurred during the last days of the tour in Casablanca. The organized tour had ended, and each traveler was free to meet with his own kin or former friends.

Alice, one of the youngest on the tour, invited me to join in her meeting with her sister, who had stayed in Morocco when all the family migrated to Israel in the 1950s. Alice asked me to escort her through Casablanca because she was afraid that she would be recognized as an Israeli; her French was poor and her Maghrebi-Arabic was not fluent. We arrived at the sister's house. It did not take long for a dispute to erupt. Alice bragged about her ability to purchase all kind of souvenirs without paying attention to their cost and about the luxurious hotels we had stayed during the tour. Joelle, her sister, repeatedly explained that she could find the same caftans as Alice bought at a cheaper price. She reminded Alice that in Morocco their family had been poor and never behaved that way. Almost the same story happened with Sami. Sami strutted like a peacock on Tahiti beach, a popular Jewish recreation site in Casablanca, with a Muslim prostitute on his arm. He loudly announced to one and all that he was unlike all the Jews there who were afraid of "taking a Muslim whore," on whom he could spend "a lot of money." One man, witnessing his flagrant behavior, called him over. "Why are you bragging? I know you and your parents . . . they came from a poor, miserable village! I know your roots!" Sami did not answer, he turned around and left. Indeed, he departed for Israel before everyone else as he ran out of money and could no longer pay for his hotel.

Both incidents, like many others I witnessed in Casablanca, demonstrate a repetitious dynamic in which Moroccan Israelis emphasized their *present* status, their ability to spend money, not to be afraid of Muslims, and so on. Moroccan Jews, on the other hand, pointed to the *past* of the travelers, reminding them of how they, or their parents, used to be.

These interactions revealed several disturbing paradoxes. One worth mentioning was that the Moroccan Jews' claims to authenticity over the past were accepted by the tourists. Because of the symbolic authority of those fixed in Morocco, the travelers recruited their improved present to save face. Ironically, their face-saving efforts prevented them from reconnecting with their past in Morocco. Indeed, the travelers' attitude towards the Jews living in Morocco was deeply ambivalent. The travelers used an accusing tone in conversations with Moroccan Jews about their reluctance to emigrate to Israel. Yet, it may be that Moroccan Jews were troubling in a more personal way. The Jews who chose not to leave Morocco represented for the travelers a sort of hypothetical biography: what would have happened had they not "become Israelis." To put it a bit differently, the travelers saw in those Moroccan Jews a present-day manifestation of their own past lives that took an alternate course.

Leaving Morocco was the *only* reasonable course for Jews. Suddenly, the finality of that decision was put into question. Here they are, real live, present-day Jews in Morocco! So unsettling was the provocation posed by them that many travelers suggested that the Jews remaining in Morocco must be either mentally unbalanced, greedy, or physically ill, and they treated the Jews they encountered as marginal, odd people, or irresponsible.

In sum, Israeli Moroccans in encounters with Moroccan Jews evoked a national discourse based on the dichotomy of homeland and diaspora. This national discourse portrays a historically constant and symbolically unidirectional relationship privileging the homeland as the focal point of longings, identifications, and aspirations. At the other side of the dichotomy stand the dispersed groups that maintain ties with their symbolic center.

The very decision of Jews in Morocco to stay put questioned the entrenched national discourse negating Jewish exile and destabilized the travelers' assumed position of belonging to a center-cum-homeland. By participating in a journey to Morocco, Israeli Moroccans confirmed the sanctity of its soil. They confirmed the symbolic centrality of Morocco, and thus they reversed, if only momentarily, the homeland-diaspora model. Throughout their journey, the travelers dug themselves ever deeper into this national Israeli model, and in doing so they precluded their ability to go back home to diaspora.

NOTES

1. This chapter is based on my ongoing interest in the complex relationships Moroccan Jews have with their dispersed communities all over the globe. Academically my research begun with my Master's study in 1986, where I followed a group of Moroccan-born Israelis revisiting their natal land. My deepest thanks to Fran Markowitz, who encouraged me to "travel back" to this early study by inviting me to participate in a panel on "homecomings" at the centennial meeting of the American Anthropological Association and contribute this chapter. Her comments were critical to this chapter. I am also grateful to Anders Stefansson for his careful reading and useful comments.

2. On the veneration of tsaddiqim amongst Moroccan Jews in Morocco see: Ben-Ami, 1988. For an analysis of this phenomenon in contemporary Morocco see: Levy, 1994. On hagiolatry in Israel see: Ben-Ari and Bilu, 1987; Bilu, 1987; Goldberg, 1992; Levy, 1991.

3. I should emphasize, however, that by using words like "intimate" and "close" I wish to evade idealization of these relations. Jews were, after all, a religio-ethnic minority under the rule of Islam.

4. Albert Memmi (1973) expresses the tragic situation in which Jews were caught when describing the double trap of the colonialism.

5. Many historical documents and personal memoirs treat this period in Morocco's Jewish lives. For a Zionist perspective of this activity see: Bensimon, 1993; Segev, 1984). For an attempt to present an uninvolved perspective see: Stillman, 1991.

6. Eisenstadt's *The Absorption of Immigrants* (1954) declared an incommensurable dichotomy between traditional Jews of the Middle East and the modern state of Israel. His sociology informed Israel's immigration policies. In its implementation, Moroccan Jews were "Orientalized."

7. On the Zionist reconstruction of the past see: Zerubavel, 1995, especially chapter 2.

8. The popularization of the spring celebration of the Mimuna in Israel is only one example of this development. The Mimuna spring festival of hospitality, which takes place immediately after Pesach (Passover), exemplified the braided and enmeshed relationships between Jews and Muslims in the Moroccan reality. In past times Muslims constituted an integral part of it. Jews and Muslims exchanged gifts of food. Goldberg sees the elaborate exchange between these groups as constituting a *rite de passage* that reopened social life with Muslims after the holiday restrictions (Goldberg, 1978). The Mimuna was renewed in Israel in a different form, turning more public, using a rhetoric accentuating its being an "all Israeli" event, and including in it politicians.

9. For a critical analysis of the political protest emerging from migrants of Islamic states see Shalom Chetrit 2003 and for an explanation for voting for the Likud see: Herzog, 1987.

10. Saying that, these spaces are not undebatable. Frequently such spaces were given to negotiations, manipulations, and even conflicts about ownership of memory and, even more so, history (Herzfeld, 1991). Differences about ownership of history emerged during these travels mainly through the discussion over the proper routes to tsaddiqim. Each group or individual wished to "promote" the importance of its own tsaddiq by pushing him to the list of visits.

11. Morocco's landscape is adorned with huge slogans, made of whitewashed stones, with the words: "God, the Land, the King."

12. Interestingly, the organizers manipulatively used these feelings to explain many mishaps in the travel.

13. Here the travelers refer to the Biblical story of exodus from Egypt.

REFERENCES

Adam, André. *La population marocaine dans l'ancienne medina de Casablanca*. Rabat: Bulletin Economique et Social du Maroc, 1950.

Almog, Oz. *The Sabra: The Creation of the New Jew*. Berkeley: University of California Press, 2000.

Bahloul, Joëlle. *The Architecture of Memory: A Jewish-Muslim Household in Colonial Algeria 1937-1962*. Tranlsated by M. C. Du Peloux. Cambridge: Cambridge University Press, 1996.

Bar-Yosef, Rivka. "Desocialization and Resocialization." *International Immigration Review* 2 (1966): 27-43.

Ben-Ami, Issachar. *Saint Veneration among the Jews in Morocco*. Detroit: Wayne State University Press, 1998.

Ben-Ari, Eyal, and Yoram Bilu. "Saints' Sanctuaries in Israeli Development Towns: On a Mechanism of Urban Transformation." *Urban Anthropology* 16, no. 2 (1987): 243-72.

Bensimon, Agnés. *Hassan II et les juifs*. Tel-Aviv: Yediot Ahronot Books and Chemed Books [in Hebrew], 1993.

Bilu, Yoram. "Dreams and Wishes of the Saint." Pp. 285-313 in *Judaism Viewed from Within and from Without: Anthropological Studies*, edited by Harvey E. Goldberg. Albeny: State University of New York Press, 1987.

———. "The Sanctification of Place in Israel's Civil and Traditional Religion." *Jerusalem Studies in Jewish Folklore*. XIX-XX (1998): 65-84 [In Hebrew].

Cohen, Erik. "Changing Legitimation of the State of Israel." *Studies in Contemporary Jewry* 5 (1984): 148-165.

Combs-Shilling, Elaine M. *Sacred Performances: Islam, Sexuality, and Sacrifice*. New York: Columbia University Press, 1989.

Eisenstadt, Shmuel N. *The Absorption of Immigrants*. London: Routledge and Kegan Paul, 1954.

Entelis, John P. *Culture and Counterculture in Moroccan Politics*. Boulder, CO: Westview Press, 1989.

Feldman, Jackie. "Marking the Boundaries of the Enclave: Defining the Israeli Collective through the Poland 'Experience.'" *Israel Studies* 7, no. 2 (2002): 84-114.

Ferguson, James, and Akhil Gupta. "Spatializing States: Toward an Ethnography of Neoliberal Governmentality." *American Ethnologist* 29, no. 4 (2002): 981–1002.

Flamand, Pierre. *Diaspora en terre d'Islam: les communautés israélites du sud-marocain.* Casablanca: Presses des Imprimeries Réunis, 1959.

Goldberg, Harvey E. "The Mimuna and the Minority Status of Moroccan Jews." *Ethnology* 17, no. 1 (1978): 75–87.

———. "Potential Polities: Jewish Saints in the Moroccan Countryside and in Israel." Pp. 233–252 in *Faith and Polity: Essays on Religion and Politics*, edited by Mart Bax, Peter Kloos, and Andrianus Koster. Amsterdam: UV University Press, 1992.

Hasson, Shlomo. "Social and Spatial Conflicts: The Settlement Process in Israel during the 1950s and 1960s." *L'Espace Geographique* 3 (1981): 169–79.

Herzfeld, Michael. *A Place in History: Social and Monumental Time in a Cretan Town.* Princeton, NJ: Princeton University Press, 1991.

———. *The Social Production of Indifference: Exploring the Symbolic Roots of Western Bureaucracy.* New York: Berg 1992.

———. *Cultural Intimacy: Social Poetics in the Nation-State.* New York: Routledge, 1997.

Herzog, Hannah. The Elections Campaign as a Liminal Stage: Negotiations over Meanings. *The Sociological Review*, 35 no. 3 (1987): 559–74.

Hirschberg, Haïm Z. *A History of the Jews in North Africa.* Leiden: Brill, 1974.

Horowitz, Dan, and Moshe Lissak. *Trouble in Utopia: The Overburdened Polity of Israel.* Albany: State University of New York Press, 1989.

Jamous, Raymond. *Honnuer et baraka: les structures sociales traditionnelles dans le Rif.* Paris: Editions de la Maison des Sciences de l'Homme, 1981.

Levy, André. "Diasporas through Anthropological Lenses: Contexts of Postmodernity." *Diaspora* 9, no. 1 (2000): 137–57.

———. "Center and Diaspora: Jews in Late-Twentieth-Century Morocco." *City and Society* XIII no. 2 (2001): 247–72.

———. "Une grande Hillulah et une 'Atzeret Tshuvah': etude d'un cas." Pp. 167–79 in *Recherches sur la Culture des Juifs d'Afrique du Nord*, edited by Issachar Ben-Ami. Jerusalem: Communaute Israelite Nord-Africaine, 1991. [in Hebrew].

———. "The Structured Ambiguity of Minorities towards Decolonisation: The Case of the Moroccan Jews." *The Maghreb Review* 19, nos. 1–2 (1994): 133–46.

Memmi, Albert. *Portriat du Colonisé.* Paris: Payot, 1973.

Nora, Pierre. "Between Memory and History." *Representations* 26 (1989): 7–25.

Ossman, Susan. *Picturing Casablanca: Portraits of Power in a Moroccan City.* Berkeley and Los Angeles: University of California Press, 1994.

Rabinow, Paul. *Symbolic Domination: Cultural Forms and Historical Change in Morocco.* Chicago and London: University of Chicago Press, 1975.

Schutz, Alfred. "The Homecomer." *American Journal of Sociology* 50, no. 5 (1945): 369–76.

Segev, Shmuel. *Operation "Yakhin": The Secret Immigration of Moroccan Jews to Israel.* Tel Aviv: Misrad Ha-Bitakhon, 1984 [in Hebrew].

Shalom Chetrit. Sami *The Mizrahi Struggle in Israel: Between Identification and Integration to Contention and Alternative 1948–2002.* Tel-Aviv: Am-Oved Publishers, 2003 [In Hebrew].

Stillman, Norman A. *The Jews of Arab Lands in Modern Times.* Philadelphia: Jewish Publication Society of America, 1991.

Suleiman, Michael W. "Morocco in the Arab and Muslim World: Attitudes of Moroccan Youth." *Maghreb Review* 14, nos. 1–2 (1989): 16–27.

Tessler, Mark A. "Moroccan-Israeli Relations and the Reasons for Moroccan Receptivity to Contact with Israel." *Jerusalem Journal of International Relations* 10, no. 2 (1988): 76–108.

Zerubavel, Yael. *Recovered Roots: Collective Memory and the Making of Israeli National Tradition*. Chicago and London: University of Chicago Press, 1995.

7

From the Centers to the Periphery: "Repatriation" to an Armenian Homeland in the Twentieth Century

Susan Pattie

Mr. Boghos is a small and wiry man who uses every muscle of his expressive face to tell his story. Talking about the decision his family made to move from the Armenian villages of Kessab in Syria to Soviet Armenia[1] in 1947, he remembers that they were very impressed by the repatriation or *nerkaght* committee. Well-dressed, ebullient, and persuasive, the committee told them, "'We have better fruit in Armenia.' But, of course, they didn't have anything. I don't blame them." Mr. Boghos looks away. Today he sits at the table across from me, his eyes intense but sunken and his cheeks gaunt. He tells me that he receives a pension of 4,300 *dram* a month (roughly $8.50). He doesn't eat meat, doesn't drink or smoke. He eats about one kilo of bread a day and can't afford cakes or sweets. He doesn't look well and clothes hang on his body. His eyes have cloudy cataracts, his face is reddish and unshaven. But he moves quickly, talks clearly and intently and has a message—a sermon almost. In an hour or so of speaking he betrays no bitterness at all. "Who should I protest to?" he asks. "I forgive." In fact, he still has some hope and wishes most of all for another "repatriation" drive like the first one. He believes only that will save Armenia.[2]

At the end of the nineteenth century, the majority of Armenians were living where people who called themselves Armenians had lived for over 2,000 years. What is popularly called "historic Armenia"[3] stretched from what is now eastern Turkey to Karabagh. By the 1920s, very few remained on those lands except in one far-eastern corner, which later became the republic of Armenia. Kessab, further south, near the Mediterranean Sea, was under the French mandate of Syria and Lebanon when survivors of the 1915 genocide were able to return and rebuild their homes. It is believed that Kessab and its surrounding villages were first settled over six hundred years ago by Armenians fleeing earlier turbulence further north.[4] Pre-genocide, the villages had a population of some eight thousand people, connected by ties of kinship, dialect, religion, and attachment to a specific locale. After World War I, new ideas and geopolitics took shape, including the eventual end of empires and the rise of the nation-state as desirable for smaller groups as well as the powerful. The local became insufficient in itself, both ideologically and in practical terms. Kessab remains an important part of the complex of identity for those descending from the villages, but through the remaining years of the twentieth century, a more general Armenian identity has been fostered through education, media, church, and, especially, politics. With this came strong competition for the title of "homeland."[5]

This paper charts the hopes, dreams, and crushing reality of a quest for a modern homeland during the twentieth century. As part of the transition from local to state-based homeland, Armenians around the world were encouraged to think of the state of Armenia, then Soviet, as their homeland. In 1947, when Josef Stalin was perhaps at his most paranoid, Armenians from the Middle East were actively recruited by committees from Soviet Armenia to leave their homes and settle there. Over the span of the *nerkaght* or "repatriation," from the 1920s to the 1960s, perhaps 150,000 people answered this call, the greatest number arriving between 1946 and 1947.[6] Here we look at how some of the people who made that journey explain the decisions made along the way and how the changing focus of their narratives reflects broader issues in the understanding of immigration, refugee studies, and diaspora/homeland relations.

There is a problem with the use of the word "repatriation," which, in print, can at least be put in quotation marks. Its very use in the English translation of nerkaght helps to shape the acceptance of the state of Armenia as original homeland. It is closer to the concept of a political and moral action, rather than a simple return. Here, where possible, I will use the word "newcomers" rather than "repatriates," as it is a clearer description of their situation—to me—but that word does not adequately contain the complex of emotional pull and political decisions involved. Neither "repatriation" nor "newcomer" gives an idea of the process of attachment nor of the ways in which personal and communal narratives develop to accommodate the realities encountered in the new homeland. And therein lies the story.

ARMENIA: FROM PERIPHERY TO HOMELAND

The republic of Armenia is a small corner of the old lands and, until the twentieth century, something of a backwater. In the Caucasus, Georgia's capital, Tbilisi, had a larger and more vibrant community of Armenians than

Yerevan, the capital of Armenia. Elsewhere, Constantinople (later Istanbul) was a center of intellectual activity. Armenians identified strongly with their local towns and villages, while maintaining connections and networks with Armenians elsewhere. With the crumbling of the Ottoman Empire and its genocide of the Armenians within its boundaries, these lands were emptied. While many survivors dispersed to neighboring Arab countries or to France and the Americas, others made their way eastward to what became briefly the state of Armenia from 1918 to 1921. Though Armenia was in desperate economic straits, the people found refuge there. After three years of independence, it became a part of the Soviet Union and remained so until 1991. During these seventy years, the country grew both in its ability to support an ever-growing population and in its position and potency as a symbol of the Armenian homeland.

Since independence, the Republic of Armenia has increasingly become "the homeland." However, while part of the Soviet Union, Armenia lost its appeal for the many (probably half the diaspora) who sympathized with the political party that had led it as a free state. The Armenian Revolutionary Federation (or *Dashnaks*) in diaspora did not forgive what they saw as betrayal and campaigned against the Soviet state in a variety of ways. "Free, Independent Armenia" was the motto of the party, referring not only to the lost Ottoman territories but to the Soviet state. Arrayed against the *Dashnaks* and supporting Soviet Armenia were other political parties, the *Ramgavars* and Hnchaks who believed that this was the only way into the future. These remained in intense opposition, particularly during the Cold War period. During the 1970s the *Dashnak* party began to warm to the idea that Armenia needed protection and if Russia was willing to provide this, then it had to be accepted, even appreciated.

This later change of attitude would have seemed impossible between the 1920s and 1960. During that period, Soviet Armenia and the diaspora went through numerous changes, in their relations and in their own images and definitions. From early years, Soviet Armenia presented itself as the homeland. Its term for the diaspora is an interesting indication of the official attitude: *ardasahman*, or beyond the borders. The borders in fact are or were those of the Soviet Union, for that term is used only for those living in the diaspora outside the Soviet Union, or, as historian Claire Mouradian has put it more trenchantly, "in enemy territory in capitalist countries." Those living in Russia, Georgia, or elsewhere within the union were included in the "internal diaspora."[7] As has been shown elsewhere, the development of a strong identity with Russia and the whole of the Soviet Union was not acknowledged or perhaps realized by those in diaspora, perhaps especially not by their allies.

Attitudes towards the diaspora ("external") and relations between the diaspora and the Armenian state were influenced greatly by the changes in the teaching of history within the Soviet Union. The Soviet period began with the

Leninist insistence that all national histories take a back seat to the Soviet history in which all play a part. Languages and local histories were allowed as part of the whole. Stalin placed more emphasis on Russia as the leader, with the other peoples as minorities within the Russian world. As Velychenko points out, "After 1947 more detailed guidelines and more stringent central control restricted presentation and discussion of plurality, diversity and national conflicts to such a degree that official histories of the non-Russian republics can be classified as a species of Russian regional history." (1994: 24). Soviet Armenians, already influenced by the Russian Empire, drew closer to a particular image of civilization. Helene Carrere d'Encausse notes that the "russification" of the Armenian political cadre was particularly remarkable (1978: 56).

During the early decades of the Soviet Union, relations between Armenia and the diaspora were organized around several factors: from the side of one portion of the diaspora—a desire to aid Armenia and at the same time, to learn from the growing intellectual and cultural base there and from the side of Soviet Armenia, the drive to consolidate a position as the center with a periphery, and the apparent desire to control and, some believe, undermine the diaspora. The latter seems unlikely as the diaspora bases were, judging from recent archival findings, useful sources of information (Sanjian 2001; Mouradian 1990) Claire Mouradian makes a case for the creation of the organization Friends of Armenia (HOK) as a deliberate infiltration of the many compatriotic unions in diaspora, turning them into aid for Armenia, focusing their attention and help on their "new" villages in Armenia rather than the refugees spread around the diaspora (1990: 310, 319). Mouradian states that the purpose was to "destabilize" the diaspora and reorient it towards Armenia as the motherland. The HOK committees later evolved into a platform for persuading people to do *nerkaght*.

LOCAL BELONGINGS

In the diaspora itself, the term *spiurk* is most commonly used to gloss diaspora.[8] Strictly speaking, a large portion of Armenian people have been living outside the homeland, but nearby, for nearly a thousand years, as Zekiyan says, "on the border between 'colony' and 'diaspora.' Their capacity for integration helped them to transform dispersion into permanent and flourishing settlements, but their deep attachment to their roots never let them forget the dream of their Edenic homeland" (1999: 47). This long-standing foundation of the thriving diaspora, including the villages of Kessab, is one of the crucial elements missing from nationalist and statist rhetoric.[9]

Today Kessab and its surrounding villages are perched above the Mediterranean on the border between Syria and Turkey. Until a generation ago, the population was nearly all ethnically Armenian, but this has changed radically over the last twenty-five years. Today, in the winter, Armenians remain the large majority but summer brings a large influx of tourists and summer residents from all over Syria and indeed the Arab world. Set at a high altitude with forests and some springs, Kessab has been an attractive summer escape from the heat of the cities and lower countryside. Armenians from Damascus and Aleppo have been regular summer visitors for decades. During that period, small shops, hotels, and a few restaurants thrive, but the main source of income throughout the year is through growing fruit, especially apples. Among Armenians, Kessab is also known for its proportionately high number of doctors and teachers, the contribution of many sons to the priesthood and clergy, its mix of denominations, and good relations with neighbors.[10] Its most distinguishing feature is certainly its dialect, *Kesspeneuts* or *Kessaberen*.[11] Though similar to other villages of the area, such as Musa Dagh, it cannot be readily understood by a standard Armenian speaker. Today the dialect is still spoken in the village, though the younger generations tend towards passive understanding rather than active use. Earlier it was considered ideal to marry another Kessabtsi; today parents are pleased if their child finds another Armenian.

Towards the end of the nineteenth century, migration began towards the United States as well as nearer destinations in the Middle East. In response to increased insecurity in the region as well as a desire for some to pursue education and other opportunities, young men, married and single, began a small but steady stream of immigration. In 1909 Kessab was burned and the population forced from their homes by "Turkish irregulars from the region of Antioch," followed soon afterwards by Ottoman Turkish troops based in Aleppo (Churukian 2003: 211). Though some were killed, most families were able to escape, and after a short period they returned to rebuild their homes. However, devastation was much greater in 1915 during the period of the Armenian genocide, when Ottoman soldiers forced the villagers to join the marches into the deserts. This time many more died and the destruction was catastrophic. Some 2,300 people survived, returned, and again rebuilt. This period was followed by an increase in migration as some were able to join family members who had already settled abroad.

The beauty of the landscape, the local knowledge, attachment to family lands, ease of communication with familiar people, all are reasons given for the courageous act of remaining to do the difficult work of reconstruction. Sadly, another setback occurred not long afterward and in 1939, roughly a third of the lands of the villages were lost as borders were redrawn between Turkey and Syria as the French left the area. The recurring losses set the scene for further emigration and the difficult decisions of the mid-1940s, culminating with departure of half of the village for Armenia.

TO LEAVE OR NOT TO LEAVE . . . ?

> In the night of homeland,
> Homeleaving is a lantern.
> In the night of homeleaving,
> Homeland is a lantern.
>
> —Kaiser Albert Afif

This fragment of a longer poem submitted to the annual *Kessabtzis Directory and Yearbook*, (1998: 204) reveals the ambivalent, difficult relationship of what the poet contrasts as exile and home. Neither can be considered alone, once the choice is there.

When considering why so many people accepted the invitation to migrate to Armenia, popular interpretations and discussions almost always characterize the decision as being motivated by poverty, political conviction, or the "last chance" response of people living outside their ancestral lands. The case of Kessab includes a variety of reasons for migration but clearly demonstrates Minasyan's thesis that the primary motive was patriotism.[12] The people were still in the villages or, if in Beirut, they had the option to go back to the village. A number of the people who applied to go were from the *Dashnak* (opposition) political side.[13] The migrants included people from a variety of economic situations. Though struggling after the losses of previous decades, most at least had land to sell. The excitement of the period is difficult to fathom as we now know what awaited them upon arrival. The decision to go was taken by families, rather than by individuals, and this itself caused enormous difficulties within relationships. Not all who applied were accepted to go and it was not clear how the official decision was made.

A well-known photograph of the time shows the Soviet boat, loaded with its passengers and cargo, preparing to pull up anchor. People have lined the shore, climbed the flag poles, stood on roofs to wave off their compatriots. On board, the ship side is crowded with people. People tell me they remember that they were singing, they were so happy to be going to this promised land. As Zekiyan points out, Armenian Romanticism had a long history and intellectuals were influenced by earlier texts of the eighteenth and nineteenth centuries where Armenia (not necessarily that particular corner) was portrayed in poetry and song as paradise (1999: 47).[14] The propagandists for *nerkaght* had only to add practical points, such as the availability of free higher education for all, free world-class health care, abundant food and drink, and work for everyone and give a specific location to the Armenia of their dreams.

A journalist who had come as a young man from Kessab told me, "Kessab was a collection of villages but each one had a school. Kessab never recovered from 1947. During the last year—1946—representatives came from the

Armenian government and told lies. 'We'll give you land, cows, houses.' Kessabtzis were very *hayrenaser* (patriotic). Half the Kessabtzis left and the village was destroyed. There were no non-Armenians there at the time."

An older man, active in *Dashnak* politics, agrees with this assessment. He told me that his father had wanted to go but he, the older son, decided the family would stay. He was involved in politics and understood what the situation was in Armenia. By 1998, he was not against the *nerkaght* in principle—indeed he regularly visited and helped to support extended family members who had migrated—but, he said, "It would have been better if they hadn't ruined Kessab—if they hadn't taken so many. Now Alouites who moved in then have learned Armenian and the children go to Armenian schools."

ARRIVAL IN THE PROMISED LAND

The older man's relatives told me of how they had gone by car to Beirut to board the boat in August 1947. "People were singing and dancing. We're going to *Hayastan*[15] (Armenia)! We sat in the boat and went to (the Black Sea port of) Batum and there the people's back was broken. We were given black bread and tried to get rid of it, to give it away. The (native or *deghatsi*) people said—keep the bread—you'll be starving later and then you'll want it." Journalist Jano added that "the bread tasted like dirt. The people began to throw it out (off the boat) on arrival and women from Batum ran into the water to get it. Then we knew there was something wrong."

The migrants had been able to pack trunks of their belongings, including food for their first year. When they landed, officials checked their belongings, dividing it between what was allowed and what would be confiscated. Mrs. Marie told me that when the Kessabtzis came to *Hayastan,* they brought whatever they wanted—chickpeas, flour, bulgur, the bulgur stone, rice, *bekmez* (carob or grape syrup). Most of them had sold their land to the *nerkaght* committee to pay for their passage on the boat—and then the committee sold it. "The food lasted through the winter and then it was gone by Spring. We ate whatever there was, which was not much. We ate a lot of bulghur and still do. No Kessabtzis were destitute because they work hard and take care of each other."

The newcomers were split up. Families who had argued and discussed for months about a joint migration were sent to different corners of the country. However, people made it a priority to find each other and eventually moved to be closer. Journalist Jano remembered that one day he and his father walked forty kilometers to find family members. However, the poverty of the country and their own dispersion were not the only problems facing the newcomers. Today few have a clear idea of why Stalin approved the *nerkaght* project proposed by the head of the Armenian church, Catholicos Chorekjian. This period of deep paranoia, where returning World War II heroes were being sent to the gulags because as prisoners of war they had outside contact, saw the influx of some one hundred thousand newcomers, all of whom had outside contacts and education. One family told me of their near escape by foot across the southern border. They were caught and the father sent to Siberia, never to be seen again. Numerous others who did not try to escape still found themselves the targets of malicious gossip, being traded off for favors, or simply disappearing with no warning. The *Dashnak* sympathizers who had decided to migrate were especially vulnerable.

A poignant text by a former *nerkaght* organizer, not a Kessabtzi, tells of this. First he writes that, as "head of the caravan" of the July 1947 ship, he was asked by Soviet officers on board to write up a list of members of the group who had been educated at American, British, or French schools and who might have former business connections with capitalist countries, etc. The author states that of the forty thousand Armenians later exiled to Siberia, over half were "repatriates." He continues, "after the national tragedy of the genocide, . . . another banishment or exile was the last thing we could have expected to happen in our fatherland" (Touryantz 1987: 87).

"STRANGERS IN THEIR OWN LAND": THE NARRATIVE DEVELOPS

The multiple difficulties confronted in the early years following migration from Kessab were dealt with in several ways and on different fronts. All spoke of their efforts to repair the broken networks of family and co-villagers. This seemed a necessary first step. Beyond this, the Kessabtzis see themselves as hard-working people who were not willing to take poverty and starvation as their fate. In addition to finding or creating work, as soon as possible (post-Stalin) they found ways to build houses with gardens—or near fields where they could grow much of their own fruit and vegetables. Equally importantly, they found ways to tell the stories of their lives that lifted them above the misery of those years and gave meaning to their troubles.

The main theme of this narrative is that the newcomers, not only the Kessabtzis, saved Armenia. They sacrificed, albeit without initially realizing just how much would be required, but the end result was that Armenia grew and prospered. There are a number of different approaches to this same conclusion. In an interview with Dr. Armenouhie Bedrossian of Yerevan State University, she responded to my questions about the planning and plausibilty of *nerkaght* by saying that it was correct as a concept but not at that time. Diaspora Armenians should have been invited to make their homes in the state, but, she felt, the government should have waited until the country was in better shape. Her own research and observations brought out two reasons for the decisions: first, to weaken the diaspora, not to help Armenia. Armenia had no room at the time and it was considered that families might go to Karabakh, an ethnic Armenian enclave in Azerbaijan. *Nerkaght*, she concurred, tore the diaspora apart—communities and families. Further, many people decided to go and went to the sea and waited and nothing happened. And they had nothing to go back to. They waited for months by the sea. *Nerkaght* was organized by Moscow for immigration in general but the capital gave money, for example, to finance migration to the Ukraine. The Armenians, however, had to find the money themselves ($50 for each person, children and older people included). The money collected in each of the communities went to Soviet Armenia. The other unofficial reason, she said, was that there was talk in the 1940s of receiving land from Turkey that the newcomers would then settle.

The stories gathered from many families echoed these observations in outline but with more emotional content. Some believe that the population of Armenia was so low following World War II that Stalin was considering splitting the territory between Georgia and Azerbaijan.[16] Catholicos Chorkejian thus was inspired to organize the *nerkaght* in order to quickly repopulate the territory and was able to persuade Stalin not to dismantle the state. Others tell stories that include their observations of the poverty and lack of skills they encountered among the people upon arrival. They believe it is the hard work and new skills brought by the newcomers that enabled the country to rebuild following the devastation of World War II and the Stalin years. As Bedrossian noted above, postwar there was Armenian pressure on the Soviet Union to acquire territories from Turkey that had been promised in the Treaty of Sevres.[17] Though this never came to even proximate fruition, the possibility of repopulating lands closer still to their family homes was a great motivation—and disappointment when it did not happen. Still, those who believed it possible could tell their children with pride that they had been willing to sacrifice to bring it about.

In the telling and retelling of these stories and their many variations families began weaving their own narratives with that of the Soviet state and with that corner of Armenia. Initially the newcomers were discriminated against and called by derogatory terms. *Akhpar* denotes outsider status and can still be heard today. One common complaint from the older generation was the surprise and disappointment at feeling themselves "strangers in their own land." The interpretation of the phrase "own land" was of course influenced not only by their own desires but by the speeches of the repatriation committees. They were not migrating to a strange country but were simply going home. But it was not a home they recognized and the "family" members living in that home were not as welcoming as they expected.[18] This became less important as they became better integrated on structural levels and were able to create something more familiar in their own homes. This for many included the maintenance of religious expressions and practices, something directly at odds with the mainstream of formal society.[19] Other differences remained, including most importantly maintaining ties, in spite of difficulties, with Kessabtzis elsewhere in the world. Kessabtzis continued to speak their village dialect (Kesspeneuts) and even incoming brides learned to speak it. Like other newcomers, the Kessabtzis found ways to make their familiar foods and this too still distinguishes them from the native Armenians.[20] However, new shops and restaurants in Yerevan today are selling these popular foods to everyone.

With gradual integration, movement also began towards the core of society, away from the Middle Eastern context of their villages and towns and towards Russia and the Soviet Union. At school and through television, children learned to appreciate Russian literature and Russia's heroic history. The Soviet Union became a source of pride. The even slower process of assimilation is more a mutual process, as it is in other countries. Within a generation those who have stayed say they are firmly rooted and speak of their dedication to Armenia. They talk of continuing the contribution of their parents to the society. When Kessabtzis described the misery of their arrival and the hopelessness of the present, I wondered aloud whether they had considered returning to Kessab—about which they spoke so fondly. "Kessab? Why? Isn't it worse there?" "There is nothing to do in the village," I was told. Many people were concerned that a mosque has been built in Kessab and they expressed concern that Syria is a Muslim nation. This concern is not shared by those still living in Kessab, who were quick to tell me that Assad (father and now son) safeguarded the rights of minorities. It appears that absence does not make the heart grow fonder, but former neighbors can quickly become strangers.[21]

A number of Kessabtzis have returned to the West—or rather, have gone farther west to Los Angeles. Those who leave have different attitudes to the narrative and it becomes more a tale of betrayal than redemption. Even so, a number of people said they were open to the possibility of change in Armenia and would consider eventual reconnection if not return migration.[22] Armenouhie tends the next-door house of her brother-in-law and his family, who now have lived in Los Angeles for four years. Last year the mother-in-law joined them there because, as Armenouhie told me, it meant one fewer mouth to feed. "She felt so guilty because the children don't have enough to eat and she is not working, just sitting around." The children miss her but Armenouhie expects her to come back, with the rest of the family—as soon as there is work again. "Why should they stay there? It is so lonely!"

While in Los Angeles, I visited with an older couple who were staying with the husband's sister, whom he had not seen for fifty-one years. They emphasized that they were visiting—possibly for one year—as their own children had remained, working in Yerevan. But their story of departure is one that points up the very different narratives and the transnational links of these people, diasporans in the homeland. The cheerful wife began the story and suddenly her eyes had filled with tears. "On our last Sunday," she began, "we were asked to go to the front of the church and there the minister put his hands on us and everyone prayed for our safe journey." "Is this a Protestant church?" I asked rather unnecessarily. "Yes, there are many now," she said. She and her husband and indeed the extended family had all been Protestant when they had emigrated to Armenia but had been unable to practice openly until glasnost and independence.[23] Today a worldwide network of Protestant Armenian churches opens up new possibilities of support, resources, and information.[24]

Protestants and other non-Apostolics (Armenian national church) have suffered under the increasingly strident nationalism during glasnost and post-independence. For a period, this also became very anti-Russian. But the latter was not deep and the late 1990s saw the acknowledgement of the necessity of diplomatic and military alliance as well as academic links with Russia. However, Caroline Humphrey notes the tendency towards the regional affiliation "Eurasia," which binds the periphery and smaller states with the central Russian project. Unlike earlier times, today there are lateral as well as vertical relations and the republics seem determined to pursue these as well as their connections with the Russian center. Humphrey adds that the contrast is also found in the opening of "an ideational space for the phantasmatic rhetorical representation of the given regional culture as injecting its own values and practices into the project of 'Eurasia' as a whole." (2002: 262) What is true for the inner Asian states that Humphrey studies is also true for intellectuals in Armenia who welcome the opportunity to become part of a larger power base on terms that are more flexible and full of possibilities than the previous Soviet and Russian empires.

CONCLUSION

In the years 1998 to 2001 as I listened to people describe the hopelessness they felt in the face of massive unemployment, wholesale corruption, and lack of leadership, I wondered whether it really was the worst of all times, as they insisted. I asked if the Stalin period they had described was not actually worse. They had told me they were afraid to speak to anyone, had less food on the table than now, practiced their religion in secret, and had limited job opportunities. Some people thought this over a bit before disagreeing, others immediately said—no. Today they feel hopeless. During the Stalin period, they thought it had to get better and that in itself makes it better.

My own impression was that the overwhelming uncertainties of post-independence and post-socialism may not be very different in scale from the transition the Kessabtzis made in 1947. Their leap of faith into a new society turned out neither to resemble their old way of life or beliefs, as they, the fellow Armenians, had been led to believe it would. Nor did it resemble anything they had been promised of the brave new socialist world of impeccable morality and equality. Like now, they made the most of what was possible and waited for better times. Today remittances from far-flung relatives in Russia, Europe, and the U.S. keep families alive. Some, like Mr. Boghos, hope for another *nerkaght*. "But," he adds, "it would be necessary to have someone like (Catholicos) Chorekjian to lead and inspire it." Given the number of people who mentioned Chorekjian, I began to wonder about the power of moral rhetoric to inspire people to strive onwards in impossible times. This is something that all agree is missing in the current period. The narrative has stalled.

At the time of the great 1947 *nerkaght*, when the Kessabtzis migrated along with the largest number of Armenians to make the journey, the world was full of people crisscrossing the globe in search of better lives. The tumult of the war, the impossibility of events and deeds witnessed, the economic, physical, and social devastation of great swathes of land, must have planted the idea in many heads that a new start was necessary.[25] Empires were ending, new nation-states emerging, dreams postponed could be indulged. The Armenians who left Kessab for Armenia were part of this global movement, some attracted by ideas, others by promises of security, many by both.

What are the implications of this story for current global politics? First, that homeland-diaspora relations are guided by constantly changing dynamics and are rarely either static or controlled by one or the other entity. Though not shown in this paper, both diaspora and homeland have numerous permutations and neither is a single entity itself.[26] There are many diasporas in the Armenian case and they are not a simple periphery of the state of Armenia.

Secondly, there are implications for refugee and other migrant settlement. Where families wished to settle together and were separated by the state, much time and energy was spent until the situation was resolved. It was only at that point that people began to feel they could settle in and concentrate on being part of the society.[27]

Finally, the case of the Kessabtzis demonstrates the willingness of people to create meaningful lives even provided with the sparsest of ingredients. People who went through the Stalin period, including deportations, are still in Armenia trying to build new lives—again. If the economic situation was different, many more would be there, but the lack of any promise of employment is proving devastating. The key ingredient seems to be a sense of inclusion, whether actually rejected or not. The ideal stated in all forms of public life was that the newcomers were "at home," equal to everyone else. For all the crudity of propaganda and the overweening romanticism of nationalist poetry and song, this seems to have provided courage and motivation when little else was available.

NOTES

I am grateful to the people who read or listened to this text at various stages and for their insightful suggestions and comments. These include Levon Chilingirian, Armine Ishkanian, Ani King-Underwood, Marine Kourkchiyan, Peter Loizos, Ruth Mandel, Hratch Tchilingirian, Khachig Tololyan, and Steven Vertovec. The editors of this volume, Fran Markowitz and Anders Stefansson, have made generous and encouraging suggestions which have been especially valuable.

1. Soviet Armenia became the independent republic of Armenia in 1991.
2. This interview on the outskirts of Yerevan, Armenia, was part of research undertaken on one of several trips to the country between 1999 and 2002. Overall, the interviews and fieldwork that inform this chapter took place in Cyprus (periodically since 1983), London (since 1983), the United States and Canada, and Kessab, Syria.
3. See Zekiyan (1999: 46) for critique of utopian and "hypercritical" versions of historic Armenia. He rightly points out that one cannot accurately outline the shape of homelands, as one can a state's borders.
4. Cholakian (1995: 27–31) and Churukian discuss different possibilities of Armenian settlement of the area.
5. See Pattie 1999 for discussion of how views of an Armenian homeland have changed over time and according to political bias and geographic position. Pattie 1997 is an ethnographic case study of such changes in Cyprus over the twentieth century. See also Panossian (1998), Tololyan (2001).
6. Mouradian states that between June 1946 and the end of 1947, ninety thousand to one hundred thousand people migrated to Armenia, or approximately ten percent of the diaspora (1990: 326). Armenians from all over the world were courted by the *nerkaght* committees. Some seven thousand migrated from France, a few hundred came from the United States, but the bulk were from the communities of the Middle East.
7. The term *ardasahman* is still in common use today, though each former Soviet state has its own international borders.
8. *Hayrenik, mayrenik* (fatherland/motherland) can be contrasted with *yergir* (land) to denote degrees of politicization without losing the importance of the local land The word commonly used for communities in diaspora, *kaghout*, is thought to be from the Semitic word *galut*—exile—and there are a number of papers written on the transition from communities of exile to trade communities.
9. In addition to the main town or village of Kessab, the surrounding villages include Ekizoluk, Keorkeneh, Karadouran, Sev Aghpiur, Chakaljuk, Nerghki Kiur, Chinarjuk, and others. According to a 1911 census, Kessab had 2,770 residents while the next largest village, Karadouran, had 1,290 (Cholakian 1995)
10. During one period in the mid-1990s, the Catholicos of all Armenians was Karekin I, born in Kessab, as was the highest ranking priest in the Armenian Catholic

Church. The Evangelical (or Protestant) church has many well-known pastors born in Kessab, who are now serving around the diaspora.

11. See Cholakian (1986) for a detailed description of the dialect.

12. Minasyan lists patriotism, a desire to be a full-fledged citizen, desire for better education, concerns over insecurity and assimilation, a desire to follow preceding families, and "nostalgia" for lands lost as the inspiring motives for repatriates generally. (2001: 5). She also notes the power of the propaganda and the need of the Armenian state for labor and for settlers for the hoped-for new territories.

13. It is important to clarify that the motivating "ideas" behind the immigration were those of nationalism, not—for the great majority—communism or socialism. (see also Suny 2000: 174–75 for information on this from U.S. intelligence reports).

14. Ladislav Holy describes similar nationalist images of Bohemia: "an earthly paradise," a "heavenly landscape" (1998: 122).

15. The Armenian word for Armenia is *Hayastan*. People from the State of Armenia are called *Hayastantsis*, which enables a distinction to be made while still including the diaspora as "Armenians" or *Hayer*. *Hayastan* today denotes the republic of Armenia but it also is used to describe the older territories.

16. Minasyan also states that Armenia was in danger of being relegated to the status of autonomous republic within the newly drawn borers of Georgia if its population went below one million (2001,4)

17. Ronald G. Suny discusses the possible acquisition of the Kars and Ardahan area and the campaign by Armenians to resolve two problems with the one solution of "repatriating" Armenians from the diaspora to resettle old territories. He notes the efforts of Armenians in the United States and elsewhere in the diaspora in the lobbying of the powers involved but suggests that Stalin's willingness to press for it (initially) probably resulted from Beria's teasing insistence that Turkey had originally stolen the lands from Georgia (1993: 167–69). See also Minasyan, 2001, and Mouradian, 1990.

18. Similar problems are described for newcomers among compatriots in Hirschon (1989) and Pattie (1997). In these and other cases, the newcomers were rejected by the native people but felt themselves to be superior in terms of skills, worldly knowledge, education, and so on.

19. For example, "God willing," "Thanks be to God," "Let God guide his/her soul."

20. When Bedrossian asked native Armenians what differences they found between themselves and the newcomers, the first response was food. "*Akhparagan geragoor*" signals something delicious and includes things like Turkish coffee, olives (*zayt*), *basturma* (spicy dried beef*)*. But she then added other phrases that, even within the food realm, showed the more negative connotations surrounding the newcomers. For example, *hoom mees oudogh akhparneruh* means raw-meat-eating brothers; "*Aydzi kdiguh*" for olives, referring to their resemblance to goat droppings.

21. Though religion was not practiced freely until independence, the orientation towards Russia (and Europe) appears to have encouraged a further identification with other Christians and a mistrust of Islam. In Kessab, people continue to go to school and work with non-Armenians and observe much more variation around them than is visible from Armenia, where 97 percent or more are ethnically Armenian.

22. Since independence, a number of people who had migrated in the Nerkaght movement and later left Soviet or independent Armenia have begun to invest or begin businesses in Armenia. Others assist in charity and humanitarian efforts.

23. Kessab is unusual in that approximately one-third of its population is Protestant (all villages included). Missionaries arrived in the mid-nineteenth century.
24. For recent information and analysis on Armenian Protestants worldwide, see Tchilingirian 2000.
25. Anahit Minasyan notes for example that an opinion poll in France taken in 1946 showed that some 38 percent of young people under thirty-five wanted to leave France. (2001: 3)
26. I discuss this further in Pattie 1999, noting that the concept of homeland has many shapes, though increasingly, for Armenians, focused on the nation-state of Armenia.
27. Loizos explores similar themes and notes a fundamental point of refugee settlement: "Dislocation and destitution do not actually damage the deepest early learning or core values. Social identity, a belief in and understanding of kinship patterns, religious commitment, technical knowledge, such things normally survive." (2000: 3). He argues that these provide the "social capital" with which the newcomers can rebuild their lives and begin to integrate with the host society.

REFERENCES

Bajakian, Hovhannes. "Kessabi Nerkaghti 50 Amiagi Artiv, 1947: Mer yev Hayrenik" [On the 50th anniversary of the Kessab Nerkaght: Our fatherland as well]. *Nor Gyank* 6–7 (1998): 13.
Bedrossian, Armenouhie. Interview in Yerevan 2000.
Carrere d'Encausse, Helene. "Determinants and Parameters of Soviet Nationality Policy." In *Soviet Nationality Policies and Practices*, edited by Jeremy R. Azrael. New York: Praeger, 1978.
Cholakian, Hagop. *Kessab* vol. 1. Aleppo: Hamazkaine Press, 1995.
———. *Kessabi Parparuh* [The dialect of Kessab]. Aleppo: Toros Toranian, 1886.
Churukian, Araxie. "Kessab Folkloric Evening." Pp. 208–13 in *Kessabtzis Yearbook Directory*. Tarzana, CA: 2003.
Hirschon, Renee. *Heirs of the Greek Catastrophe: The Social Life of Asia Minor Refugees in Piraeus*. Oxford: Clarendon Press, 1989.
Holy, Ladislav. "The Metaphor of Home in Czech Nationalist Discourse." In *Migrants of Identity: Perceptions of Home in a World of Movement*, edited by Nigel Rapport and Andrew Dawson. Oxford: Berg, 1998.
Humphrey, Caroline. "Eurasia,' Ideology and the Political Imagination in Provincial Russia" Pp. 258–76 in *Postsocialism: Ideals, Ideologies, and Practices in Eurasia*, edited by Chris M. Hann. London: Routledge, 2002.
Loizos, Peter. "Are Refugees Social Capitalists?" In *Social Capital: Critical Perspectives* edited by Stephen Baron. Oxford: Oxford University Press, 2000.
Minasyan, Anahit. "The Promised Land: Armenian and Jewish Experiences in the Second Half of the Twentieth Century." Paper presented at Armeniens et Grecs en Diaspora: Approches Comparative conference. Athens, Greece, October 2001.
Mouradian, Claire. *De Staline a Gorbachev. Histoire d'une republique sovietique: l'Armenie*. Paris: Editions Ramsey, 1990.

Panossian, Razmik. "Between Ambivalence and Intrusion: Politics and Identity in Armenia-Diaspora Relations." *Diaspora* 7, no. 2 (1998) 149–96.

Pattie, Susan. *Faith in History: Armenians Rebuilding Community*. Washington, DC: Smithsonian Institution Press, 1997.

———. "Longing and Belonging: Issues of Homeland in Armenian Diaspora." In *Polar*, vol. 22, no. 2 (1999): 80–91.

Sanjian, Ara. "Homeland-Diaspora Relations Under Kruschev and Brezhnev: The Soviet Embassy in Beirut and the Armenian Community in Lebanon, 1957–1982." Paper presented at Armeniens et Grecs en Diaspora: Approches Comparative conference, Athens, Greece, October 2001.

Suny, Ronald Grigor. *Looking Toward Ararat: Armenia in Modern History*. Bloomington: Indiana University Press, 1993.

Tchilingirian, Hratch. "When Small is Big: Evangelicals Render a Century and a Half of Service." *Armenian International Magazine (AIM)*, (January 2000): 34–53.

Ter Minassian, Taline. "Les rapatriements et leurs consequences sur l'organisatoin de l'espace urbain a Erevan." Paper presented at Armeniens et Grecs en Diaspora: Approches Comparatives conference. Athens, Greece, October 2001.

Tololyan, Khachig. "Rethinking Diaspora(s): Stateless Power in the Transnational Moment." *Diaspora* 5, no. 1 (1996): 3–36.

———. "Textual Nation: Poetry and Nationalism in Armenian Political Culture." Pp. 79–108 in *Intellectuals and the Articulation of Nation* edited by Ronald G. Suny and Michael D. Kennedy. Ann Arbor: University of Michigan Press, 2001.

Touryantz, Hagop Jack. *Search for a Homeland*. New York, n.p., 1987.

Velychenko, Stephen. "National History and the 'History of the USSR': The Persistence and Impact of Categories." Pp. 13–40 in *Nationalism and History: The Politics of Nation Bulding in Post-Soviet Armenia, Azerbaijan and Georgia* edited by Donald Schwartz and Razmik Panossian. Toronto: University of Toronto Press, 1994.

Zekiyan, Boghos Levon. "The Armenian Way to Enlightenment: The Diaspora and its Role" Pp. 45–486 in *Enlightenment and Diaspora: The Armenian and Jewish Cases*, edited by Richard G. Hovannisian and David N. Myers. Atlanta: Scholars Press, 1999.

8

When Home Is Not the Homeland: The Case of Japanese Brazilian Ethnic Return Migration

Takeyuki (Gaku) Tsuda

It is now commonly acknowledged that the increasing movement of populations across national borders in a globalized world has ruptured the previously assumed connection between peoples and their territorial homelands. The deterritorialization caused by transnational migration has created many diasporic peoples who have become disconnected from their homelands as they have settled in different countries. Despite such relocations, the homeland remains important in their imaginings, even among second and third generation diasporic descendants, who continue to maintain a sense of attachment and nostalgic longing to their country of ethnic origin.

Transnational migration and territorial dispersion have also created the need to distinguish between *homeland* (a place of origin to which one feels emotionally attached) and *home* (a stable place of residence that feels secure, comfortable, and familiar). Although the concepts are often used interchangeably in the literature (the assumption being that home is located in the homeland), the two places frequently do not correspond for transmigrants and diasporic peoples. Despite being territorially detached from their homelands, many immigrants have settled long-term or permanently abroad, have grown accustomed to life in their host countries, and feel well-situated and comfortable living in self-contained immigrant communities with their families and acquaintances. In other words, they have created a "home away from homeland." Transnational migration therefore not only introduces a disjuncture between peoples and their homelands, but also between their homelands and their homes, which have become different places for migrants.

This disconnect remains important even for diasporic peoples who have been "returning" to their ethnic homelands. The volume of such ethnic return migration has increased considerably in the past few decades as millions of people of German, Italian, Spanish, and Jewish decent living in Eastern Europe and Latin America have migrated back to their ethnic homelands of Germany, Italy, Spain, and Israel (e.g., see Münz and Ohliger 2003; Pastore 2001; Remennick 1998). In East Asia, over half a million people of Korean and Japanese descent scattered across South America (mainly Brazil, Peru, and Argentina) as well as Russia and China have return migrated to South Korea and Japan (Lee 2003; Louie 2000; Roth 2002; Tsuda 2003; Yoo 2002). Even for such ethnic return migrants however, homeland and home may remain distinctly different places (see Anteby-Yemini; Holsey; Markowitz; Pattie; this volume). Although they have returned to their ethnic homeland, their diasporic homecomings are often ambivalent, challenging their previously nostalgic feelings of attachment to their country of ethnic origin. For such ethnic return migrants, therefore, their ancestral homeland may not feel like a homeland. However, I argue that this does not always prevent it from becoming a new immigrant home.

This chapter will explore the often contradictory relationship between homeland and home by analyzing the ethnic return migration of second and third generation Japanese Brazilians from Brazil to Japan. Although they are *nikkeijin* (Japanese descendants born and raised outside of Japan) who had expressed strong attachment to Japan in Brazil, they are ethnically excluded and socially marginalized as foreigners in their ethnic homeland because of what the Japanese perceive as the Brazilian cultural differences they have acquired while living abroad for generations. As a result, the Brazilian nikkeijin are alienated from their country of ethnic origin, making it difficult for them to experience it as a homeland. Despite this "loss" of their ethnic homeland however, they have made themselves "at home" in Japan by becoming long-term immigrant settlers and by creating self-contained and cohesive immigrant enclave communities that have facilitated their lives and compensated for their ethnic and social alienation in Japan. In this manner, this chapter will examine how an alienating place that does not feel like a homeland can still become a home.

Because of a severe Brazilian economic crisis and a crippling shortage of unskilled labor in Japan, the Japanese Brazilians began return migrating to Japan in the late 1980s as temporary migrant laborers and found work primarily in factories of small and medium-sized Japanese companies. Although they are relatively well educated and mostly of middle class background in Brazil, they earn five to ten times their Brazilian salaries in Japan as factory workers. Currently estimated at over 280,000, the Brazilian nikkeijin have become the second largest population of foreigners in Japan after the Chinese and their numbers continue to increase at a steady pace.[1] Although most of them migrate with the intention of returning to Brazil in a couple of years, many have called over their families and the process of long-term settlement has already begun (see Tsuda 1999; Yamanaka 2000).

This chapter is based on over twenty months of fieldwork and participant observation in both Japan and Brazil from 1993 to 1995. Nine months were first spent in Brazil among two separate Japanese Brazilian communities in the cities of Porto Alegre (Rio Grande do Sul) and Ribeirão Preto (São Paulo). During my one-year stay in Japan, I conducted fieldwork in Kawasaki (Kanagawa prefecture) and Oizumi/Ota cities (in Gunma prefecture), where I worked for four months as a participant observer in a large electrical appliance factory with about ten thousand workers, of which one thousand were Japanese Brazilians. Close to one hundred in-depth interviews (in Portuguese and Japanese) were conducted with Japanese Brazilians and Japanese workers, residents, employers, and officials.[2]

AMBIVALENT HOMECOMINGS

Cultural Differences and Ethnic Marginalization in Japan

Although the Japanese Brazilians have been officially welcomed by the Japanese government, which has granted them special renewable work visas as Japanese descendants, they are ethnically rejected as foreigners and socially marginalized in Japan because of their cultural differences. In this manner, despite being admitted to Japan because they are racially Japanese, they do not speak Japanese very well and have become culturally Brazilianized to various degrees. As a result, most Japanese I interviewed in Japan viewed them as quite culturally foreign and did not ethnically accept them as Japanese, indicating the exclusionary nature of Japanese ethno-national identity. The remarks of one local resident were quite representative of this general Japanese reaction:

> There's a lot of *iwakan* [sense of incongruity] towards those who have a Japanese face but are culturally Brazilian. If they have a Japanese face, we interpret this to mean they are Japanese, so we initially approach the nikkeijin this way. But then when we find they are culturally different, we say they are foreigners.

In fact, the Japanese Brazilians are constantly called "*gaijin*" (foreigners) by the Japanese.

Because of their status as culturally different foreigners, most of my Japanese Brazilian informants felt socially excluded in Japan. In fact, according to one research survey, 44.3 per cent of the Brazilian nikkeijin in Japan report that they have almost no social contact with the Japanese and 15.8 percent have only minimal contact (Kitagawa 1996). For instance, Martina, a younger *nisei* (second-generation nikkeijin) who had been living in Japan with her husband for a long time, had this to say:

> I have no social relationships or friendships with the Japanese, only with other Brazilians, and remain very isolated from them at work and where ever I go. It's because we're foreigners in Japan. If a group of Japanese are sitting and talking, they don't let you into the conversation—they don't even give you a chance. Because you're a foreigner, they just let you sit there and simply forget about you. Occasionally, someone might ask you a brief question, but that's about it.

Although most of the Brazilian nikkeijin are not phenotypically distinct from the Japanese, at the factory where I conducted participant observation (which I will call Toyama), they wore different uniforms from the Japanese as temporary workers contracted from outside labor broker firms. As a result, they were "ethnically visible" on the factory floor and immediately subject to social exclusion by the color of their uniforms. Although they cannot be as readily distinguished outside the factory, language becomes the ethnic marker that identifies the nikkeijin as foreigners. Some of my Japanese Brazilian informants emphasized the social separation they would experience as soon as the Japanese discovered they were culturally different foreigners who cannot speak Japanese well. According to an older nisei man living in Oizumi:

> Once the Japanese find out you aren't fluent in Japanese, they realize to their surprise that you aren't Japanese and therefore distance themselves. They completely sideline you and you can't become part of their group. As a foreigner, you are treated like an object in Japan. My [Japanese] neighbors have therefore decided not to say a single word to me and remain completely separate.

When my Japanese informants at the Toyama factory were asked about their ethnic reluctance to interact with the Brazilian nikkeijin, they commonly stressed the difficulty they have relating to foreigners who are culturally different. A young Japanese who worked next to me on the assembly line elaborated as follows:

> Because we live in an ethnically homogeneous society, the Japanese are simply bad at dealing with foreigners they don't know well and can't communicate effectively with. We don't cope well with ethnic diversity and are not used to people who are different, like the nikkeijin. We have no way to react and adapt to foreigners in our midst, so we just prefer to stay away. Some will stop to help foreigners if they need assistance, but most just look at them and ignore them.

Language was obviously the most significant cultural barrier that discouraged the Japanese from interacting with the Japanese Brazilians. At Toyama, many Japanese workers did not even attempt to speak with their nikkeijin coworkers because they were afraid the nikkeijin would not be able to communicate in Japanese, leading to an awkward situation. Others attempted to start conversations with the Brazilian nikkeijin, but were quickly discouraged when faced with difficulties. One Japanese worker shared his experiences with me:

> When there's a Japanese Brazilian working next to me, I sometimes exchange a few words with him. They seem to comprehend, but they can't say a whole lot in Japanese or just tell me they didn't really understand. It's no use because we can't really communicate very well. So I just figure there's really no need to talk to them since we can get by just as well without saying anything to them.

As a result, most of the Japanese at Toyama had learned to react to the Japanese Brazilians with detached indifference.

This social separation and marginalization of the nikkeijin as ethnic outsiders on the basis of cultural difference was also a reflection of general group dynamics at the factory, where any means of social differentiation seemed to produce mutually exclusive social groups constituted according to insider/outsider distinctions. I was repeatedly struck by how the Japanese workers generally remained within their own separate social groups structured by differences of gender, factory section, company affiliation, or length of employment. Most notable was the social separation and relative lack of interaction between men and women, who always stood apart when they congregated for the morning *cholei* (assembly) and sat at different tables during break and lunch. Although men and women were dispersed on the assembly line, they would converse mainly along gender lines and generally did not initiate extended cross-gender interactions, except for supervisors delegating work tasks to the female workers and those with romantic or flirtatious interests (primarily men).[3] The Japanese workers also segregated themselves according to work sections. I constantly noticed that those workers who were temporarily transferred to a different section (called *oen*) did not speak to those around them and always returned to their own sections during break. Likewise, newly hired Japanese employees would initially be socially isolated from the others and would only be gradually incorporated into the work group. In addition, temporary Japanese workers contracted from outside broker firms confronted the same social isolation at Toyama as the nikkeijin. "When a Japanese worker from an outside subcontracting firm enters our section wearing a different uniform, we look at them like they are different people," a Toyama employee remarked. "We don't make social contact with these people."

In other words, the social separation between the Japanese and the Japanese Brazilians is not simply a process that occurs only between culturally different ethnic groups but is a specific manifestation of a broader pattern of social group segregation. The social exclusion of the Brazilian nikkeijin by the Japanese is a "normal" reaction of in-group members to "outsiders," which is simply exacerbated in this case because the group differences are much greater.

During my fieldwork, it also became apparent that the ethnic avoidance behavior of the Japanese is not just based on exclusionary group dynamics or simple reluctance to overcome barriers of cultural difference. At times, it seemed motivated by latent prejudice toward the nikkeijin, which is based on negative preconceptions of their migration legacy, social class status, and Brazilian cultural behavior.[4] Many of my Japanese informants viewed the Brazilian nikkeijin as descendants of originally poor and uneducated Japanese of low social class background who could not survive or endure economic difficulties in Japan and thus abandoned their own country and emigrated to Brazil. This ethnic perception of the nikkeijin is further worsened by their current return migration to Japan as migrant workers. Since most of my Japanese informants associated migrant workers with poverty and did not know that the Japanese Brazilians are of middle-class background in Brazil, they saw the nikkeijin as poor people who could not survive economically in Brazil and were thus forced to come to Japan to earn money. Therefore, the nikkeijin migrants are subjected to a double stigma—the descendants of those who initially fled to Brazil because they supposedly could not survive in Japan have now returned to Japan because they could not survive economically in Brazil either. This image of migrant poverty is exacerbated by a generally low perception of Brazil itself as a poor and underdeveloped Third World country. Few of my Japanese informants were aware that most nikkeijin come from developed and modernized Brazilian cities.

There is also considerable social class stigma attached to the unskilled factory jobs that the Japanese Brazilians perform in Japan, which are generally known as *kiken* (dangerous), *kitanai* (dirty), and *kitsui* (difficult). The social stigma attached to such "3K" working class jobs in Japanese society has grown in recent years as an increasingly better-educated populace has come to actively shun such degrading and demeaning work. However, even my Japanese informants who were part of this stigmatized working class looked down on nikkeijin migrants as members of an even lower social class than themselves. Because immigrants seem to evoke images of economic desperation in Japan, I was surprised by the number of Japanese factory workers who seemed to assume that the Japanese Brazilians live very poorly in Japan, earning low wages and confined to miserable housing.[5] Finally, the Japanese I interviewed generally had negative opinions of the "Brazilian" cultural behavior of the nikkeijin, both within the factory and in public, and were ethnically disappointed because they expected even Japanese descendants born abroad to retain more Japanese culture.

The economic marginalization of the Japanese Brazilians as a flexible and readily disposable migrant labor force also socially marginalizes them on the factory floor. Since most Brazilian nikkeijin are informal, temporary contract workers who are "borrowed" from outside labor broker firms, they are not employees who belong to the companies where they work and are therefore separated from regular Japanese employees. In addition, as a casual and disposable workforce, they are constantly transferred by their labor broker from one company to another depending on changing production needs. As a result, most of the Japanese Brazilians at Toyama did not stay in the factory for more than a few to several months. Most Japanese workers did not bother to associate with such migrant laborers who are outsiders to the company and constantly circulate in and out. "You might try to befriend a nikkeijin worker," a Toyama employee explained, "but then they suddenly disappear the next day without warning. So I just don't bother with them anymore." On their side, the Japanese Brazilians found little use in establishing meaningful and long-term relationships with Japanese workers because of their status as transient outsiders who could leave at any time. In this manner, the economic confinement of migrant workers to the peripheral labor market becomes a significant social barrier that makes both migrants and their hosts unwilling to interact with each other (cf. Roth 2002: 7).

Feelings of Alienation in Japan

The socioeconomic marginalization that Japanese Brazilian immigrants experience in Japan is quite disconcerting for many of them who in Brazil had a strong identification with Japan and therefore expected an ethnic homecoming in Japan.[6] Although few expect to be embraced just like another Japanese, many hope to be socially accepted. As a result, when such expectations are sorely disappointed by their ethnic exclusion and social separation in Japan, the result is a profound sense of social alienation, which was manifested in reactions of discontent, displeasure, and even dismay bordering on outrage.

A good number of my informants claimed that they did not expect such strong social separation between themselves and the Japanese and felt quite deceived. Those with even stronger prior expectations of social acceptance and inclusion in Japan referred to their social marginalization as foreigners not only as a surprise, but as a "shock," indicating a more powerful experience of social alienation. My roommate, Rodney, was certainly one of them:

> In Brazil, we were always proud of our Japanese ancestry and our ties to Japan and thought of the Japanese people in positive ways. Although I don't speak Japanese that well, I thought the Japanese would accept us because we are Japanese descendants. Coming to Japan and being treated as a foreigner despite

my Japanese face was a big shock for me, a shock I'll never forget. I think it's unfair that we are not socially accepted here simply because we've become culturally different.

I was also struck by the number of times the Brazilian nikkeijin referred to their social separation in Japan as "discrimination" or even used the more ethnically charged term of "racism." For example, consider the comments of an older nisei man:

> The Japanese always keep us separated from them because of the prejudices that they have. I was offended when I first saw the social separation at Toyama. There are some Japanese who simply don't like us and don't trust us because we are Brazilian. If you don't understand Japanese culture and act just like the Japanese, they discriminate against you and you can't enter their group. The Japanese are racists, so even the [Japanese] Brazilians experience discrimination here. In Brazil, this type of discrimination exists only toward blacks.

In this manner, a majority of my informants were quite bothered and disturbed by their ethnic exclusion in Japan, indicating an acute awareness of a state of social isolation typical of the alienated individual.[7] Such feelings of alienation make it impossible for many Japanese Brazilians to continue identifying with Japan, leading to a loss of their ethnic homeland. A homeland is not simply a country of origin in an objective sense—it must be imbued with positive emotional affect as a place of desire and longing to which the individual feels a strong sense of personal attachment and emotional affiliation. Because return migration has caused the Japanese Brazilians to feel socially alienated, Japan has become a place of detachment and estrangement instead of attachment and identification and no longer evokes the feelings of affiliation and fondness that make homelands subjectively meaningful.

MAKING ONESELF AT HOME

The Settlement of Japanese Brazilian Immigrants in Japan

Although Japan certainly does not feel like a homeland for the Japanese Brazilians, it is starting to feel a lot like home for a number of them. The main reason for this is that a good number of them have made Japan their long-term, if not permanent, residence. This indicates that the social alienation of ethnic return migrants in their ancestral homelands does not necessary prevent them from making it a stable home because immigrant settlement is determined by other economic, familial, and social reasons and not by whether immigrants develop an emotional attachment to the host country.

Although a good number of the Brazilian nikkeijin will remain sojourners and "target earners" who will return in the near future to Brazil, a sizable portion of the immigrant population is settling long-term and permanently in Japan.[8] Although virtually all of the Japanese Brazilians initially migrate to Japan as sojourners, research surveys indicate that 41 percent have already been in Japan for over 3 years, 40 percent intend to remain in Japan for over three more years or did not know, and roughly 50 percent wish to settle long-term in Japan (Kitazawa 1997: 104, 142, 148).[9] Surveys conducted in the early nineties show that perhaps 20 to 30 percent had already decided to remain indefinitely or permanently in Japan (Japan Statistics Research Institute 1993; Kitagawa 1992, 1993).

Most Japanese Brazilians have decided to prolong their stays in Japan because of economic reasons. Although they initially intend to return to Brazil in a couple of years after they have amassed considerable savings, most find it difficult to save money because of the high cost of living in Japan. In addition, the decade-long Japanese economic recession has decreased their incomes by reducing hourly wages and overtime, forcing many to extend their stays in Japan in order to save the desired amount of money.

In addition, despite the serious recession in Japan, the Japanese Brazilians have been able to continue to find lucrative employment because the demand for their immigrant labor has become structurally embedded in the Japanese economy. Since the early 1980s, Japan has suffered from an acute labor shortage caused by decades of unprecedented and unbridled economic expansion, unfavorable demographic changes (a declining birth rate and aging population), and the increasing unwillingness of better educated and socially mobile Japanese youth to do unskilled jobs.[10] In addition, rural labor supplies were depleted, further large increases in the employment of women and elderly became unfeasible, and labor-saving mechanisms such as automation and further rationalization of production had begun to show serious limitations. As a result, labor deficient firms became dependent on foreign workers as the only realistic and cost-efficient source of labor power. The labor shortage has persisted despite the prolonged recession, especially in small and medium-sized firms in the manufacturing section where many Brazilian nikkeijin are employed.

Because nikkeijin migrant labor has become a structurally necessarily component of the Japanese economy, the country's severe and prolonged recession has had only a relatively mild effect on the Japanese Brazilians and has not provoked a mass exodus from Japan. They have not been laid off en masse and those who have lost their jobs have been able to find other employment (even if it is at lower wages with worse working conditions). In addition, the Brazilian nikkeijin have been generally insulated from the recession's worst effects because of their privileged position on the immigrant labor market. They are one of the few groups of legally admitted, unskilled foreign workers in Japan and are the most ethnically preferred among all immigrant workers because of their Japanese descent and presumed cultural affinities with the Japanese.[11]

Meanwhile, a gradual improvement in the Brazilian economy has not encouraged the Brazilian nikkeijin to return home in significant numbers either. Since the implementation of the Plano Real by the Brazilian government in 1994, inflation has been brought under control and the economy has become more stable, compared to the crisis years of the 1980s. Nonetheless, economic uncertainty has definitely continued in Brazil with the persistence of low wages and limited employment opportunities, an increase in the cost of living for the middle class (Martes 2000: 64), as well as two major currency crises in recent years. Regardless of short-term improvements in the Brazilian economy, many of my nikkeijin informants in Japan remained quite pessimistic about their long-term economic prospects back home and felt more economically secure in Japan because of the much greater employment opportunities at much higher wages.

Because of the continued availability of jobs in Japan and economic uncertainty in Brazil, most Japanese Brazilians have remained in the country despite the recession. In fact, their total immigrant population continues to increase, indicating that a growing number of nikkeijin are making Japan a long-term and stable immigrant home. It is important to remember, however, that immigrant settlement is not simply a result of economic factors. Over time, immigrants also become "socially embedded" in the host country, making it less likely they will quickly, if ever, return home.

As the Japanese Brazilians have prolonged their stays in Japan because of economic reasons, an increasing number of them have brought their families to Japan. Others are now migrating to Japan with their families in anticipation of longer stays. In 1990, 35 percent of the immigrants were already living with their families. A few years later, the figure had risen to 60 per cent and remains at the level.[12] The presence of the family produces a greater social commitment among immigrants to the host society, therefore making them more willing to become settlers and permanent residents. As their children attend Japanese schools and acculturate to Japanese society, many Brazilian nikkeijin have increased their social connections and involvement in the surrounding Japanese community. Since a good number of their children have forgotten Portuguese and know nothing about Brazil, many have become reluctant to repatriate since they realize their children will have serious problems readapting to Brazilian society. As they face the prospect of an extended stay in Japan with their families, the Japanese Brazilians have also become less willing to endure long working hours and economic austerity in an effort to maximize their earnings and have instead begun to desire more socially fulfilling lives in Japan. This shift from purely economic to social priorities therefore reduces their incomes and increases the cost of living, making it even more difficult to save the amount of money necessary to return home. As an increasing number of Japanese Brazilian immigrants settle in Japan for these various reasons, the country has become a long-term, stable home to them.

The Development of Immigrant Ethnic Communities

In addition to their immigrant settlement, Japan has increasingly become a home for many Japanese Brazilians because of the emergence of cohesive and self-contained immigrant ethnic communities, which has made them more accustomed and comfortable living in Japan (cf. Roth 2002: 5–6). These immigrant communities are especially prominent in areas where the nikkeijin are highly concentrated, and are supported by a vast array of Brazilian restaurants, snack shops, food stores, entertainment centers, clothing stores, barbers, boutiques, and nikkeijin churches. Large labor brokers as well as nikkeijin assistance centers are especially active in such communities, providing extensive employment, housing, and other social services, mainly in Portuguese. Local governments in cities with large nikkeijin populations have also been very receptive to the Japanese Brazilians, providing many services for them, including national health insurance, Japanese language classes, guidebooks in Portuguese, counseling and other personal services, as well as assistance (in Portuguese) with alien registration and even job placement. In addition, nikkeijin with families in Japan have been strongly encouraged to enroll their children in Japanese schools and those with large numbers of nikkeijin students have created special Japanese classes for them and special teachers have been hired as personal tutors and assistants. The Japanese Brazilians have also been welcomed by Japanese Christian churches and a good number have joined their congregations.

Such cohesive, full-service immigrant communities have greatly facilitated the lives of the Brazilian nikkeijin in Japan. Even if they are ethnically segregated and socially alienated from Japanese society, many of them have become very accustomed to living in Japan by making themselves at home in these "Little Brazils" that allow them to conduct their lives in ethnically and culturally familiar surroundings reminiscent of their home country of Brazil. In fact, most of the Japanese Brazilians' occupational, consumer, informational, and recreational needs can be met within these self-contained immigrant communities without much contact with Japanese society. More than a few of my informants living in Oizumi remarked that they do not really feel like they are living in a foreign country since much of their daily interaction takes place among compatriots, often in familiar Brazilian cultural settings, enabling them to maintain their former lifestyle to a certain extent.

In addition, an active ethnic mass media has developed among the Japanese Brazilians in Japan which center around three weekly Portuguese newspapers: the *International Press, Folha Mundial,* and *Tudo Bem.* One survey found that 80 percent of nikkeijin immigrants read one of these papers all or some of the time (Nomoto et. al. 1993). Not only is news from Brazil and Japan featured in these papers, they also publish stories about activities, incidents, problems, and personal experiences among Japanese Brazilians in various parts of Japan. The papers also contain business and service announcements, entertainment guides, information about upcoming events, job ads, and a section in which readers' questions are answered. In addition to newspapers, Portuguese radio programs, broadcast from stations in Shizuoka, Tokyo, and Nagoya, have also become part of the immigrant mass media. These broadcasts feature programs and news, Brazilian music, and replies to letters from Japanese Brazilians experiencing difficulties in Japan. Brazilian television has also become part of the immigrant mass media in Japan. Brazilian news programs, soap operas, comedies, and variety shows are recorded on videotape and sent to nikkeijin-owned stores in Japan for rent. Starting in October 1996, Brazilian satellite television has also become widely available for the nikkeijin in Japan through a digital multichannel broadcasting service called "PerfecTV." By March 1998, nineteen thousand nikkeijin households had subscribed to this service (Sellek 2001: 135). Brazilian newspapers, magazines, and music are also readily available through nikkeijin food stores in Japan. Although many Japanese Brazilians do not live in geographically concentrated immigrant communities and are scattered throughout Japan in towns and cities where they are a very small minority, most of them have ready access to such ethnic media and can therefore remain connected to a larger imagined community of nikkeijin immigrants in Japan.

In addition, even if they do not reside in one of Japan's "Little Brazils," most Brazilian nikkeijin are part of cohesive, ethnic network communities of family, relatives, friends, and acquaintances, which make them feel at home by countering the social alienation they experience in Japan. Most important in this regard is the presence of the family in Japan. Those nikkeijin who were single sojourners in Japan frequently complained of the loneliness, homesickness, and social isolation they experienced as a result of separation from their families, relatives, and friends who were left behind in Brazil. In addition, many continue to be personally and emotionally attached to their home country of Brazil as they worry about the welfare of their families back home, remit money to support them, and are concerned about the upbringing and education of their children who are being raised with a missing parent. In fact, close to 60 percent of the Japanese Brazilians cite *saudade* (homesickness/longing) as the biggest social problem they experience in Japan (see Kitagawa 1992; Japan Statistics Research Institute 1993). However, once they bring over their families to Japan, such emotional difficulties and problems subside and they feel less personally attached to their home country. As their longing and homesickness for Brazil attenuate and they come to feel more well-situated and comfortable living in Japan, it starts to feel much more like home than before.

The family also provides the Brazilian nikkeijin with socially meaningful and intimate familial relationships that help neutralize the negative experiences they have in Japan as a socioeconomically marginalized immigrant minority. A number of my nikkeijin informants spoke about how the presence of their families at home allows them to air their complaints and grievances in Japan, thus relieving them of the frustrations that accumulate in their daily lives. One Japanese Brazilian in Kawasaki-city spoke of this crucial role of his family as follows:

> I would have nothing here in Japan without my family. With them, it becomes much easier to neutralize the bad sentiments from the outside that we have living in Japan. We can separate out our Brazilian lives in the family from the outside and complain about the Japanese and help each other out. I spend a lot of time with my wife talking about the problems we encounter here in Japan.

Another individual informant had similar experiences:

> It is much easier to overcome our problems in Japan with the family. We can release our frustrations instead of keeping them inside and can talk about difficulties at work and what we don't like about the Japanese. We end up feeling that our problems have been alleviated. With the family, we can protect ourselves more. Without my wife here, I would be more influenced by the bad experiences I have outside [in Japanese society].

The family also serves as a source of status, prestige, and respect that allows the Brazilian nikkeijin to distance themselves from their low occupational status as unskilled immigrant workers outside the home. Regardless of the socially degrading nature of their factory jobs, the Japanese Brazilians can be treated with proper respect according to their own cultural standards of judgment within their families, thus preserving their social self-esteem. Intact and cohesive families provide a context for the Japanese Brazilians to perform their respected social roles as father or mother, fulfill their duties and obligations as economic providers and caretakers, and serve as proper role models for their children. As the Brazilian anthropologist, Roberto DaMatta notes (1991: 64, 66), proper social roles and hierarchies based on respect and consideration are maintained inside the home (*casa*), in contrast to the struggle, work, and harsh reality of life in the outside world of the street (*rua*).

Many Japanese Brazilians are also able to rely on cohesive networks of relatives, friends, and acquaintances that serve a similar function as the family by alleviating the social segregation and alienation they feel from Japanese society. A number of my informants felt that there was greater cohesion and unity among themselves in Japan than in Brazil because previous differences in social class, economic wealth, and educational level are not openly apparent. Since over 90 percent of the Brazilian nikkeijin are employed as unskilled factory workers in Japan, they live in a relatively egalitarian and homogeneous community, performing the same type of manual labor, wearing the same uniforms, earning comparable wages, and living in similar apartment complexes.

This sense of increased collective solidarity and unity among the Japanese Brazilians produced by their social commonalities in Japan was expressed most directly by one informant:

> In Brazil, we were less cohesive and integrated because there were lots of differences among us. We tended to associate only with those of the same social level and from the same region. Here, we are all united. We are all Brazilians, doing the same work and subordinate to the Japanese. We have similar experiences and suffer from the same problems living in a foreign country. When I see fellow [Japanese] Brazilians in Japan, I feel like going over and greeting them. In Brazil, it was never like this.

A number of Brazilian nikkeijin specifically mentioned the greater ease of social relationships and friendships with other nikkeijin in Japan compared to Brazil because status differences no longer interfere. "In Brazil, an educated, rich [Japanese Brazilian] doctor from São Paulo would never interact with a less educated farmer from the countryside," one of them noted. "But here in Japan, we don't care about such things because we're all equals who all face the same difficulties in Japan and are all in the same boat. So we are all united and socialize more freely."

Despite the itinerant and temporary nature of most of the Japanese Brazilians and their long hours in the factory (including overtime on weekends), the amount of socializing that occurs among them in local communities is quite remarkable, especially in cities with high nikkeijin immigrant concentrations. Informal gatherings in apartments were frequent, especially on weekends, when relatives and friends would congregate for no specific purpose except to socialize and talk. Sometimes, when I conducted interviews, other nikkeijin would be gathered at the same apartment or would be summoned for the occasion. At other times, small parties, dinners, or informal meals, and even *churrascos* (Brazilian barbecues), were arranged. Gatherings at local Brazilian restaurants or eateries were also quite frequent and the most popular restaurants in Oizumi would frequently be packed beyond capacity on weekends.

In this manner, although the Japanese Brazilians are separated and excluded from Japanese society, they can rely on their own cohesive immigrant communities and ethnic networks through which they are able to obtain the companionship and social support necessary to overcome their social marginalization in Japan. By conducting their lives almost exclusively in familiar settings with family and co-ethnics in their neighborhoods, factories, associations, and residences, they have created a socially secure and comfortable home for themselves in an alienating society.

CONCLUSION: TRANSNATIONAL MIGRATION, ALIENATION, AND HOME

The recent interest in transnational migration has led some critics of the approach to openly wonder what is so new about transnationalism (e.g., see Foner 1997; Mintz 1998). Of course, the constant movement of peoples across national borders as well as the development of transnational communities has been occurring for centuries (Glick Schiller, Basch, and Blanc 1995; Foner 1997; Mintz 1998; Portes and Rumbaut 1996). Undoubtedly, transnational migrant communities have been fundamentally reconfigured by the advent of better communications and transportation technologies, which have increased the speed, efficiency, and volume of transnational flows across national borders (cf. Foner 1997: 362). Although this does make current transnational communities appear different from past ones (cf. Mintz 1998: 124), the difference is mainly a matter of degree and not of kind.

Instead, what is new about the transnational perspective is its emphasis on the subversive, counterhegemonic, and liberating nature of such cross-border processes (e.g., see Appadurai 1996; Basch, Glick Schiller, and Blanc 1994: 290; Glick Schiller and Fouron 1998; Guarnizo 1997; Kearney 1991; Portes 1996). Transnational practices and processes such as international migration are frequently seen as empowering because they provide sites for resistance, struggle, and adaptive responses that subvert the dominant hegemonic order. For instance, the transnationalism of subordinated migrant groups is sometimes seen as the basis for social movements and struggles of resistance against the nation-state and global capital (see Basch, Glick Schiller, and Blanc 1994: 290). In a similar vein, Arjun Appadurai (1996) claims that "postnational imaginaries" emerge from transnational practices, producing new forms of allegiance, social organization, and discursive consciousness that escape and transcend the hegemonic confines of the nation-state, making possible an emancipatory postnational political order. For Aihwa Ong (1999), the practice of flexible citizenship on a transnational scale in which individuals obtain political rights and residential basis in multiple countries is a personally advantageous adaptation to the vicissitudes of global capitalism and shifting international political conditions. Likewise, Roger Rouse argues that transnational migrant communities, by allowing individuals to maintain active social relationships over large geographical distances, enable them to respond effectively to changing economic constraints and limited opportunities in various locales by constantly circulating between these places (1991: 13–14).

In this manner, the emergence of transnational studies seems to be connected to the desire for an emancipatory politics, causing some scholars to celebrate the liberating potential of transnationalism, even if the transmigrants themselves do not have any political motives or conscious intentions to resist their subordination (Guarnizo and Smith 1998: 5). The Japanese Brazilian case indicates that the increasing flow of peoples across national borders is not always empowering. It can also produce disorienting experiences of unrootedness, ungroundedness, and social alienation, resulting in a loss of stable identities and a firm sense of place (cf. Portes and Rumbaut 1996: 158–159). Before the Japanese Brazilians return migrated to Japan, many of them emphasized their Japanese descent and heritage and retained a strong sentimental attachment to their ancestral homeland. As we have seen, however, when they actually return migrate to Japan, Japan does not feel like an authentic homeland. Instead of an expected "homecoming" befitting Japanese descendants who have returned to their ancestral roots, they confront ethnic rejection and marginality as foreigners because of their different cultural practices, exclusionary dynamics of Japanese ethnicity and social groups, ethnic prejudice, and their low socioeconomic status. Because return migration results in alienation from the ethnic homeland, it has now become impossible for the Japanese Brazilians to nostalgically imagine an idealized ancestral land on which to base their sense of ethnic rootedness. Indeed, feelings of ethnic disorientation caused by the dislocations of migration were frequently expressed by my informants in Japan. Transnational migration can be destabilizing and disorienting as much as it can be enabling and emancipatory.

Of course, such deterritorialized instability is now regarded as a permanent condition of postmodernity. In terms of migratory groups, the concept of diaspora is now increasingly invoked to describe the movements and distribution of ethnic populations around the world in order to capture the qualities of dispersal and dislocation, unboundedness and unrootedness. The constantly shifting and territorially transgressive nature of diaspora is understood to destabilize and challenge territorial spaces, national borders, and bounded cultural discourses. Others have taken this notion of diasporic unrootedness further, arguing that the transnational connections that keep diasporic communities together need not be articulated primarily through a real or symbolic homeland but through shared experiences of displacement, suffering, and resistance (Clifford 1997: 249–250). According to Clifford, diasporas are thus decentered and based on shifting multilocal attachments (1997: 248-2–49). Likewise, a number of scholars have claimed that migratory movements have destabilized the notion of a fixed "home," which has become a constantly shifting or imagined habitat that is no longer a singular, coherent place confined to specific territorial boundaries (Chambers 1994:

4–6; Gupta and Ferguson 1992: 9–11; Jackson 1995: 1–6; Malkki 1992: 25; Massey 1992: 12–15).

The transnational perspective is therefore characterized by an inherent tension. If transnational mobility is destabilizing and disorienting, how could it also be liberating and emancipatory? The irony is that it is precisely displacement and unrootedness that makes transnationalism empowering. Because deterritorialized transmigrants constantly uproot themselves and refuse to be spatially confined, they are supposedly freed from the hegemony of territorialized nation-states, allowing them to obtain multiple citizenships, residences, and homelands, become culturally hybrid and adaptable cosmopolitans, free their imaginations and practices from hegemonic processes, and resist the domination of global capital.

This chapter suggests that the emphasis on the territorially destabilizing and liberating aspects of transnational migration is a bit misplaced because it is based on a tendency to conflate the concepts of homeland and home. Migration certainly entails a disorienting loss of the natal homeland as migrants move away from their country of birth. In addition, ethnic return migrants often experience a loss of their ethnic homeland when they find themselves alienated strangers in the country of ethnic origin. However, this does not mean that they are also deprived of a stable and familiar place of residence that they regard as a home. Even though Japan does not feel like a homeland for the Japanese Brazilians, this does not preclude them from making it their home as they have decided to settle in the country because of economic and familial reasons and are able to conduct their lives in supportive and familiar settings by relying on cohesive social networks of co-ethnics in well-developed immigrant communities (cf. Margolis 1994; Markowitz 1993). Undoubtedly, a place does not have to be experienced as a homeland for it to be considered a home. While the Brazilian nikkeijin will definitely remain "homeland-less" in Japan, they will by no means remain "home-less" in Japan. In addition, in response to their alienation in their ethnic homeland, they strengthen their emotional ties to Brazil and end up realizing that their country of birth is their true homeland (see Tsuda n.d.).

Therefore, although transnational migration and deterritorialization may lead to a sense of *up*rootedness caused by a loss of homeland, it does not necessarily produce a permanent state of *un*rootedness, since many migrants are able to create stable and comfortable new homes for themselves in foreign countries and thus *re*territorialize themselves in these new locales. When viewed from that perspective, transnational migration appears much less destabilizing and deterritorializing than on first sight. Although transnational mobility may not always liberate migrants from territorializing hegemonies, it does attest to their ability to create homes in alienating, foreign places, making them resilient against the social segregation, degradation, and homesickness that many may experience. Ethnic homecomings therefore blur the boundaries of where one's home, heart, and hearth lie.

NOTES

The research for this chapter was made possible by a Fulbright-Hays Doctoral Dissertation Research Abroad Fellowship, a Wenner-Gren Predoctoral Grant, and fellowships from the Social Science Research Council and the Center for U.S.-Mexican Studies at UC San Diego. I would like to thank Fran Markowitz and Anders Stefansson for their detailed and insightful comments on an earlier draft, which were critical in improving the chapter.

1. This is excluding the approximately 650,000 Korean Japanese who are still registered in Japan as "foreigners." Although 80 percent were born in Japan, they are not granted Japanese citizenship and many have not naturalized.

2. See Tsuda (1998) for a self-reflexive analysis of the methodological implications of my fieldwork experiences in Japan as an ethnically ambiguous anthropologist.

3. It is interesting to note here that gender segregation generally did not exist among the Brazilian nikkeijin.

4. See Tsuda (2003: chapter 2) for an extensive analysis of Japanese ethnic prejudice toward the nikkeijin.

5. Again, this is a mistaken perception—the nikkeijin earn high wages and are generally provided with quality housing.

6. See Tsuda (2003: chapter 1) for an analysis of the transnational affiliation the Japanese Brazilians in Brazil have developed with their ethnic homeland.

7. As Marilyn Ivy notes (1995: 10), the recovery of a precious object of nostalgic longing (the homeland in this case) can be an unwelcome experience.

8. See Tsuda (1999) for an in-depth analysis of the settlement of nikkeijin immigrants in Japan.

9. Both of the questionnaire surveys conducted by JICA (1992) and the Japanese Institute of Labor (1995) report that only 2 to 3 percent of the Brazilian nikkeijin came to Japan because they wanted to make Japan their permanent home.

10. The birth rate had declined by almost 32 percent from 2.14 children per family in 1965 to 1.46 in 1993—the world's lowest fertility rate. Japan has the fastest growing elderly population among industrialized countries. The proportion of the population over the age of sixty-five grew from 7.1 percent in 1970 to 10.3 percent in 1985 and then jumped to 14.5 percent in 1995.

11. Japan has a large illegal immigrant population of probably well over 300,000. In addition, there are a good number of unskilled foreign workers who enter the country with various professional visas (as "entertainers," language "students," and "trainees") but actually work as manual laborers (or in Japan's sex industry). Most of Japan's immigrants are from other East Asian countries (mainly China and Korea) and various Southeast Asian countries.

12. These figures are from surveys conducted by Kitagawa (1993, 1997) and the Japan Statistics Research Institute (1993).

REFERENCES

Appadurai, Arjun. *Modernity at Large: Cultural Dimensions of Globalization.* Minneapolis: University of Minnesota Press, 1996.
Basch, Linda, Nina Glick Schiller, and Cristina Szanton Blanc. *Nations Unbound: Transnational Projects, Postcolonial Predicaments, and Deterritorialized Nation-States.* Amsterdam: Gordon and Breach Publishers, 1994.
Chambers, Iain. *Migrancy, Culture, Identity.* London: Routledge, 1994.
Clifford, James. *Routes: Travel and Translation in the Late Twentieth Century.* Cambridge, MA: Harvard University Press, 1997.
DaMatta, Roberto. *Carnivals, Rogues, and Heroes: An Interpretation of the Brazilian Dilemma.* Notre Dame, IN: University of Notre Dame Press, 1991.
Foner, Nancy. "What's New About Transnationalism? New York Immigrants Today and at the Turn of the Century." *Diaspora* 6, no. 3 (1997): 355–75.
Glick Schiller, Nina, Linda Basch, and Cristina Szanton Blanc. "From Immigrant to Transmigrant: Theorizing Transnational Migration." *Anthropological Quarterly* 68, no. 1 (1995): 48–63.
Glick Schiller, Nina, and Georges Fouron. "Transnational Lives and National Identities: The Identity Politics of Haitian Immigrants." Pp.130–61 in *Transnationalism from Below, Comparative Urban and Community Research*, vol. 6, edited by Michael Peter Smith and Luis Eduardo Guarnizo. New Brunswick: Transaction Publishers, 1998.
Guarnizo, Luis Eduardo. "The Emergence of a Transnational Social Formation and the Mirage of Return Migration Among Dominican Transmigrants." *Identities: Global Studies in Culture and Power* 4, no. 2 (1997): 281–322.
Guarnizo, Luis Eduardo, and Michael Peter Smith. "The Locations of Transnationalism." Pp.3–34 in *Transnationalism from Below, Comparative Urban and Community Research*, vol. 6, edited by Michael Peter Smith and Luis Eduardo Guarnizo. New Brunswick: Transaction Publishers, 1998.
Gupta, Akhil and James Ferguson. "Beyond 'Culture': Space, Identity, and the Politics of Difference." *Cultural Anthropology* 7, no. 1 (1992): 6–23.
Ishi, Angelo A. "Burajiru Nikkei Dekasegi Rodosha to Nihon no Shinzoku" (Brazilian *Nikkei Dekasegi* Workers and Japanese Relatives). *Mare Nostrum* 5 (1992): 69–72.
Ivy, Marilyn. *Discourses of the Vanishing: Modernity, Phantasm, Japan.* Chicago: University of Chicago Press, 1995.
Jackson, Michael. *At Home in the World.* Durham, NC: Duke University Press, 1995.
Japan Institute of Labor. *Nikkeijin Rodosha no Jukyu Shisutemu to Shuro Keiken* [the demand/supply system and employment experiences of Nikkeiin workers]. Tokyo: Japan Institute of Labor, 1995.
Japan Statistics Research Institute (Nihon Tokei Kenkyujo). *Tokei Kenkyu Sanko Shiryo no.38: Nikkei Burajirujin Shuro/Seikatsu Jittai Chosa* [Statistical research reference: Survey of Brazilian *Nikkeijin* employment and living conditions]. Tokyo: Nihon Tokei Kenkyujo (Hosei University), 1993.

JICA (Japan International Cooperation Association). *Nikkeijin Honpo Shuro Jittai Chosa Hokokusho* [Report on the survey of the Nikkeijin working in our country]. *Kokusai Kyoryoku Jigyodan*, 1992.

Kearney, Michael. "Borders and Boundaries of State and Self at the End of Empire." *Journal of Historical Sociology* 4, no. 1 (1991): 52–74.

Kitagawa, Toyoie. *Gunma-ken Oizumi-machi ni Okeru Nikkeijin Rodosha Hiaringu Chosa: Eijyuka Shikou to Ukeire Kibanseibi* [Survey hearing of Nikkeijin workers in Gunma-ken, Oizumi-machi: The intention to become permanent and the fundamental framework for their acceptance]. Pp.89–154 in *Hito no Kokusaika ni Kansuru Sogoteki Kenkyu: Tokuni Gaikokujin Rodosha ni Kansuru Chosa Kenkyu o Chushin ni* [General survey on the internationalization of people: Especially focusing on the survey research about foreign workers]. Tokyo: Toyo University, 1992.

———. *Hamamatsu-shi ni Okeru Gaikokujin no Seikatsu Jittai/Ishiki Chosa: Nikkei Burajiru/Perujin o Chushin ni* [Survey of living conditions and consciousness of foreigners in Hamamatsu city: Focusing on Nikkei-Brazilians and Peruvians]. Hamamatsu Planning Section/International Exchange Office, 1993.

———. "Hamamatsushi ni Okeru Nikkei Burajirujin no Seikatsu Kozo to Ishiki: Nippaku Ryokoku Chosa o Fumaete" [The lives and consciousness of the Brazilian Nikkeijin in Hamamatsu city: Based on surveys in both Japan and Brazil]. *Toyo Daigaku Shakai Gakubu Kiyo* (Bulletin of the Department of Sociology at Toyo University) 34, no. 1 (1996): 109–96.

———. "Burajiru-taun no Keisei to Deasupora: Nikkei Burajirujin no Teijyuka ni Kansuru Nananen Keizoku Oizumi-machi Chosa" [Diaspora and the formation of Brazil-town: A continuing seven-year Oizumi-town survey about the settlement of Brazilian Nikkeijin]. *Toyo Daigaku Shakai Gakubu Kiyo* (Bulletin of the Department of Sociology at Toyo University) 34, no. 3 (1997): 66–173.

Lee, Jeanyoung. "Korea's Policy for Koreans Overseas."*Korea Focus* 11 no. 4 (2003): 108–32.

Louie, Andrea. "Re-territorializing Transnationalism: Chinese Americans and the Chinese Motherland." *American Ethnologist* 27, no. 3 (2000): 645–69.

Malkki, Lisa. "National Geographic: The Rooting of Peoples and the Territorialization of National Identity Among Scholars and Refugees." *Cultural Anthropology* 7, no. 1 (1992): 24–62.

Margolis, Maxine, L. *Little Brazil: An Ethnography of Brazilian Immigrants in New York City*. Princeton, NJ: Princeton University Press, 1994.

Markowitz, Fran. *A Community in Spite of Itself: Soviet Jewish Emigrés in New York*. Washington, DC: Smithsonian Institution Press, 1993.

Martes, Ana Cristina Braga. *Brasileiros nos Estados Unidos: Um Estudo sobre Imigrantes em Massachusetts* [Brazilians in the United States: A study about immigrants in Massachusetts]. São Paulo, Brazil: Editora Paz e Terra, 2000.

Massey, Doreen. "A Place Called Home?" *New Formations* 17 (1992): 3–15.

Mintz, Sidney. "The Localization of Anthropological Practice: From Area Studies to Transnationalism." *Critique of Anthropology* 18, no. 2 (1998): 117–33.

Münz, Rainer and Rainer Ohliger. *Diasporas and Ethnic Migrants: Germany, Israel, and Post-Soviet Successor States in Comparative Perspective*. London: Frank Cass, 2003.

Nomoto, Hiroyuki, Satoshi Oga, Miyoko Goto, Regina Miyazaka, Kazunari Matsuo, Motoyasu Nakamura, Kazushi Yoshida, and Mioto Kato. *Zainichi Nikkeijin Oyobi sono Kazoku no Seikatsu Jittai to Nihongo no Gakushu ni Kansuru Chosa Hokoku* [Survey Report of the Living Conditions of the resident Nikkeijin and their families and their study of Japanese]. *Nagoya Kyoiku Kenkyu Nenpo* (Nagoya Educational Research Annual Report) 10 (1993): 136–95. Nagoya: Nagoya University Department of Education Social Education Research Center.

Ong, Aihwa. *Flexible Citizenship: The Cultural Logics of Transnationality*. Durham, NC: Duke University Press, 1999.

Pastore, Ferrucio. "Nationality Law and International Migration: The Italian Case." Pp. 95–117 in *Towards a European Nationality: Citizenship, Immigration and Nationality Law in the EU*, edited by Randall Hansen and Patrick Weil. London: Palgrave, 2001.

Portes, Alejandro. "Global Villagers: The Rise of Transnational Communities." *The American Prospect* 2 (1996): 74–77.

Portes, Alejandro and Rubén G. Rumbaut. *Immigrant America: A Portrait*. Berkeley: University of California Press, 1996.

Remennick, Larissa. "Identity Quest among Russian Jews of the 1990s: Before and After Emigration." Pp. 241–58 in *Jewish Survival: The Identity Problem at the Close of the Twentieth Century*, edited by Ernest Krausz and Gitta Tulea. New Brunswick, N.J.: Transaction Publishers, 1998.

Roth, Joshua. *Brokered Homeland: Japanese Brazilian Migrants in Japan*. Ithaca, NY: Cornell University Press, 2002.

Rouse, Roger. "Mexican Migration and the Social Space of Postmodernism." *Diaspora* 1, no.1 (1991): 8–23.

Sellek, Yoko. *Migrant Labour in Japan*. New York: Palgrave, 2001.

Tsuda, Takeyuki. "Ethnicity and the Anthropologist: Negotiating Identities in the Field." *Anthropological Quarterly* 71, no. 3 (1998): 107–24.

———. "The Permanence of 'Temporary' Migration: The 'Structural Embeddedness' of Japanese-Brazilian Migrant Workers in Japan." *Journal of Asian Studies* 58, no. 3 (1999): 687–722.

———. *Strangers in the Ethnic Homeland: Japanese Brazilian Return Migration in Transnational Perspective*. New York: Columbia University Press, 2003.

———. Migration and Alienation: Japanese Brazilian Return Migrants and the Search for Homeland Abroad. Center for Comparative Immigration Studies Working Paper, no. 24 (www.ccis-ucsd.org/PUBLICATIONS/working_papers.htm).

Yamanaka, Keiko. "'I Will Go Home, But When?' Labor Migration and Circular Diaspora Formation by Japanese Brazilians in Japan." Pp.123–52 in *Japan and Global Migration: Foreign Workers and the Advent of a Multicultural Society*, edited by Mike Douglass and Glenda S. Roberts. London: Routledge, 2000.

Yoo, Myungki. "Dilemma of Joseon People: Ethnicity vs. Nationality." *Korea Focus* 10, no. 6 (2002): 99–113.

9

Promised Land, Imagined Homelands: Ethiopian Jews' Immigration to Israel

Lisa Anteby-Yemini

The children of Ethiopian Jewish villages used to look up in the sky when the storks flew by every year, returning from their migration, and sing in Amharic:

> *Shimela, shimela andiet allah?*
> *yä-yerusalem säwotch dehna natchäw?*
>
> [Stork, stork! How are you?
> Are the people of Jerusalem doing well?]

These birds were believed to bring good omens and this song expressed the fervent yearning and legendary dream of reaching Jerusalem, a fabulous land and a mythic city, both intertwined in the imagination of the Ethiopian Jews[1].

The Jews of Ethiopia, better known under the designation of Falashas, inhabited the Ethiopian highlands until their mass emigration, mainly via Israeli government–sponsored airlifts in the 1980s and 1990s. The quasi-totality of the community is now living in Israel, numbering close to eighty-five thousand individuals. Even though in 1975 the Rabbinate of Israel recognized the Falashas as Jews descending from the lost tribe of Dan, allowing them to immigrate to Israel under the Law of Return, the origins of this group still remain obscure. Recent studies situate the emergence of this community only around the fifteenth century (Kaplan 1992 and Quirin 1992). But the Jews of Ethiopia, who called themselves by the name Beta Israel or "House of Israel," claim to be an ancient Jewish exiled group and considered themselves as strangers in Ethiopia. Indeed, myths of return to Biblical Israel, their Promised Land, widely circulated in this group's century-long dream of reaching their "ancestral homeland." After several attempts to reach Jerusalem, the recent emigration of the community to Israel confronts its members with the harsh reality of resettlement, with orthodox Judaism, with the discovery of new racial categories, and with the practice of Israeli citizenship.

As they integrate into their new society, Ethiopian Jews also begin to develop ties with their country of origin. Growing transnational practices rebuild an "Ethiopian" culture in Israel and recreate an imaginary space of what was "home" for this displaced population, shaping Ethiopia into a "reconstructed homeland." At the same time, the immigrants are more and more influenced by global culture conveyed through audiovisual and electronic media; a minority even develops traits of an emergent Black Diaspora, making these nonlocalized cultural sites into a "virtual homeland." These various dimensions of the Ethiopian Jews' homecoming experience challenge the very notion of "home" as well as that of Jewish returnees coming back to their "ancestral homeland."

A PROMISED LAND

The myth of a promised land is a fundamental narrative in many identity constructs. Whether it be an imaginary place or a real country, a mythic elsewhere always presents itself in the image of a lost paradise, a land of abundance and a better world. Over the generations the Jews of Ethiopia have kept alive the myth of "return" to their ancestral home and the hope of one day reaching Jerusalem, their Promised Land. This mythology of a distant homeland was perpetuated through prophecies, stories, myths of origin, and constructions of identity as others in a foreign land. Indeed, numerous Ethiopian Jews felt that they did not belong in Ethiopia and strived to reach the original homeland that their ancestors had left centuries ago.

Dreaming of Jerusalem

As in all oral traditions, versions of the group's history have been changed and reinterpeted over the centuries. Ethiopian Jews' contact with Western Jewry and their immigration to Israel have profoundly transformed the ways by which they construct their identity and perceive their origin myths. During their first encounters with Europeans, the Falashas claimed that they were the descendants of the priests and the sons of notables from Jerusalem chosen by Solomon to escort his son Menelik back to Ethiopia. A more recent version that they tell makes them the descendants of Egyptian Jews who had either migrated to Ethiopia during the Exodus from Egypt or after the destruction of the First Temple of Jerusalem (in 586 B.C.). Another legend that they sometimes invoke makes them originate from an Israelite group that would have escaped to Ethiopia after the destruction of the Second Temple of Jerusalem (70 A.D.). Thus, different versions circulate and modify themselves according to the period and the contexts, giving way to a history constantly reinvented and erecting new narratives as foundation myths of the group.[2]

However, similar origin myths also existed among the dominant Amhara group, which complicated the Falashas' claim of "return to their homeland" since Christian Ethiopians *also* see themselves as the descendants of the Solomonic lineage.[3] In effect, the links between Ethiopia and Jerusalem date back to the legend of King Solomon and the Queen of Sheba. The national Ethiopian saga, the *Kebra Nagast* (Glory of the Kings), tells the story of Menelik, the son of King Solomon and the Queen of Sheba, who became king of Ethiopia, as well as that of the transfer of the Ark of the Covenant from Jerusalem to Axum, a city in the north of Ethiopia. This epic positions the Ethiopian emperors as direct heirs of the Solomonic dynasty and endows the Ethiopian people with the status of "Israelites." In fact, they claim, in many ways, to be the Chosen People in possession of the key symbol of Zion, the sacred Tabernacle. Axum is often called the Second Jerusalem because legend has it that the Holy Ark is hidden in one of its churches. In addition to the Ethiopian Christians' pilgrimages to Jerusalem, the Ethiopian church entertains narrow ties with the holy city where two Ethiopian churches are established, one of them on the roof of the Holy Sepulcher in the Old City. The site of Lalibela, in the Lasta region, has also been considered a place of pilgrimage, especially since the thirteenth century, when the road to Jerusalem was blocked. Moreover, the river that runs through this "Jerusalem of Ethiopia" is named *yardenus*, as in the River Jordan, or *yarden* in Hebrew. Therefore, the sacred geography that Jerusalem represents also possesses a value no less metaphorical in Ethiopian Christian life.[4]

The national Ethiopian saga thus poses an obvious problem for the origin myths and the identity constructs of the Falashas who claim to be the "real" Israelites. This situation creates a struggle for the legitimacy of descent as a Jewish group in a Christian Ethiopia that itself claims to be of "Israelite" origin. The Falashas, therefore, had to articulate various distinctions to reproduce the collective memory of and the group's self-definition as the "House of Israel" while differentiating themselves from the foundation myth of the Ethiopian nation.

This ideology of difference was sustained in particular through ethnoreligious borders in the spheres of food, slaughtering practices, strict purity rituals, and separation from the local Christian Amhara population (Kaplan 1992; Quirin 1992). In addition, the Falashas only used the Old Testament, in Geez, the Ethiopian liturgical language, and followed its festivals, including strict observance of the Sabbath. Tsaggay, a young man in his twenties, told me, "All the elders of the village knew the direction of Jerusalem for the prayers. I remember that my grandfather always spoke about Jerusalem, even before he knew the state of Israel existed." Certain rituals, such as the direction of prayer, faced Jerusalem, and before an animal was slaughtered, its head was turned towards Jerusalem. Prayers and blessings mentioned the sacred city several times and the return to Zion. Lastly, the opening lines of liturgical texts invoked the "God of Israel" (*Amlakä Esra'el*). But this utopic place that the Ethiopian Jews dreamed of was first and foremost a product of the imagination. Like all spaces associated with a name, Marc Augé writes that some places "only exist by the words that they evoke, in a sense nonplaces (*non-lieux*) or rather imaginary places, banal utopias, clichés. The word, here, does not dissociate between daily uses and lost myths: it creates the image, produces the myth and as a result makes it function" (1992: 120).

In fact, the very name of Jerusalem represented a mythical evocation and evoked a magical power. As Joseph Halevy, the first Western Jew to have met the Falashas in 1867, wrote:

> The name of Jerusalem, which I had accidentally mentioned, changed as if by magic the attitude of the most incredulous. A burning curiosity seemed all at once to have seized the whole company. "Oh, do you come from Jerusalem, the blessed city? Have you beheld with your eyes Mount Zion, and the House of the Lord of Israel, the holy Temple?" . . . I told them that the Jewish inhabitants of the Holy City were plunged in misery; and that a mosque stands on the site of the ancient temple. They were grieved at the news, as they had no correct idea of the actual state of the Holy Land; most of them believed that it belonged to Roman Christians. (1877: 215–16)

In effect, the isolation of the Falashas had left them thinking that they were the only Jews in the world, and it was only in 1865, with the arrival of the first Christian missionaries, that they began to change their own self-perception and think of themselves as members of world Jewry (Kaplan 1992). Their encounter with white Jewish emissaries, such as Joseph Halevy, a few years later, led to an even deeper redefinition of the group's collective identity, as is illustrated in their first reaction upon learning that he was himself a Jew. "'What! You a Falasha! A white Falasha! You are laughing at us! Are there any white Falashas?' I assured them that all the Falashas of Jerusalem, and in other parts of the world, were white" (Halévy 1877: 215). These quasi-kinship links with "white" Jews would soon give the Falashas a feeling of belonging to a wider Jewish "imagined community" and would renew their hope of immigrating to Israel (Seeman 2000). Indeed, for the Ethiopian Jews, the myth of the Promised Land represented a religious quest: Jerusalem is seen as the Israel of the ancient Hebrews and takes on Jewish eschatological models. The Falashas believed that Biblical prophecy would realize itself and that the time would come to return to their original homeland.

Prophecies and Visions

In a climate of messanic fervor inspired by the reign of Emperor Theodoros II (1855–1868), a name that the Ethiopian Jews associated with the Messiah (Leslau 1957: 58), and facing the threat of conversion by Protestant missionaries, a false Falasha prophet announced that the time had come to leave for the Promised Land. Inspired by his prophetic ardor, in 1862 thousands of Falashas abandoned their homes and began walking towards Jerusalem following the charismatic figure of Abba Mahari, a Falasha monk. As Abba Mahari arrived at the Takazé River (in the north of Ethiopia), he, like Moses facing the Red Sea, pointed his stick towards the river to part the waters. In vain. Stricken by diseases and hunger, hundreds perished and the survivors slowly made their way back to their villages.[5] However, like many messianic prophets, Abba Mahari's failure only renewed in the group's collective memory its dream of reaching the Promised Land.

At the beginning of the twentieth century, Jacques Faitlovitch followed in the steps of his teacher Halevy and made several trips to Ethiopia. In 1908, however, Rabbi Haïm Nahoum headed a countermission and concluded that there are no similarities between Falashas and the Jewish world. He recommended against establishing Jewish schools among the Falashas and discouraged their immigration to Palestine. In response, Faitlovitch redoubled his efforts and devoted the rest of his life to the cause of the Falashas. He endeavored first to draw the Falashas closer to normative Judaism by introducing rabbinic practices and a Hebrew liturgy. This "normalization" of the Falashas' Judaism meant abolishing their sacrifices, their institution of monasticism, and the purity rituals as they were practiced. Likewise it meant adopting the normative Jewish calendar of festivals, the dietary laws, and the Hebrew language of prayer. Faitlovitch opened a network of schools to educate the children and sent youngsters to Jewish communities in Europe and Palestine to form a Western-trained elite. Finally he mobilized the international community by creating pro-Falasha committees in Europe and the United States, and campaigning for the repatriation of the community to the land of Israel. However, for reasons linked to the political situation in Ethiopia, where Emperor Haile Selassie was not ready to let them leave, and in the new state of Israel, which did not then recognize them as Jews, the Falashas could not yet fulfill their dream.

The Falashas, however, had developed for the first time a diasporic conscience that went beyond the local level and linked them to a global Jewish community that remained nevertheless imagined and distant for most of them. But how had it come about that the Falashas were incorporated, in less than a century, into Jewish history after having been at the margins of Judaism for so long? The construction of a historic, religious, and ethnic Jewish belonging goes back to the encounter with the West, first with Protestant missionaries and then with Jewish emissaries who endowed the Falashas with new identity discourses and narratives that linked them to the Jewish world and created from a particular local group an "Ethiopian Jewish" diaspora. Furthermore, the idea of "rescuing" the Falashas and regenerating their Judaism fit into the Zionist-religious discourses at the time of the creation of the state of Israel, which called for the "ingathering of the exiled" (*kibbutz galuyot*) as one condition for the coming of a Messianic era. In fact, in Israel in the 1940s and 1950s, particularly during the presidency of Itzkhak Ben-Zvi, a renewal occurred in this movement in favor of conversions and searches for lost Jewish communities (Trevisan-Semi 1999). In the Falasha case, their status as *nidhe Israel* (dispersed tribe of Israel) and their possible return to the Promised Land were seen as the accomplishment of the Zionist dream and the realization of a prophetic message leading to the redemption of the entire Jewish people. Thus, in 1955, some twenty young Falashas were sent to Kfar Batya in Israel in order to return to their villages upon completion of their studies as teachers. At the same time (1953–1958) the Jewish Agency established a network of schools in Ethiopia's Gondar region. Jewish tourists and researchers also visited the Falashas during those years and presented them with the liturgical books, prayer shawls (*tallith*), and Torah scrolls in Hebrew that had been unknown to them, while introducing the Star of David as a specifically Jewish symbol. In 1974, just one year before the Israeli rabbinate officially recognized the Falashas as full-fledged Jews, the Marxist-Leninist régime of Mengistu Haile Maryam came to power and put an end to the Falashas' contacts with world Jewry. Mass immigration would only begin years later.

Migration and Redemption

It was with the famine and the political unrest that fell upon the Horn of Africa from 1983 to 1984 that the first mass exodus of Ethiopian Jews began. Under Mengistu's regime all emigration was prohibited, and very few Ethiopian Jews managed to reach Israel. As a flow of Ethiopians fleeing from the famine started, the Falashas also decided to walk towards Sudan. Their hope was to reach Israel. Often whole villages decided to depart. They abandoned everything and left at night, so that their Christian neighbors would not notice their exodus. In other places, only the young adults and the children fled, sometimes leaving behind parents and grandparents. In yet other instances, the youth escaped at night without telling their parents or their peers and joined other groups of Ethiopian Jews traveling by foot. Ethiopian guides led them towards the Sudanese border, in some cases robbing them of their last belongings or leaving them to their own destiny in the middle of the wilderness.

Not only were there shortages of water and food during the trek, but also the danger of robbers, wild animals, Ethiopian and Sudanese soldiers, and deadly diseases. Refugee camps in Sudan offered precarious conditions and an estimated four thousand Ethiopian Jews perished en route to Israel. They had to hide their Jewish identity in Sudan and often refused the food or the pills the rescue teams were distributing for fear of ingesting impure food. Most of their traditional religious practices, such as purity rituals and burial ceremonies, could not be pursued.

With the deterioration of the situation in the camps, Israeli authorities organized a first airlift code-name "Operation Moses." Between 1984 and 1985 it secretly evacuated some 6,700 Jews to Israel. The revelation of this rescue operation put an end to this immigration because of Sudan's membership in the Arab League.[6] As any voyage to a promised land implies a process of selection, the numerous deaths among Ethiopian Jews' were seen as the price for migration to Israel via Sudan. In fact, once they arrived in Israel as new immigrants, Ethiopian Jews compared their journey through Sudan to the biblical Exodus from Egypt and to the forty years that the Israelites spent in the desert before entering the Promised Land. They explained that only the "chosen" or "the just" were granted the chance to reach Israel, as they rationalized the suffering and the deaths along the journey (Ben-Ezer 2002). Some even saw the migration path as a purification process, considering those who arrived in Israel as having gone through a renewal or rebirth that gave them the strength to go on.

Interrupted following the 1973 Yom Kippur war, diplomatic relations between Ethiopia and Israel were renewed in 1989. The opening of an Israeli embassy in Addis-Ababa allowed for legal, albeit very limited, immigration to Israel. Despite the Ethiopian government's restrictions on exit visas, hundreds of Falashas left their villages and streamed into the Ethiopian capital city, and by 1990 there were close to twenty thousand residing around the embassy of Israel in the hope of emigrating. In the spring of 1991, while the rebel forces of the northern Tigray province were at the doors of Addis and the regime of Mengistu was on the verge of collapsing, the Israeli government decided to take the opportunity of this political disarray to launch a massive rescue plan, code-named Operation Solomon. Within forty-eight hours, 14,200 people were airlifted from Addis Ababa to Ben-Gurion airport in Israel.

Here, once again, with the Biblical code names of Moses and Solomon, Zionist and messianic discourses framed the narratives of these rescue operations. Ironically, perhaps, it was also the centrality of Biblical metaphors in the immigrants' construction of a distant utopia that would lead to their coming disappointments. For the danger of trying to reach a promised land lies in its very failure: the end of the journey can shatter a centuries-long yearning.

THE PARADOXES OF PARADISE

In fact, when the miracle of homecoming did happen, myth and reality confronted each other for the first time, and the Ethiopian Jews felt more than ever displaced and alienated in time and space. Indeed, the disillusionment and the disenchantment that awaited the immigrants were not to be long in manifesting themselves. Like the storks in their oral tradition, it was in "birds of steel" that they left the universe of illusions in which they lived to land in a world that was to shatter, in various ways, their utopic visions.

Tsaggay remembers with nostalgia that in Ethiopia he was told that Israel would be like the Garden of Eden; Lemlem recalls that her parents always told her that it would be a country where all was green with plenty of water. Many believed that Israel would be a land of milk and honey, just like the Bible described it, where all the inhabitants would be observant Jews.[7] Some elders remember hearing from their parents that in Jerusalem no one would become sick and that no one ever died there![8] These representations of the Holy Land in the collective imaginary of the immigrants could only disappoint their expectations. Finally, other adults also recalled how, as children, they were told that they would become white when they reached this mythic land! However, not only did their skin color not change, but they discovered with surprise that they were the only black-skinned Jews in the Jewish homeland.

A painful discovery was also made when the Ethiopian Jews learned that the Temple of Jerusalem that appeared in so many of their prayers and religious texts was no longer standing, and that its remnants only consisted of a Wailing Wall. Dawit, a young adult, added that he always thought Jerusalem (or *Yerussalem*, as he pronounced it) was the whole land of Israel and had not known that there were other cities. In fact, when the immigrants first landed and some were directed to absorption centers in Jerusalem, many could not believe that this was the Holy City! If a transitional period in Addis Ababa acclimated this rural population to city life, their encounter with a new urbanity that intertwined thousand-year-old stones and cosmopolitan postmodernity deeply disoriented these new immigrants.

Exotic Returnees

Upon arrival the Ethiopian Jews at first received a warm welcome from the host population. Day after day, in an immense expression of solidarity, crowds of excited Israelis brought huge quantities of toys, clothes, shoes, and even home appliances to absorption centers where the new immigrants were housed for the first year (and often more) under the auspices of the Jewish Agency. The media's depiction of the Jews of Ethiopia as "poverty-stricken refugees" in need of all basic necessities was confirmed by the comments I heard around the integration centers: "Look at them, they are so unfortunate (*miskenim*)!" "Poor people, they have suffered so much." "See, they're barefoot, they don't even own shoes." This empathy seemed mostly directed toward the children, whom the host population pitied the most and overwhelmed with gifts. But this image of Jewish suffering, so emotionally ridden, recalled in the collective national memory the arrival of survivors from the concentration camps and touched Israeli citizens' conscience in a most profound way. If they welcomed these "black brothers" with the utmost hospitality, this gesture also heightened their own image of themselves.

Indeed, the strong media coverage of Operation Solomon and its effects offered to Israeli citizens, who were yearning for a renewed ideology, the feeling of having lived out a historical episode of the "return of the exiled" to the Promised Land. It reendowed Zionism with its primary meaning and reconfirmed the legitimacy of the Jewish state that had otherwise been undergoing a deep identity crisis. Many citizens actually felt they had personally rescued these "Biblical Jews" and accomplished a humanitarian mission, as if, in a way, they were the real heroes of this saga. In the Israeli imagination, the fascination about these new immigrants came, in part, from the pride and emotion that accompanied the spectacular return of this "lost tribe" to its ancestral homeland. Only later would the host population's attitudes change to disinterest and indifference, and in certain cases outright racism.

A Religious Clash

The first conflicts that the Ethiopian immigrants encountered were in the religious sphere, and in particular, in their confrontation with orthodox Judaism. When they chose to leave everything behind in Ethiopia, many adults emphasized that they did so first and foremost for religious reasons, even if economic or political factors also played a role in their decision to emigrate. No persecution per se haunted their daily lives in Ethiopia, but they often encountered stigmatization as an outcast group. During the Marxist-Leninist regime of Mengistu, Ethiopian Jews could not freely display their support for Israel; some were jailed for Zionist activities. Upon arriving in Israel, however, the personal Jewish status of the immigrants was questioned by the Israeli rabbinate. Even though it had recognized the Ethiopian immigrants as a Jewish community, the rabbinate demanded symbolic conversions on an individual basis to eliminate any doubt of illegitimacy (*mamzerout*) because of marriage, divorce and conversion procedures that did not conform to rabbinic Judaism.[9] This is also the avowed reason why the religious authority of

Ethiopian Jewish spiritual leaders (*the qesotch*) was not recognized in Israel, and until this day they are not permitted to perform legal weddings, burials, or divorces for community members.[10]

At the same time, the Ethiopian Jews were confronted with an Israeli population that is not, in its majority, religiously observant and with behaviors that go against their laws of ritual purity. In Ethiopia, Falashas were considered impure if they touched a dead body, an animal's carcass, or a non-Falasha, and women were considered impure during the menstrual period and after childbirth. According to their degree of impurity, these individuals were confined in a hut outside the village and after the required period (from one day to eighty days) they immersed themselves in a river and washed their clothes before coming back purified to their home. The new immigrants were therefore startled that Israeli women were not isolated during menstruation and that Israeli men could touch a corpse without undergoing seclusion and purification rites (Anteby 1999). Because of their isolation in Ethiopia, the Falashas had been unaware that since the destruction of the Temple of Jerusalem rabbinic Judaism reformed many of these rituals. The newcomers also discovered post-Biblical festivals that had been unknown to them, dietary laws (such as not mixing milk and meat) that they had not practiced, and slaughtering meat in a way that they claimed differed from their own ritual. Many of the new immigrants still observed their own distinct slaughtering, kept specific holidays of the community, and endeavored to maintain some of their purity rituals, particularly concerning women, elaborating a rhetoric of purity that distinguishes them from the presumed impurity of the Israelis (Anteby-Yemini, forthcoming). Those who continue to uphold their Ethiopian Jewish practices thus consider themselves as the authentic Jews and see the Promised Land as an impure place (Trevisan Semi 1985).

Homecoming and Its Discontents

However, soon after their arrival, the harsh reality of resettlement and the daily difficulties of material life came to preoccupy the immigrants. Housing was a major concern for families who were living in integration centers and caravan sites (mobile homes). Thanks to a special government subsidy program, launched in 1993, the "Operation Solomon" wave of Ethiopian immigrants was able to purchase apartments in middle-class neighborhoods. However, most decided to live together, voluntarily creating ethnic enclaves. Language was another issue that the returnees had to deal with, since none of them knew Hebrew and most were illiterate in their mother tongue Amharic, or Tigrinya. After a ten-month state-sponsored intensive Hebrew class (*ulpan*), many of the adults had not succeeded in learning the language and acquiring literacy, and they remained, as they put it, "without a tongue" (*melas*, the organ of the mouth). Integrating into the work force was also problematic. Most of the newcomers had made their living from agriculture and pastoralism, and in addition to their poor Hebrew skills, had no qualifications for the Israeli job market. If the majority of young adult men did find employment, it was at the bottom of the occupational hierarchy. Many women and elders lived from payments from government unemployment and social security funds and family allowances. But the most difficult adjustment was to a free-market economy and a consumer society where one needs money for everything. As many people told me, money is necessary "to pay the rent, the food, and even the water!"

During their first year in Israel, all the Ethiopian children were sent to schools and boarding schools belonging to the state religious network (*mamlakhti-dati*) and until this day the majority are still educated within this framework. The state religious network offers a limited choice of institutions, which are often considered of a lower level than secular schools. Ethiopian students are overrepresented in these schools, and they sometimes constitute more than 25 percent of the student body. Finally, family patterns were deeply transformed by new spatial arrangements limiting housing for extended families, by the loss of authority of parents over their children, and by the new freedom women had from their husbands' control. Thus, research on Ethiopian immigrants speaks of spatial segregation, social marginalization, domestic violence, the emergence of an occupational underclass, and a population living under the poverty line.

Yet, as opposed to immigrant groups in many other parts of the world, Ethiopian Jews have presumably benefited from "optimal conditions" for integrating into their host society: they have received full citizenship rights upon arrival, enjoy preferential policies in the areas of housing (loans and subsidies), education (affirmative action and after-school programs), and vocational training and are the recipients of considerable financial investments to insure a smooth "absorption." Furthermore, as Jewish returnees to their homeland, they have no plans to return to Ethiopia and are encouraged to melt into Israeli society and identify with the ethnoreligious nationality of their new state. Finally, even with the realities of the Promised Land, its ritual impurity and its sometimes racial prejudices, all the newcomers consider Israel their home and wish their children to integrate into the social, political, and economic life of the country.

Indeed, in a short period of time both children and adults began entering Israeli society through the schools, army service, employment, politics, and their reliance on health, legal, and welfare institutions. Gradually they have constructed a new identity as Israeli citizens. For the younger generation, the educational system represented their first formal socialization experience; even if their scholastic achievements are still fairly poor in comparison with the Israeli average and the dropout rate is on the rise, school is a place of integration. In common with other Israelis, Ethiopian men and women serve their compulsory army duty and, even though discrimination and racist treatment have sometimes been reported, on the whole the army experience appears to strengthen their Israeli identity and increases their feeling of belonging to the Israeli nation (Shabtay 1995). On the national level, Ethiopian Jews rapidly built a tight network of associations and organizations to promote the community's demands for education, culture, and welfare. Moreover, they have developed various "indigenous media" in Amharic, state-subsidized television and radio programs, and a monthly magazine. Often under the auspices of the umbrella organization United Organization of Ethiopian Jews, Ethiopian Israelis have successfully staged strikes and large demonstrations to claim their rights as Israeli citizens. The clearest expression of their citizenship rights by far is the way that these homecomers have participated in Israeli civil society and political life by massively voting in national elections. At the local level, Ethiopian Jews have also been candidates in various municipal elections, though none has been elected to office. In sum, a local and national citizenship is developing and a national Jewish Israeli identity is being affirmed as these returnees undergo mechanisms of reterritorialization.

But since they have found themselves for the first time as a black minority in a "white" society, it is their encounter with new racial categories that is becoming a major theme in the integration process of the Ethiopian immigrants in Israel. More and more frequent usage among the immigrants of a racial discourse in their condemnation of Israeli policies as daily discrimination and institutional racism situates them at once in an interracial relation rather than an interethnic one vis-à-vis the host society. At the same time, they are also constructing new models of ethnicity and the emergence of identity references based less on religion or on Ethiopian features than on skin color. This awareness of a color line goes hand in hand with the marginalization and the exclusion many feel as second-class Israeli citizens. This process of ethnicization of color establishes a "Black Jewish" ethnicity that can be considered as an instrumental identity, socially and politically constructed (Anteby 1997). It is in fact mainly strategic, since the Ethiopians have forged no ties with other black communities in Israel such as the Black Hebrews (see Markowitz in this volume) or African foreign workers. Herein might lie the very paradox of the Promised Land: striving to remain Ethiopian while becoming Israeli, being black and Jewish, being citizens yet feeling racial discrimination, living in the Jewish "homeland" yet considering it to be in an impure space, and having dreamt of a better world while surviving at the bottom of the socioeconomic hierarchy.

How does one thus maintain the myth of the Promised Land *and* in the words of French anthropologist André Mary (2000) "postpone hope" in the face of "failure of success"?

REIMAGINED HOMELANDS

In the face of contradictions they encountered in Israel, where they feel both at home and not at home, some Ethiopian Jews endeavor today to find new promised lands by constructing alternative mythologies of dreamed elsewheres. Avtar Brah, asks, "Where is home? On the one hand, 'home' is a mythic place of desire in the diasporic imagination. In this sense, it is a place of no return, even if it is possible to visit the geographical territory that is seen as the place of 'origin'. On the other hand, home is also the lived experience of a locality" (1996: 192). This double tension gives rise to processes that Brah defines as *homing of diaspora and diasporizing of home*. In the case of the Ethiopian Jews, one indeed observes the "homing" of Ethiopia and the "diasporizing" of Israel, since Israel appears at once as a Promised Land and a diasporic land and Ethiopia as the native country and the country of exile.

Dreaming of Ethiopia

One means of postponing the return to a mythic homeland is by traveling back to the old country and perpetuating the feeling of being in exile. And in effect, today thousands of Ethiopian-Israelis make trips to their native country, resembling in a way a new form of pilgrimage. They all travel for short visits of leisure, to cure health problems, conduct business, and visit family members. No one has ever moved back permanently to Ethiopia.

In Addis Ababa, the capital, these Ethiopian-Israelis encounter an African urban society that they had never had access to as villagers and that deeply remodels their representation of Ethiopia. Ethiopian Jews reinvent this city as a "home" locality and its urban culture is reappropriated as their culture of origin, leading to a process of "homing Addis Ababa." While participation in this newly discovered homeland culture is mainly a male experience, those who do not travel become consumers of this popular Ethiopian culture through the cultural traffic between Ethiopia and Israel.

Stories of the trips and descriptions of Addis that the travelers relate in great detail also enable those who remain in Israel to reconstruct new images of their home country. In addition, circulation of commercial videotapes and music cassettes from Ethiopia, and in particular the landscapes seen in the movies, are alternative ways of reenvisioning the homeland from their Israeli living rooms. This (re)creates an idealized image of the native country that is often distant from reality (Anteby-Yemini, forthcoming). The consumption of video movies is in fact a common practice among various migrants, enabling them to be "there" and "here" at once. Memories of Ethiopia are also maintained through stories, comments, and conversations among the viewers about how beautiful their country is and how green it looks. These films' romantic scenery produces an imaginary and mythical reconstruction of the native land (Steen Preis 1997 for a similar phenomenon among Sri-Lankan refugees). The adults usually refer to Ethiopia as "our country" (*agäratchin*) and often discuss how much cattle they owned, how much food they produced, how good the *ingera* pancakes tasted, how pure the air felt, how good the water was, how healthy they were, etc., blatantly idealizing in a nostalgic mode their own past. This *ethnoscape*—what Arjun Appadurai (1996) has called the native country reinvented in the imagination of deterritorialized groups—becomes an additional solution for making the myth of a lost paradise linger on. It is also these links to the native land, Ethiopia, that maintain in Israel the collective identity of the group, a common feature of diaspora communities.

If we can speak of Ethiopia as a reimagined "homeland," what are we to make of the traveling culture of this homecoming population making return trips back to its country of origin? For the imported home culture that is currently emerging in Israel is nothing else than a diasporized Ethiopian culture. And what does it mean to watch, almost daily, videos of Ethiopia when one is settled in Israel, the so-called ancestral homeland? The image of the native country, Ethiopia, is being reconstructed *here* and may come to represent home for immigrants who are considered returnees to their Promised Land. This leads to the issue of the homing of Ethiopia and thus the emergence of an Ethiopian diaspora in Israel or, in other words, the diasporization of the Promised Land.

An Imagined Black Diaspora

A similar process is also occurring among the youth of Ethiopian origin in Israel, albeit with a different location. A minority of youngsters adopt African American identity models and black international symbols (music genres, hairdos, dress) conveyed through electronic media to the extent that some researchers are already speaking of a black counterculture in the midst of Israeli society (Anteby-Yemini forthcoming). Some teenagers even dream of traveling to the United States, especially to see how blacks live, as well as to Jamaica, mostly for its reggae music (Shabtay 2001: 213–15). This identification with a Black Diaspora thus offers, in a symbolic way, alternative modes of belonging to the myth of an imaginary land. Finally, the attraction, through music, to Rastafarianism among some young Ethiopian-Israelis enables them to rediscover their home country as the source of inspiration for this movement.

But these identifications are based on the influences of global culture, transmitted by "virtual" connections; furthermore, identifying Ethiopian immigrants with a Black Diaspora could seem paradoxical for Jewish returnees to their homeland. Here one seems to encounter a virtual homeland, since it is not always located geographically and is reconstructed through imaginary links.

CONCLUSION

The itinerary of a historical, religious, and ethnic incorporation of a group at the margins of Judaism has illustrated here how the Falashas "succeeded" in being considered as Jews and being repatriated to their "homeland" in Israel. But from the contradictions of the Ethiopian Jews' return, it seems that the quest for a promised land is doomed to failure. Is not any homecoming experience bound to disappoint expectations and reveal the paradoxes of "the return to the homeland"? It might be the very nature of the myth of a dreamed homeland to remain unachievable. This example of the Ethiopian Jewish returnees goes further and brings up an additional question: What are the reactualized forms that the myth takes when the prophecy is not realized? In other words, how does one preserve the myth of Israel as the Promised Land, when discrimination and baffled purity laws continue to haunt the homecomers? What strategies allow for maintaining the dream of a utopia when daily reality points to the opposite? The question that lingers in the background pertains to new forms of utopias that emerge when the prophetic project fails or vexes century-long yearnings. These alternative mythologies may lead to new narratives of identity that remain to be seen in the next generation.

As this chapter has attempted to show with the case of the Ethiopian Jews, the appropriation of new identity models, often taken from global culture (such as "black diasporas") or from transnational ties (such as those created between Ethiopia and Israel), offers a new geography of imagined homelands. One indeed observes more and more that the representations of the promised lands of tomorrow are generated by a flow of images and narratives conveyed through multimedia communication or international travel. Ethiopian Jews who do not even enter into contact with African Americans can create myths through mediated encounters that make them belong to imagined worlds, or to use Appadurai's formulation, to *mediascapes*.

These questions of home, belonging, and identity and these contradictions of and between diasporic location and dislocation are, as Avtar Brah discusses, "intrinsically linked with the way in which processes of inclusion and exclusion operate and are subjectively experienced under given circumstances. It is centrally about our political and personal struggles over the social regulation of 'belonging.' As Gilroy (1993) suggests, it is simultaneously about roots and routes" (1996: 192). This chapter has argued that even though Ethiopian Jews, as returnees to Israel, are included in the nation and benefit from all the rights of its citizens, they do not always feel quite at home in their homeland, as they are still negotiating their belonging in the wider sense of the term. This questions their very definition as Jewish returnees or *olim*, those who ascend spiritually to Israel, who are supposed to have come home. As such, their experience challenges the very meaning of homeland when it is both here, in Israel, there, in Ethiopia, and, for some, elsewhere in the black global diaspora.

NOTES

I wish to thank the editors of this volume for their comments on an earlier draft of this chapter and particularly Fran Markowitz for her thorough linguistic editing.

1. This song, already recorded in a Falasha village more than sixty years ago by M. Griaule (1935: 71) during the Dakar-Djibouti expedition, has remained the same until today, making a few years ago a hit song, "Shimela," in Hebrew by an Ethiopian immigrant children's choir (Shlomo Grunig and Makelat Shva).
2. For an account of these mytho-legends see J. Abbink (1990).
3. The Amharas are Christian Ethiopians who dominated and "amharized" the northern part of Ethiopia, spreading Orthodox Christian religion and Ethiopia's official language, Amharic.
4. On Jewish influences in Ethiopia, cf. E. Ullendorff (1968).
5. On this episode that has remained alive in the Ethiopian Jews' oral tradition, cf. S. Ben-Dor (1987).
6. For a Sudanese point of view of this rescue operation, see A. Karadawi (1991).
7. An excellent book edited by A. Kamoun (1996) about the first group of Ethiopian Jews who came to study in 1955 in an Israeli institution (Kfar Batya) opens with a chapter intitled "Jerusalem," which presents the first reactions and impressions of these young Ethiopian students arriving in Israel. See also G. Ben-Ezer (2002).
8. See also R. Westheimer and S. Kaplan (1992: 116).
9. A *mamzer* or "illegitimate child" is a child born from prohibited marriages because they are considered incestuous or adulterous according to the Bible or the Talmud. For example, if a Jewish woman is not religiously divorced, the child that she would have with another man would be considered illegitimate.
10. In Israel, these institutions are under the jurisdiction of the Rabbinate since religion and state are not separated.

REFERENCES

Anteby, Lisa. "Blood, Identity and Integration: Reflections on the Ethiopian Jews in Israel." Pp. 262–83 in *Ethiopia in Broader Perspective: Papers of the 13th International Conference of Ethiopian Studies*, vol. 2, edited by Katsuyoshi Fukui. Kyoto: Shokado Booksellers, 1997.

———. "There's Blood in the House: Negotiating Female Rituals of Purity among Ethiopian Jews in Israel." Pp. 166–86 in *Women and Water: Menstruation in Jewish life and Law*, edited by Rahel Wasserfall. Hanover, NH: Brandeis University Press and University Press of New England, 1999.

Anteby-Yemini, Lisa. *Les paradoxes du paradis: chronique de la vie des juifs éthiopiens en Israël*. Paris: CNRS Editions, forthcoming.

Abbink, Jan. "The Enigma of Beta Esra'el Ethnogenesis: An Ethno-historical Study." *Cahiers d'Etudes Africaines* 30, no. 120 (1990): 392–449.

Appadurai, Arjun. *Modernity at Large: Cultural Dimensions of Globalisation*. Minneapolis: University of Minnesota Press, 1996.

Augé, Marc. *Non-lieux: introduction à une anthropologie de la surmodernité*. Paris: Seuil, 1992.

Ben-Dor, Shoshana. "The Journey to the Land of Israel: The Story of Abba Mahari." *Pe'amim* 33 (1987): 5–31 (in Hebrew).

Ben-Ezer, Gadi. *The Ethiopian Jewish Exodus: Narratives of the Migration Journey to Israel 1977–1985*. London: Routledge, 2002.

Brah, Avtar. *Cartographies of Diaspora: Contesting Identities*. London: Routledge, 1996.

Griaule, Marcel. *Jeux et divertissements abyssins*. Paris: Ecole des Hautes Etudes et Librairie E. Leroux, 1935.

Halévy, Joseph. "Travels in Abyssinia." in *Miscellany of Hebrew Literature*, edited by A. Lowy. London: Wertheimer, Lea and Co., 1877.

Kamoun, Azriel, ed. *The First Bridge: Testimonies of Jewish Students of Ethiopian Origin at Kfar Batya 1955–1995*. Ramat Efal: Yad Tabenkin, 1996 (in Hebrew).

Kaplan, Steven. *The Beta Israel (Falasha) in Ethiopia: From Earliest Times to the Twentieth Century*. New York: New York University Press, 1992.

Karadawi, Ahmed. "The Smuggling of the Ethiopian Falasha to Israel through Sudan." *Journal of Modern African Studies* 29, no. 4 (1991): 557–81.

Leslau, Wolf. *Coutumes et croyances des Falachas (Juifs d'Abyssinie)*. Paris: Institut d'Ethnologie, 1957.

Mary, André. "Voyage visionnaire et errance prophétique: du nomadisme à la fondation." *Social Compass* 47, no. 1 (2000): 77–92.

Quirin, James. *The Evolution of the Ethiopian Jews: A History of the Beta Israel (Falasha) to 1920*. Philadelphia: University of Pennsylvania Press, 1992.

Seeman, Don. "The Question of Kinship: Bodies and Narratives in the Beta-Israel-European Encounter (1860–1920)." *Journal of Religion in Africa* 30, no. 1 (2000): 86–120.

Shabtay, Malka. "The Experience of Ethiopian Soldiers in the Israeli Army: The Process of Identity Formulation within the Military Context." *Israel Social Science Research* 10, no. 2 (1995): 69–80.

———. *Between Reggae and Rap: The Integration Challenge of Ethiopian Youth in Israel*. Tel Aviv: Tcherikover, 2001 (in Hebrew).

Steen Preis, Ann-Belinda. "Capsized Identities and Contracted Belonging among Sri Lankan Tamil Refugees." Pp. 86–100 in *Siting Culture: The Shifting Anthropological Object*, edited by Karen Olwig and Kirsten Hastrup. London: Routledge, 1997.

Trevisan Semi, Emanuela. "The Beta Israel (Falashas): From Purity to Impurity." *Jewish Journal of Sociology* 27, no. 2 (1985): 103–14.

———. "Universalisme juif et prosélytisme. L'action de Jacques Faitlovitch, 'père' des Beta Israel (Falashas)." *Revue de l'histoire des religions* 216, no. 2 (1999): 193–211.

Ullendorff, Edward. *Ethiopia and the Bible.* London: Oxford University Press, 1968.

Westheimer, Ruth, and Steven Kaplan. *Surviving Salvation: The Ethiopian Jewish Family in Transition.* New York: New York University Press, 1992.

IV
CONTENTIOUS HOMECOMINGS

10

Transatlantic Dreaming: Slavery, Tourism, and Diasporic Encounters

Bayo Holsey

Mr. Nguah[1] is a Ghanaian businessman in the Ghanaian town Cape Coast who operates a tour company that specializes in kinship tourism. He explained to me that through this operation, he helps Africans in the diaspora trace their roots. Mr. Nguah proudly told me of one particular client, an African American man whom he helped to reunite with his long-lost Ghanaian relatives. This man knew the name of the family from which he believed he descended, so he employed Mr. Nguah's company to locate this family and to reunite him with them. Mr. Nguah located the family, and the man promptly traveled to Ghana to meet them. When he arrived, he was taken to their village where he was met by a man who was to take him to the family's house. When the man saw him, he simply stared in disbelief. The American asked him what it was, but the other man simply replied, "wait and you will know." As they walked through the village, other people stopped and stared. Again the man became curious, but his companion repeated, "wait and you will know." When they finally reached the house of the family that he believed to be his relatives, a group of people emerged from the house, and the man discovered that he looked remarkably similar to all of the members of the family. They welcomed him, having no doubt that he was indeed their kin.

   This story is similar to others that, having circulated throughout both Ghana and the United States many times, have lost their specific referents, and operate instead as a fantasy trope of transatlantic reunion. Here, phenotype functions as absolute proof of a familial relationship, providing an idealized, dreamlike notion of a seamless transatlantic connection. In contrast to these dreams, in real life, most such connections are much more fraught with tension and misunderstanding. The complexity of these encounters is due to the fact that African Americans, especially those with the means to travel abroad, and Ghanaians occupy radically different positions within the global economy. Their respective experiences of late capitalism determine the dissimilar ways in which they understand the meanings of each other and of slavery as the root of their separation.

In what follows, I examine African American tourists' constructions of Ghana as home and homeland. Through their travel, these tourists seek to encounter remnants of the slave trade and to visit the point of dispersal of the African diaspora. They imagine and conduct their trips as pilgrimages. But such pilgrimages are contested by many local residents because the slave trade, as the diaspora's origin, occupies a marginalized and stigmatized place in public memory. Instead, for Ghanaians, these tourists conjure images of wealth and mobility that fuel their imaginations of homes elsewhere that they have little chance of ever experiencing. Thus, I argue that both African Americans and Ghanaians participate in simultaneous yet reverse imaginative processes or transatlantic dreamings that converge within sites of painful memories of slavery's past. This encounter provides an apt example of the "power geometry" of late capitalism, which, as Massey notes, describes not only differential access to travel but also varying levels of control over the nature and meaning of that travel (1994: 149).

The analysis provided in this chapter is based on twelve months of fieldwork during 2001 in Cape Coast and Elmina, two coastal towns in Ghana that have become key sites of diaspora tourism because of their infamous slave forts. Elmina Castle was built by the Portuguese by 1482 and used by the Dutch as their base of operation for the slave trade until the late nineteenth century, while Cape Coast Castle was originally built by the Swedish in 1653 and quickly turned over to the British who used it for the same purpose. Both castles contain dungeons where slaves were kept before they were shipped to the New World, which have become the primary focus of diaspora tourists who visit the castles. During my fieldwork, I observed visitors at these sites in addition to interviewing African American tourists, Ghanaian residents, as well as tour guides and other tourism officials. Through their discussions of tourism, slavery, and each other, African Americans and Ghanaians revealed their divergent notions of "home."

DREAMING OF "HOME"

Recent studies of longings for a coherent "home" in the late capitalist era have associated it with the postmodern condition. Massey (1994) argues that a recourse to place as a source of authenticity is a response to the disorienting effects of time-space compression and in particular the movement of formerly colonized populations into European metropoles (see also Appadurai 1996). But Massey notes that the sense of dislocation as a new phenomenon is a white/First World perspective that ignores earlier dislocations (see also Clifford 1997; Gilroy 1993; Gupta and Ferguson 1997; and Lavie and Swedenburg 1996). She concludes that at least in the case of Africans in diaspora, the temporal distance of their dislocation makes the concept of home less salient to them. In writing of Toni Morrison's description of American slavery in her novel, *Beloved*, Massey argues that the text "undermines for ever any notion that everyone once had a place to call home which they could look back on, a place not only where they belonged but which belonged to them, and where they could afford to locate their identities" (1994: 166).

In opposition to Massey's claim, Gupta and Ferguson argue that the concept of homeland retains significance for displaced peoples of all kinds: "'Homeland' in this way remains one of the most powerful unifying symbols for mobile and displaced peoples, though the relation to homeland may be very differently constructed in different settings" (1997: 39). Further, they argue that this idea adheres even when "home" is distant or its relationship to the displaced population is complex (see also Bisharat 1997; Malkki 1997; Markowitz et al. 2003; and Smith 2003). In a similar vein, I argue that for many African Americans, Ghana functions as an imagined homeland even in the absence of a genealogical certainty of their connection. Many African American tourists articulate an almost mystical sense of belonging upon their arrival on Ghanaian soil, a sense of spiritual connection that requires no further proof. Renée Kemp, an African American journalist, describes this feeling, "I understand, with my first whiff of Ghanaian air, that absent of any proof to the contrary, this is where my family's history begins" (2000: 17). Thus, contrary to Massey's conclusion, the notion of an African homeland remains significant for African Americans in the so-called "postmodern" age, but as I discuss below, the conditions of late capitalism infuse both the experience of this homeland as well as their reception by Ghanaians.[2]

Over the course of the past decade, the tourist industry in Ghana has attempted to capitalize on this longing through the development of its diaspora tourism industry, known alternatively as "roots tourism" or "heritage tourism." Diaspora tourism seeks to attract Africans in the diaspora by suggesting Ghana's particular significance among West African nations as a departure point during the Atlantic slave trade. As the site of two of the largest slave castles in West Africa, Ghana's slave history has received a disproportionate amount of attention, and has led to the belief that the bulk of enslaved Africans in the United States departed from Ghana, when in actuality,

Ghana only accounted for approximately 13 percent of North American slave imports (Gomez 1998: 29).

This construction has been widely successful due in no small measure to Ghana's status as an English-speaking, politically stable West African nation, and therefore the perfect destination for African American tourists. Senegal receives numerous diaspora tourists, especially to the infamous Goree Island, another former slave warehousing site. But because Senegal is a French-speaking nation, undoubtedly many American tourists choose Ghana over Senegal to experience this history. In addition, Nigeria plays an important role in the African American imaginary of homeland because many of the African-based religious beliefs and practices of African Americans are derived from Nigerian religions (Matory 1999). Dominance in the realms of religion and literature notwithstanding, Nigeria's political instability has discouraged diasporic travel to this popular religious homeland.

Many African American professionals traveled to Ghana during the 1960s and 1970s because of its status as the first sub-Saharan African nation to achieve independence and the popularity of Kwame Nkrumah's socialist ideals as well as his prominence in the Pan-African Movement.[3] Although Ghana never saw an organized movement of African Americans like the Back-to-Africa Movement that brought hundreds to Liberia and Sierra Leone, since the late 1950s Ghana has become the African nation to receive the largest numbers of African Americans intending to permanently settle in Africa (Jenkins 1975: 151). As of 2000, this population is estimated at one thousand individuals (Zachary 2001). African American professionals who resettled in Ghana immediately following its independence had experienced loss of faith in the possibility of equality in American society that led them to embrace Ghana and Nkrumah's socialist ideals as an alternative political sphere (cf. Markowitz, this volume). They imagined Ghana as a permanent home in which they could escape from the twin forces of racism and capitalism that ensured their marginalization in the United States (Jenkins 1975 and Lake 1995).

The sense of being out of place that drove them to move to Ghana in the sixties and seventies continues to lead African American professionals to Ghana, although most of these travelers today are not permanent migrants; rather, they are tourists, and their travel has very different meanings. Earlier expatriates revoked their American citizenship and aligned themselves with a nation in which few of its citizens have the privileges enjoyed by those in the United States. Thus, their act served as an open contestation of the inequalities created by world capitalism. In contrast, the travel of today's diaspora tourists reaffirms the existing power geometry that gives middle class Americans the freedom to travel for pleasure. U.S. and European ownership of major hotels in Ghana demonstrates one of the ways in which tourism in Africa serves to maintain Western dominance of the global economy. The hegemony of the world capitalist system is such that even the history of the slave trade has become a commodity that can be bought and sold.[4]

Diaspora tourism is the main focus of the tourist industry in Cape Coast and Elmina. In particular, the tourist industry has sought to encourage diaspora tourism through the conservation of the slave castles and dungeons as well as through the launching of Panafest in 1992, a biannual Pan-African tourist festival. In addition, in 1998, former President Rawlings launched the celebration of Emancipation Day in Ghana after witnessing the same celebration in Jamaica. This celebration included the reinterment of the remains of two slaves from the United States and Jamaica in Ghana, thereby symbolizing the return of the diaspora to its rightful "home" (cf. Huseby-Darvas, this volume, Verdery 1999). Now an annual declaration of Emancipation is held at Cape Coast Castle. Thousands of tourists travel to Ghana each year to attend these events in addition to a general increase in tourists throughout the year to visit the newly conserved castles and dungeons. Today, in contrast to an estimated one thousand African Americans who reside in Ghana, ten thousand African American tourists visit Ghana each year (Zachary 2000) constituting approximately 12 percent of the total recreational tourists, a significant percentage of the tourism market.[5] The importance of this segment of the tourist market is noted in the tourist development plan for the Central Region:

> A special interest market for the Central Region are African Americans whose ancestors originated in West Africa and were sent overseas from the slave-trading castles and forts along the Ghana coast. Sometimes called Roots Tourism, this specialized tourist market has already commenced to develop in Ghana and the Central Region. (1996: 41)

Through these events, the tourist industry has established Ghana's preeminence as a top destination for African American tourists looking to explore their African "roots."

DREAMING OF THE PAST

The popularity of diaspora tourism among African American tourists reflects the centrality of the slave trade in African American collective memory. The television miniseries *Roots*, based on the book by Alex Hailey, is largely responsible for its growth.[6] In addition, Toni Morrison's critically acclaimed novel about slavery, *Beloved*, published in 1987, won the Pulitzer Prize, and Morrison went on to win the Nobel Prize for fiction. As these two outstanding examples show, although the history of slavery is complex and often contested with many silences in different arenas within various communities, the artistic traditions of African Americans is replete with representations of it, demonstrating that slavery forms a salient part of their historical imagination.

As a result, African American tourists have already encountered powerful representations of the slave trade before setting foot in Ghana. In writing about an African American heritage tour to Goree Island, a departure point for slaves in Senegal similar to Ghana's Cape Coast and Elmina castles, Ebron notes that the site "captured an already strong African American 'structure of feeling'" (2002: 201). Indeed, the power of slave sites lies in the fact that they fit well within preexisting imaginings about the slave trade. These imaginings are part of the historical dreaming process. Here, however, the dreams are nightmares. In this way, diaspora tourism is similar to Jewish Holocaust tourism (see Kugelmass 1994), and Cape Coast and Elmina Castles, similar to the status of Auschwitz within Holocaust tourism, are the key sites for African diaspora tourism. Though quite different from the common understanding of tourism as a quest for pleasure, this type of tourism, which involves exploring historical atrocities, has gained popularity because of its role in creating a sense of group identity as well as providing a sense of personal and collective catharsis.

Below, I describe some of the key features of African American responses to the slave dungeons. The dank, dark spaces of the dungeons become theaters of memory in which visitors imagine the experiences of their ancestors. As they connect to the spirits of long-dead forbears, they regard the dungeons as sacred space. At Cape Coast Castle, visitors enter the male slave dungeons by walking down a steep sloping tunnel into an open space. The dungeons are located underground and consist of three different rooms. The only light comes from small windows placed high above the dungeons to ensure that captives could not reach them. The rooms are almost completely dark. Lighting has been added in order to allow visitors to see, but tour guides will briefly turn out the lights so that they can experience the actual conditions that captives faced.

Not only are the dungeons dark, but a dank, unpleasant smell fills the small, underground rooms. Visitors are told that this is the smell of the blood, sweat, feces, and corpses that rotted for centuries in this place. The tour guide then tells them to look down at the floor, which they find is not the floor at all but what appears to be mounds of packed, layered dirt. He points out that the floor is covered by dirt, waste, and human remains. The guide then explains that up to one thousand men were kept in the dungeons at a time, and the ones who had tried to escape were chained to the walls. Food was indiscriminately thrown down to the men, who were forced to eat, sleep, and relieve themselves all on the floors of these cramped rooms. The female slave dungeons are equally dank and oppressive. The tour guide's account of the rape of female slaves by their captors renders these spaces even more horrific.

One of the most common responses of African American tourists to being in the dungeons is intense anger. Tour guides at both castles often tell tales of African Americans becoming enraged on tours and occasionally attempting to attack a white tourist. I repeatedly witnessed tourists stomp and feign spitting on the grave of the British governor, which is located within the courtyard at Cape Coast Castle. Bruner similarly describes such attacks and the desire, as one woman stated after visiting the castle, "to go out and strangle a white person" (1996: 296).

A second common emotion is that of pathos. Many visitors cry while in the dungeons. Their extreme emotional responses suggest a deep sense of connection to the suffering of captives who were kept there. Miss Violet is a seventy-two-year-old woman originally from Jamaica who now lives in Florida. She discussed her desire to understand what slaves suffered in the dungeons as an embodied experience. She describes entering the slave dungeons:

> My very first step down, I felt a sort of queasiness and my hair rose up on my head and shiver went through my body. And I can't put the rest of it in words, I just can't. . . . I felt that I could hear the moaning, I could hear the moaning and I could see the filth and I could smell it. And it's not until now that I want to cry, I didn't want to cry then but now I want to cry. How in the world could human beings survive in something like that? I think that's when I really, really felt what they must have felt. . . . I could feel the flesh falling off of my body.

She describes the experience of recalling this past as one of literal dismemberment, (the flesh falling off her body), collapsing the slave's experience with her own, or in other words, the experience recalled with the experience of its recalling. This description also suggests that the physical experience of the dungeons allows visitors not just to recall the past, but to divine it, or to make it real and present before them, a theme that is addressed in the film, *Sankofa* (Gerima 1993) in which the main character, while inside one of the slave dungeons, is transported back in time and space and finds herself a slave on a New World plantation.

After their dismemberment by the unbearable weight of the past, these visitors remember themselves as survivors.[7] Ella, a middle-aged woman from Dallas, described her experience of catharsis,

> I was overwhelmed at first and very saddened by the fact, but I came away with strength! I came away with strength knowing that if my ancestors, if I survived all that through my ancestors, I'm a very strong person. I came from a very strong stock to have survived the capture and the entrapment and the dungeon and took through the middle passage and another four hundred some years through just abject poverty and beaten, I mean I survived all that and I claim all that? I am so strong! Nobody in this world I can claim is stronger than I am and

that's what I went away with, with a sense of strength, and my daughter said too, we analyzed and my daughter said they're the strongest of the strong, they're the strongest of the strong and if my ancestors can survive that, certainly I can survive what I'm going through no matter what it is, I have no excuse. None.

Her return itself becomes a triumph over the ghastly experience of enslavement that she has just imagined. Ultimately, visits to the castles seem to provide a cathartic experience for many African American visitors. They express a sense of pride from the ability of their ancestors to survive their enslavement. The castles provide a transformative experience through the communion with the spirits of the dungeons, the cathartic experience of grief and anger, and the recognition of the strength and courage of their ancestors.

The experiences of African American tourists in the slave dungeons suggest that the dungeons serve as a space in which they negotiate their relationship to a painful past. Though a sometimes agonizing process, it is an ultimately positive experience from which they return home to the diaspora strengthened with the knowledge that their ancestors' courage continues to dwell in them. This homecoming to Africa experience helps them to negotiate their relationship both to the past of slavery and to its lingering presence in their ongoing experiences of racism.

FORGING FORGETFULNESS

In contrast to African Americans' insistence on remembering the slave trade, traditionally, in Ghana, the topic of slavery is strictly sequestered from discourse. This restriction results from the character of slavery in Ghana, which was quite different from its character in the New World. In Ghana, prisoners of war and victims of slave raids, most from the northern regions of the country, were sold into slavery, both locally and abroad. In Cape Coast and Elmina, domestic slaves served primarily as skilled artisans and laborers, and in many ways, had the same status as other servants.[8] Over time, they were incorporated into the families that owned them, and their children were considered to be full-fledged members of those families.[9] This process of assimilation was necessary in order to incorporate strangers into the lineage system. Eventually, their ancestry was, if not forgotten, then ignored, and mention of their slave ancestry became taboo. Bringing it up is an outright insult because it questions their inclusion in their families, rendering them kinless and therefore exceedingly vulnerable. Slave ancestry is therefore a stigma to which few in Ghana would willingly lay claim, and mentioning slave ancestry is prohibited by customary law.[10] Because of its problematic nature, the slave trade is not part of a popular historical memory.[11]

As a result, in contrast to its wide treatment by African American writers, there are few literary treatments of the slave trade in Ghana.[12]

Given this context, many Ghanaians are baffled by African Americans' insistence on slavery remembrances. I focus here primarily on Ghanaian youth in Cape Coast and Elmina, who have come of age in the midst of the tourist industry's popularization of the slave trade in their towns. In particular, I interviewed several senior secondary school girls about their views of diaspora tourism, and of Emancipation Day in particular. This generation's perspectives are fruitful for an analysis of the impact of an emerging popular memory of the slave trade on the development of political consciousness among Ghanaians in the post-Independence era.

One teenage girl expressed her negative opinion of the remembrance of the slave trade, "I think Emancipation Day should be cancelled because it reminds us of all that our ancestors went through and all the bad things they went through and it's like the visitors, the African Americans who come, they usually feel so bad, they cry and all that." Her schoolmate added,

> So what is the use of coming here to remember your past? It's only just going to make you feel like you are more inferior and inferior and inferior. And you have that thing in your mind, oh god they treated me like this, and they treated me like this, I must be very inferior for them to have seen me in this way.

These comments include themes that were often repeated by other local residents. They express the fact that for slave descendants to remember their slave past only serves to remind them and the rest of society of their inferiority. It reactivates a stigma that they might otherwise escape. In contrast to the organizing principle that drives most African American tourists who participate in Panafest and Emancipation Day, namely that remembrance of the slave trade can lead to a meaningful catharsis that is ultimately positive, many Ghanaians express the belief that the history of the slave trade has no redeeming quality.

THE EXTRAVAGANCE OF MEMORY

The difference between African American tourists and Ghanaians' perspectives regarding the slave trade results of course from the fact that whereas in Ghana, slave ancestry can be successfully hidden, in the United States, black racial classification serves as an indelible marker of a slave past. Thus, it could be argued that African American tourists in Ghana acknowledge their slave past precisely because they have no hope of escaping from it, and seek to redefine it from stigma to a source of pride.

On the other hand, many Ghanaians do not understand the workings of race within the United States in which black subjects are always already stigmatized regardless of their personal relationship to their slave ancestry. As a result, African Americans' embrace of their slave ancestry suggests to them their lack of vulnerability to stigmatization. In other words, it suggests to them that African Americans occupy a position of such security within their society that the discussion of their slave ancestry poses no threat to them. Thus, their acknowledgement of their slave past strikes Ghanaians as an act of privileged subjects.

In addition, most of these tourists stay in expensive hotels, travel around on tour buses, buy souvenirs at exorbitant prices, and attend entertainment events that Ghanaians complain they cannot afford. The extravagance of African American tourists' remembrance practices, combined with their lavish displays of wealth, create a conspicuous contrast to Ghanaians' own relative insecurity within the global economy. Ghanaians have watched their nation's economic decline since the 1980s. Ghana's joining of the Highly Indebted Poor Nations Initiative, an international plan to provide a measure of debt relief to countries with troubled economies, made their economic woes a particularly salient issue in the minds of many Ghanaians. As a result, Emancipation Day and similar commemorations serve to highlight the distance between African Americans and Ghanaians' places in the global economy. This evaluation leads Ghanaians to critique African Americans' inattention to this difference, and in essence, to critique their failure to address the economic conditions of Ghanaians. Georgina, another student in Cape Coast, expressed this sentiment:

> It's okay, Emancipation Day is fine with us, but then, we don't want to remember what happened to our ancestors so I think they should not celebrate it. . . . But even when they want to celebrate it, they should put down some aims and objectives to help Africans come up on the economy. They shouldn't just come here and just celebrate, celebrate and not do anything about our plight. I think after they celebrate, they should try and do something for Africans.

Many Ghanaians express the belief that if African Americans feel a historical connection to their towns, then they should also feel an obligation to aid in their development. Sharing wealth is after all a key requirement of family members in Ghana; it is part of the making of kinship. But African Americans' travel to Cape Coast and Elmina has led to very few instances of meaningful investments. Another resident who had often observed tourists at the castles stated, "They come, they cry, and they leave," arguing that ultimately, their expressions of emotion and grief are hollow; they do not result in a higher level of activism.

The structure of Emancipation Day, which focuses on a spiritual connection rather than an economic one, is also a point of critique. In particular, the relocation of the remains of the two slaves to Ghana was greeted with a degree of skepticism and perplexity by many Ghanaians. Yaw and Kweku are two young teachers whom I met while they were touring Cape Coast Castle. I asked them what they thought about the reburials, to which they responded,

> *Y*: It's okay, but personally I think that is not so important. The harm has been done already. Many of the Africans died there. Their bodies have not been brought here. But the fact that all Africans who are alive are coming together is an indication that we don't want to forget our roots. We are one people; I think that is rather of more importance. Those bones being brought here will not do us anything, unless there are certain religious rites attached to it. If not, I don't see the significance.
>
> *K*: They should have brought goods, rather. That compartment that their bodies were brought in could have held goods for us!

Many Ghanaians view activities aimed at remembering the slave trade as bearing little or no relationship to those that are aimed at improving their welfare. Indeed, the catharsis that many tourists experience in the castles is an intensely personal experience, and often does not translate into a firmer sense of community that includes both African Americans and Ghanaians. In fact, many African American tourists leave Ghana having established a sense of connection to their imagined Ghanaian ancestors, but without having established a sense of connection to contemporary Ghanaians.

Another one of the students, Anne, critiqued Emancipation Day's lack of efficacy in Ghanaian development:

> I believe that before . . . they thought that it would do some good, but since it is just the same, I mean, it is not bringing any development, I think it's better if they stop, because even when they do that, it brings about memories of what happened and you keep on hurting them, so if you're not going to do anything to help the situation, so why bring about this Emancipation stuff and all that? It even makes the case worse.

Her classmate, Yaa, reinforced this point, stating, "[Emancipation Day] still doesn't make any sense to me. It hasn't brought about any positive change. I think they should . . . stop . . . giving lip service and start materializing objectives instead of just talking."

While many African American tourists hand out money on the streets and contribute in other small ways, restructuring the Ghanaian economy is not their primary objective. Their travel to Ghana is temporary, while they remain permanents residents of American communities where they commit a large percent of their resources. In contrast to the Independence era during which, for African American expatriots, their spiritual, political, and economic commitments were located concomitantly within African nations, for today's African American tourists, these commitments are often unfastened from one another and are situated within multiple geographic locations. The unmooring of these commitments is itself a key feature of late capitalism.

Because of their limited understanding of racial politics in the United States, many Ghanaians fail to recognize the importance of African Americans' cathartic experiences in the slave dungeons. As a result, they express confusion with regard to visitors' emotional outpourings. I was often asked why African Americans cry so much in the dungeons, perhaps because I myself am an African American, though I was not a tourist. What these perplexed Ghanaians failed to realize is that the tears that African Americans shed in the slave dungeons are as much for themselves and their personal experiences of racism as they are for the slaves who were kept there. But while they seek catharsis and name themselves pilgrims, they ultimately remain tourists who stay in hotels and travel around on air-conditioned buses. Their desire to travel to Ghana, a sort of spiritual home that they lack in the United States, while enjoying all of the comforts of their physical home, demonstrates their entanglement within the logic of late capitalism as a celebration of deterritorialization. Their search for roots entails a desire to become cosmopolitan subjects. In other words, it is simultaneously a celebration of the rootedness and routedness of their identities.

DREAMING OF ESCAPE

At the same time, Ghanaians' critiques of diaspora tourism turn on its inability to improve their position in the global economy. The tourist industry provides few jobs in Cape Coast and Elmina. Because most tourists stay at hotels outside of the towns and only enter the towns briefly to visit the castles, few residents benefit directly from their presence. At the same time, neither Cape Coast nor Elmina has any major industries, and many youth travel to Accra, Takoradi, or other larger cities within Ghana to find work. As a result, youth in Cape Coast and Elmina, who grew up after the hopefulness of the Independence era had been destroyed by the economic downturn of the 1980s, read diaspora tourism through the lens of their marginalization within contemporary national and global economies. In their eyes, diaspora tourism serves to confirm the success of U.S. capitalism, with African Americans as its agents. But their critique is not primarily a critique of the world capitalist system; rather, it is a critique of their unfavorable position within it. In other words, they seek access to travel as well as to flows of capital and goods that they see tourists enjoying. In this way, they demonstrate a similar entanglement within the logic of late capitalism, but from a position of much greater disadvantage.

This analysis of U.S. wealth, of course, does not take into account racial politics of capitalism within the United States that have severe implications for the economic lives of African Americans, even those who have reached the middle class. Instead, many Ghanaians do not make a distinction between white and black tourists, viewing them all as (privileged) foreigners, or *buronya* (singular: ob*runi*). One man, in pointing to the opportunities that tourists are seen to represent, spoke of Ghanaians' interest in linking themselves "to these black Americans, white, whatever as long as you're foreign." This categorization of foreign blacks results from the fact that given the limited amount of knowledge that most people have regarding the nature of the transatlantic slave trade, if people think about blacks in the diaspora at all, they tend to think that they, like slaves in Ghana, were incorporated into the families of their white owners. This explains comments about the "positive" outcomes of slavery like one made by a woman who told me, "But now you are there [in the United States] so it is bad, but there is some good from it too, don't you think?" The images of blacks that they receive, as movie stars and famous musicians, in conjunction with the diaspora blacks that they meet as tourists, who are almost all middle class or better, confirm their assumption that blacks in the diaspora are well-to-do, and therefore the process of incorporation must have proceeded well. Therefore, many Ghanaians often do not make a significant distinction between foreigners of European descent and those of African descent.

The nature of tourism helps to maintain the status of African American tourists as strangers. Many tourists, particularly those on package tours, stay at luxury hotels and travel to and from their hotels on large tour buses; thus, they have little contact with local residents outside of the ones that are directly involved in the tourist industry. Children often approach these tourists with a chant that enacts an imagined conversation with them, "Obruni, how are you? I'm fine. Me too." This chant reveals the familiarity of the sight of foreigners in Cape Coast as well as the excitement they inspire, but it is also telling of the nature of the relationship between residents and tourists: the child must carry on both sides of the conversation because the foreigner rarely answers back.

Some residents, particularly adolescents, have learned to mobilize a discourse of connection with these visitors, such that many tourists are greeted as they descend from their tour buses and approach the castles with shouts of "Welcome to your homeland!" But besides these savvy youth who employ the language of homeland strategically in their panhandling endeavors, to most residents, the imagined geography of diaspora and homeland has little reality to them. In addition, the imagined ties between African Americans and Ghanaians do not perform the central function of international links according to Ghanaians: they rarely lead to trips abroad. The intellectual construction of homeland and diaspora relies not only on practices of travel but also, as Clifford (1997) has noted, on practices of dwelling. In this vision, people residing in the homeland are required to remain in place, to have a certain fixity to their location that then becomes the object of desire for those who have left. The extreme difficulty for Ghanaians of obtaining a visa for travel supports this conception. Indeed, because of their inflexible citizenship[13] that confines them within national borders, travel is one of the most commonly expressed desires of Ghanaian youth. Thus, while many African Americans travel abroad in search of roots in Ghana, Ghanaians are searching for routes out of it.

Their fantasies of travel demonstrate the desperation felt by many Ghanaians who see few avenues to both travel and economic advancement. This sentiment leads to frequent critiques of their position within the global economy. Discussions of the slave trade often arise in a cynical comparison to the lack of opportunities in Cape Coast and Elmina. I often heard people say that if a slave ship were to dock off the coast of Ghana today, bound for America, and Ghanaians were told that they could get on, but that they would have to endure the same conditions that the slaves did, the boat would still be full of volunteers. These comments index the marginalized position in which Ghanaians find themselves with regard to the global economy. While they are no doubt said for their shock value, they nonetheless illustrate a view of entrenchment in place as itself a form of enslavement in the new millennium from which many Ghanaians seek escape by any means.

Diaspora tourism as a transatlantic encounter between African Americans and Ghanaians reveals the tensions within the construction of homeland. The notion of returning "home," even if this return takes the form of a temporary pilgrimage, remains important for African Americans for whom the United States remains in many ways an inhospitable abode. But their status as tourists complicates Ghanaian readings of their presence. The Americans' apparent wealth as well as their ability to embrace the history of the slave trade, an act that few Ghanaians would even contemplate, suggests to Ghanaians their high status in American society, leading to many misunderstandings in their encounters. In addition, young Ghanaians' often-thwarted desires to travel affect their readings of the mobility of tourists. Thus, while African American tourists dream of "home" as a place of spiritual renewal and mourn their placelessness, Ghanaians dream of leaving home and bitterly lament their entrenchment in place. In the end, for contemporary black subjects, whether they view themselves as rootless or as ensconced, the racial politics of late capitalism make their homes and homecomings unsettling experiences.

NOTES

1. Names of individuals have been changed throughout the chapter.
2. African American tourism to West Africa is the subject of a growing body of literature. Ebron (2002) provides important accounts of African American experiences,

while Bruner (1996) and Hasty (2002) discuss of various aspects of Ghanaians' responses to it. These articles also discuss issues related to the tourist industry's representation of the slave trade.

3. Nkrumah encouraged African American teachers, engineers, doctors, etc to move to Ghana and use their skills to help build the new nation. Many prominent African Americans also traveled to Ghana during this period, including W.E.B. Du Bois, Malcolm X, Maya Angelou, and Richard Wright. See Gaines (1999), Jenkins (1975), Meriwether (2002), and Walters (1993) for a discussion of African Americans and Ghana during the Independence era.

4. Indeed, in Ebron's study of diaspora tourism to Senegal and Gambia, not only are the tourists apolitical, but the tour itself is sponsored by McDonald's. She explains the context in which McDonald's could become the sponsor of an African American homeland tour, "Oppositional identities no longer appear autonomous from global commerce, even to their most radically passionate adherents; instead, they are inescapably intertwined" (2002: 211).

5. The tourism development guide projected 83,000 recreational tourists in 2000.

6. When *Roots* aired in 1977, it became a hit, claiming the highest ratings record for an entertainment program at that time. The *Roots* record was broken in 1983 by the series finale of *M*A*S*H*.

7. I draw here on Jennifer Cole's definition of remembering as both recalling the past and remembering or reconstituting that which has been dismembered (2001: 21).

8. See Yarak (1989) for a discussion of slavery in Elmina.

9. Rattray (1929) discusses this feature of Akan slavery. Klein (1989) and Robertson (1983) also discuss the incorporation of slaves into families, although Cooper (1979) challenges the idea that slaves would revoke all ties to their original families in favor of incorporation. Nevertheless, incorporation remains an important ideal within local understandings of West African slavery.

10 Akosua Perbi (1996) discusses examples of court cases resulting from accusations of slave ancestry.

11. As opposed to its place within secret ritual discourses. See Baum (1999), Rosenthal (1998), and Shaw (2002) for examples throughout West Africa of memories of the slave trade within ritual.

12. See Opoku-Agyemang (1992) on this issue. Important exceptions include the works of Aidoo (1970), and Armah (1979) and Opoku-Agyemang's own work (1996).

13. This idea draws on Ong's (1999) discussion of flexible citizenship.

REFERENCES

Aidoo, Ama Ata. *Anowa*. London: Longman Drumbeat, 1970.

Appadurai, Arjun. *Modernity at Large: Cultural Dimensions of Globalization*. Minneapolis: University of Minnesota Press, 1996.

Armah, Ayi Kwei. *Two Thousand Seasons*. London: Heinemann, 1979.

Baum, Robert M. *Shrines of the Slave Trade: Diola Religion and Society in Precolonial Senegambia*. Oxford: Oxford University Press, 1999.

Bisharat, George E. "Exile to Compatriot: Transformations in the Social Identity of Palestinian Refugees in the West Bank." Pp. 203–33 in *Culture, Power, Place: Explorations in Critical Anthropology*, edited by Akhil Gupta and James Ferguson. Durham: Duke University Press, 1997.

Bruner, Edward M. "Tourism in Ghana: The Representation of Slavery and the Return of the Black Diaspora." *American Anthropologist* 98, no. 2 (1996): 290–304.

Clifford, James. *Routes: Travel and Translation in the Late Twentieth Century*. Cambridge: Harvard University Press, 1997.

Cole, Jennifer. *Forget Colonialism?: Sacrifice and the Art of Memory in Madagascar*. Berkeley: University of California Press, 2001.

Cooper, Frederick. "The Problem of Slavery in African Studies." *Journal of African History* 20, no. 1 (1997): 124–25.

Ebron, Paulla A. *Performing Africa*. Princeton: Princeton University Press, 2002.

Gaines, Kevin. "The Cold War and African American Expatriate Community in Nkrumah's Ghana." Pp. 135–58 in *Universities and Empire: Money and Politics in the Social Sciences During the Cold War*, edited by Christopher Simpson. New York: New Press, 1998.

Gerima, Haile. *Sankofa* [film]. Washington, DC: Myphedus Films, 1993.

Gilroy, Paul. *The Black Atlantic: Modernity and Double Consciousness*. Cambridge: Harvard University Press, 1993.

Gomez, Michael. *Exchanging Our Country Marks: The Transformation of African Identities in the Colonial and Antebellum South*. Chapel Hill: University of North Carolina Press, 1998.

Gupta, Akhil and James Ferguson. "Beyond 'Culture': Space, Identity, and the Politics of Difference." Pp. 33–51 in *Culture, Power, Place: Explorations in Critical Anthropology* edited by Akhil Gupta and James Ferguson. Durham: Duke University Press, 1997.

Hasty, Jennifer. "Rites of Passage, Routes of Redemption: Emancipation Tourism and the Wealth of Culture." *Africa Today* 49, no. 3 (2002): 47–76.

Jenkins, David. *Black Zion: Africa, Imagined and Real, as Seen by Today's Blacks*. New York: Harcourt Brace Jovanovich, 1975.

Kemp, Renée. "Appointment in Ghana: An African-American Woman Unravels the Mystery of Her Ancestors." *AARP* July–August, 2002.

Klein, Martin A. "Studying the History of Those Who Would Rather Forget: Oral History and the Experience of Slavery." *History in Africa* 16 (1989): 209–217.

Kugelmass, Jack. "Why We Go to Poland: Holocaust Tourism as Secular Ritual." Pp. 175–83 in *The Art of Memory: Holocaust Memorials in History*, edited by James Edward Young. New York: Prestel, 1994.

Lake, Obiagele. "Toward a Pan-African Identity: Diaspora African Repatriates in Ghana." *Anthropological Quarterly* 68, no. 1 (1995): 21–36.

Lavie, Smadar and Ted Swedenburg. "Introduction: Displacement, Diaspora, and Geographies of Identity." Pp. 1–25 in *Displacement, Diaspora, and Geographies of Identity*, edited by Smadar Lavie and Ted Swedenburg. Durham: Duke University Press, 1996.

Malkki, Liisa H. "National Geographic: The Rooting of Peoples and the Territorialization of National Identity among Scholars and Refugees." Pp. 52–74 in *Culture, Power, Place: Explorations in Critical Anthropology*, edited by Akhil Gupta and James Ferguson. Durham: Duke University Press, 1997.

Markowitz, Fran, Sara Helman and Dafna Shir-Vertesh. "Soul Citizenship: The Black Hebrew and the State of Israel." *American Anthropologist* 105, no. 2 (2003): 302–12.

Massey, Doreen. *Space, Place, and Gender.* Minneapolis: University of Minnesota Press, 1994.

Matory, J. Lorand. "The English Professors of Brazil: On the Diasporic Roots of the Yorùbá Nation." *Society for Comparative Study of Society and History* 41, no. 1 (1999): 72–103.

Meriwether, James H. *Proudly We Can Be Africans: Black Americans and Africa, 1935–1961.* Chapel Hill: University of North Carolina Press, 2002.

Ministry of Tourism. *Tourism Development Plan for the Central Region, Draft Final Report* 1996.

Ong, Aihwa. *Flexible Citizenship: The Cultural Logics of Transnationality.* Durham: Duke University Press, 1999.

Opoku-Agyemang, Kwadwo. "A Crisis of Balance: The (Mis)Representation of Colonial History and the Slave Experience as Themes in Modern African Literature." *Asemka: A Literary Journal of the University of Cape Coast* 7 (1992): 63–77.

———. *Cape Coast Castle: A Collection of Poems.* Accra: Afram Publications, 1996.

Perbi, Akosua. "The Legacy of Indigenous Slavery in Contemporary Ghana." *FASS Bulletin* 1 (1996): 83–92.

Rattray, R.S. *Ashanti Law and Constitution.* Oxford: Clarendon Press, 1969 [1929].

Robertson, Claire C. "Post-Proclamation Slavery in Accra: A Female Affair?" Pp. 220–42 in *Women and Slavery in Africa*, edited by Claire C. Robertson and Martin A. Klein. Madison: University of Wisconsin Press, 1983.

Rosenthal, Judy. *Possession, Ecstasy, and Law in Ewe Voodoo.* Charlottesville: University Press of Virginia, 1998.

Shaw, Rosalind. *Memories of the Slave Trade: Ritual and the Historical Imagination in Sierra Leone.* Chicago: University of Chicago Press, 2002.

Smith, Andrea. "Place Replaced: Colonial Nostalgia and Pied-Noir Pilgrimages to Malta." *Cultural Anthropology* 18, no. 3 (2003): 329–64.

Verdery, Katherine. *The Political Lives of Dead Bodies: Reburial and Postsocialist Change.* New York: Columbia University Press, 1999.

Walters, Ronald W. *Pan Africanism in the African Diaspora: An Analysis of Modern Afrocentric Political Movements.* Detroit: Wayne State University Press, 1993.

Yarak, Larry W. "West African Coastal Slavery in the Nineteenth Century: The Case of the Afro-European Slaveowners of Elmina." *Ethnohistory* 36, no. 1 (1989): 44–60.

Zachary, G. Pascal. "Tangled Roots: For African Americans in Ghana, the Grass isn't Always Greener: Seeking the 'Motherland,' They Find Echoes of History and a Chilly Welcome." *Wall Street Journal* 14 March 2001.

11

Leaving Babylon to Come Home to Israel: Closing the Circle of the Black Diaspora

Fran Markowitz

The Black Diaspora began with the violence of uprooting. Torn from their homes, ripped from their families, millions of men and women were shackled and shipped across the ocean where, if lucky enough to survive, they were forced into slavery. Rerooted in a strange land, Africans in America were given new names, a new God, and a new language while they were stripped of what the signers of the U.S. Declaration of Independence called the inalienable rights to "life, liberty and the pursuit of happiness."

For some four hundred years African Americans have had no other homes than the ones that they were born into in the no-longer-strange land of America. In the year 2004, nearly one and a half centuries after Emancipation, one might even say that the United States is African Americans' only homeland. Yet by virtue of an unrelenting color line that construes black people as misplaced in America, their homes have always been, and may still be, tenuous. Familial homeplaces—those shacks, shelters, apartments, and houses that constitute domestic space and provide islands of safety, respect, and esteem—have long served African Americans as refuge from dehumanization in the wider (white) world where racism can disrupt and negate whatever sanctuary the American homeland has to offer. These spaces, however, have always been porous and vulnerable to intrusions of "terrifying whiteness," those constantly present dangers that threaten the sacredness and security of hearth and home (hooks 1990).

Semiotician Yuri Lotman (1990: 171–91, esp. 185) has noted that the moral and spatial opposition between home—a safe, divinely sanctioned and life-giving place—and the anti-home—alien, satanic, and life-threatening space—is a universal theme of world folklore. Despite crosscultural demands for a clear divide between home and anti-home, symbolic, not to mention physical, overlaps often occur between these mutually exclusive moral domains, creating what amount to irresolvable cultural problems. Lotman notes that although they, and the anxieties that they produce, never disappear from the mundane world, many religious rituals manipulate key symbols and settle these problems. He notes as well that journeys abroad are another means of escaping the vexation of homes impinged upon by anti-home. Yet these too fail to produce resolution, for although travelers may return with the satisfaction of finding that "there's no place like home," that home remains the same troublesome place from which their journeys began.[1]

Over the ages, the desire to overcome such spatiomoral ambiguities has inspired literary works of astounding genius. Lotman highlights Dante's *Divine Comedy* and Bulgakov's *The Master and Margarita* as masterpieces that pivot on the yearning for an absolute home/anti-home opposition in a less than perfect world. Homi Bhabha, however, points to the novels of African American writer Toni Morrison to underscore the harrowing fact that many contemporary homes may be just as life-threatening as they are life-giving. Rather than decry this cruel irony as debilitating, Bhabha joins with Lotman in noting that "in the stirrings of the unhomely [at home] another world becomes visible" (1997: 45). This visualized other world, where anti-home can never cross over the threshold into home, offers a utopic vision of better times and more hospitable places. Incongruous intrusions of alien space into homeplace, they agree, only strengthen longings for a home that is completely consecrated and utterly secure.

Stepping outside of literature into the experiential results of historical contingencies, David Scott (1991) has claimed that the trauma of the initiatory *event* of diaspora has overshadowed and overpowered the importance of *place* in the collective memory of New World blacks. Consequently the line demarcating the homeland from which they were extracted from the new, unhomely American homeland has been blurred, rendered almost moot, and so too have the unique memories associated with each place. Throughout history Americans of African descent responded to this incomprehensible plight by envisioning alternatives to the unfreedom of enslavement and the diseases of racism and second-class citizenship. They passed on these visions from one generation to the next through a wide array of cultural productions, in sayings, songs, and in their prayers (Lawrence-McIntyre 1987; Levine 1997), through their labor and in their crafts (Gilroy 2000: 200), and increasingly from the nineteenth century onward, inscribed in literature and scholarly writings. During the twentieth century such yearnings also took programmatic form as social movements. Some, like Marcus Garvey's Back to Africa initiative (Burkett 1978; Jenkins 1975) and Muhammad Elijah's Nation of Islam (Lee 1996), aimed at resurrecting a long-ago golden age by returning homeward via prediaspora traditions, if not physically to the ancestral homeland.

From amidst the mid-1960s diversity of integration and civil rights movements, antiwar and antipoverty groups, black cultural organizations, and calls for black power, the Black Hebrews of Chicago emerged from an earlier black Hebraic congregation to assert their vision and place in the world. Unlike several contemporaneous black separatist groups that demanded territory from and within the United States for an autonomous black nation free of terrifying whiteness (Cunnigen 1999; Hall 1978; Van Deburg 1992; Zangrando and Zangrando 1970), the Hebrews completely rejected America as their homeland. They equated the debilitating racism that black people daily encountered there with the biblical anti-home of Babylon and pushed to the side whatever homely feelings they had for their cities, neighborhoods, and family residences. Resolving to affirm their lives by putting the humiliations of exile behind, their goal was to exit America, retrace the route of their exile, and come home to the Holy Land of Israel.

Rather than search for answers to "who we are as a people" in the public domain of white Christian America, where they were demeaned, the Black Hebrews turned instead to the Old Testament to reveal the hidden truth of their history. Piecing together what they had once disregarded as quaint folk sayings from their elders, like "A small black nation will rise out of the east," with the wisdom of the Bible, this group of young, radicalized black men and women determined that they were the descendants of the biblical Israelites and that the land of Israel was their original home. Ben Ammi, the group's leader, teaches that prior to the construction of the Suez Canal, Israel and all of the Arabian Peninsula were part of Africa, "Israel was formerly composed of a Black race, just as the nations of Egypt, Libya and Ethiopia are comprised of Blacks" (1990: 116).[2] Conceived of as an unambiguously nurturing northeast African land, they looked forward to resettling there, relearning and speaking their Hebrew native tongue, and practicing their preexilic Israelite culture. The Black Hebrews anticipated that resettlement in the Holy Land of Israel, now revitalized as the newly formed state of Israel, would be the ultimate homecoming. Reconciling home with homeland and the past with the future; body, soul, and identity would converge unambiguously, once and for all (see Ben Ammi 1990; Prince Gabriel Ha-Gadol 1993).

The Black Hebrews' homecoming was not, however, a happily-ever-after story of instant resolutions. Instead of inclusion in the Israel that they had envisioned, the men and women of the Black Hebrew Israelite Community (later, the African Hebrew Israelite Community, or AHIC) encountered a set of laws and policies legislated by the government of the state of Israel that placed them outside the Jewish nation and beyond Israel's citizenry (see Markowitz, Helman and Shir-Vertesh 2003). All that notwithstanding, several hundred people came to dwell in Israel where they contended with and strove to overcome the final test of their long-sought homecoming. During the 1970s and 1980s as illegal aliens in the dusty towns of the Negev Desert, they were what Virginia Dominguez (1989: 178) has called a "tolerated presence." Ineligible for any and all social, health, and welfare benefits, instead of giving up and returning to the fleshpots of Babylon, contributions were solicited from African Americans and Israelis to support the community's fledgling health and educational institutions while most adults eked out a living doing what they had always done—temporary agricultural, factory, and construction work and domestic service.[3] Had the Black Hebrews' myth of return and social program for homecoming simply resulted in the substitution of one unhomely home for another?

Had this essay been written before the 1990s, the answer would have been yes (cf. Ben-Yehuda 1975; Singer 1979). But the story of the Black Hebrews' homecoming does not end there. In its portrayal of how the Black Hebrews stayed steady in asserting their Bible-based claims to a home while altering their rhetoric to conform with the demands of the Israeli state, this chapter offers an ethnohistorical analysis of the AHIC's ongoing homecoming to Israel, extending into the present. It presents the community's struggle to understand their past and resolve the vexing home/anti-home overlap that they experienced in America as the enactment of an alternate vision aimed at closing the circle of black people's exile, namelessness, and identity loss by returning home.

The Black Hebrews' rejection of an ambiguous home, America-as-Babylon, for what they have determined to be their authentic home, Israel, illustrates the success of a group that refuses to accept others' definitions of who they are and where their home must be. This chapter, then, presents a challenge to those who would contend that "roots and home will be felt progressively less in the world . . . [for] there's no cultural home to go back to" (Mathews 2000: 196–97; see also Rapport and Dawson 1998) and raises serious questions about the potential of diasporas to overcome fixed categories of race, religion, and geography (Bhabha 1990; Gilroy 2000). In the final analysis, as this chapter will show, the Black Hebrews' homecoming confirms both the power of self-defining groups to implement their visions *and* the authority of nation-states to make home, land, language, culture, and hope converge into one.

AFRICA AND ISRAEL IN BLACK DIASPORIC IMAGININGS OF HOME

Ever since the seventeenth century, African Americans sporadically undertook voyages back to Africa, but homecomings did not begin in earnest until late in the eighteenth century, after the rise of American evangelical Christianity which black people made their own (Raboteau 1997).[4] Charismatic but often unschooled preachers, in ecstatic revival meetings, taught that every man and woman, rich or poor, black or white, could get the spirit, transcend the woes of the world, and find favor in God's eyes.

Finding in the Christian notion of redemptive suffering a way to interpret and cope with the pain of slavery and the disappointments of its aftermath, many New World blacks concluded that their (ancestors') capture, transport to America, and forced labor comprised the path that God had chosen for bringing them into his fold. Those black Christians who became overseas missionaries took this lesson even further, and they returned to Africa to spread the Gospel and save its inhabitants from the doom of paganism.[5]

During the 1920s, Marcus Garvey's United Negro Improvement Association intertwined religious passions with civic concerns and rallied millions of supporters with the idea of rejecting dependency and second-class status in America by returning to live as fully enfranchised, contributing men and women in Africa (Burkett 1978; Jenkins 1975). Although this repatriation scheme ultimately failed, Garveyism—as well as a homeland in West Africa—captured a central place in the black diasporic imaginary.

By the latter part of the twentieth century black Americans increasingly traveled to Mother Africa—often on *Roots* tours or pilgrimages to the slave castles, cities, and villages on the continent's west coast (e.g., Bruner 1996; Ebron 2002: viii–x; 189–212; Holsey, this volume). Very few, however, stayed for the long term. Those who did seek to live in countries where they believed that they would be part of the majority's racial and cultural heritage repatriated to the West African states of Liberia, Ghana, Nigeria, and Sierra Leone (see Lake 1995).

As the foregoing discussion illustrates, in popular discourse, mainstream American history, and in the immigration and citizenship policies of many African states, it is widely accepted—indeed a point of doxa—that the west coast of Africa is the ancestral homeland of black Americans (Ebron 2002). Nonetheless, as Andrew Apter (2002: 234) reminds us, "the problematic notion of origins continues to haunt African diasporic research and motivate its debates."

Africa's east coast, in particular the ancient civilizations of Egypt and Ethiopia, has long held an honored place in the imagination and scholarly writings of the Black Diaspora (see Bernal 1987; Howe 1998). During the nineteenth century the biblical verse, "Princes shall come out of Egypt and Ethiopia shall soon stretch forth her hands unto God" (Psalms 68: 31), began circulating with regularity, offering to disenfranchised Americans of African descent noble origins as well as the promise of better times. Ethiopian sects arose in the early twentieth century to rival mainstream and evangelical Christianity (Fauset 1974), while later in the century Jamaican-born Rastafarianism, which designates Ethiopia as Zion and equates the Black Diaspora with exile to the fleshpots of Babylon, spread into North America and Great Britain (Nelson 1994). In their websites, brochures, and especially in reggae music, Rastas urge black repatriation to Ethiopia, the "birth place for human life on earth, the original home for black men, and the promised land."[6]

African Americans' identification with the hope and glory of Ethiopia more than likely derives from their encounters with Christianity (Raboteau 1997: 103–104). Although white masters and overseers initially forced this religion upon African slaves, the slaves' own interpretations of the messages of the Bible shaped their Christian beliefs and practices. Jesus lent solace by embodying their suffering and promising redemption. The Old Testament, however, provides numerous illustrations of *this-worldly* deliverance and a vehement message that human freedom is the will of God (Levine 1997: 98). And no Bible story resonated more strongly than that of the Hebrews' exodus from slavery in Egypt to freedom in the Promised Land. "In the ecstasy of worship," writes historian Albert Raboteau (1995: 33–34), "time and distance collapsed, and the slaves *became* the children of Israel." This often forgotten and severed theme of African American Christianity later became an important historical source for the Black Hebrews' identity assertions and their homecoming claims in the state of Israel.

THE BLACK HEBREWS

The African Hebrew Israelite Community and Nation—the Black Hebrew group I've become acquainted with over the past ten years—emerged in the mid-1960s in Chicago from an older Hebraic sect during the height of the civil rights and black pride/black power movements.[7] It was not, of course, the first black group to search for answers to "who we are as a people" in the sacred texts of the Bible, to claim that they were God's Chosen, or to claim that the Israelites were black, and that Israel, their historical homeland, is situated in the northeastern corner of Africa. Black Judaic sects that blended Christian messianic theology with claims for being the descendants of biblical Israel sprang up in urban America from at least the beginning of the twentieth century (Baer and Singer 1992; Brotz 1964; Chireau 2000; Fauset 1974; Landes 1967).[8] But the African Hebrew Israelite Community was certainly the first, and remains the only one, to have transformed a diasporic mythography into a social program (Appadurai 1996: 6) by executing an exodus out of America and coming home to Israel.[9]

Today over two thousand men, women, and children reside in the community's Village of Peace in Dimona, Israel, and we will return to them shortly. At this juncture it is important to underscore that a good part of the Black Hebrews' social program is directed at exposing the disasters of diaspora to the wider black community—"We were disconnected from our very soul," writes Ben Ammi (1990: 155), "a non-people seeking to be every race except our own"—and advocating the rectitude of return. It is their belief that when the long-lost children of Israel reclaim their heritage and live according to God's laws in God's land they will have established the kingdom of God on earth. In major American cities, the men and women of the AHIC provide a window onto the kingdom by offering alternative health care and tasty vegan substitutes for high-fat, meat-based dishes; operate day-care centers for children and inviting meeting places for adults; conduct Bible study and African Hebrew history classes, and run boutiques where attractive, colorful, and modest garments made from natural fibers are for sale.

Rallying the consciousness of African Americans to accept the knowledge that they are the descendants of the Biblical Israelites while urging them to change their lifestyle, dress, diet, identities, and beliefs—to say nothing of leaving Babylon to come home to Israel—poses a great challenge to the Black Hebrews. Everyone knows that the ancestors of black Americans came from Africa's west coast (Ebron 2002), and that the Jews are the people of Israel (see Budick 1998). Two women who embraced the community in the early 1970s, first Batya, who had flitted from one black cultural group to another in her native Detroit, and then Tumaya, who at the time was a student at Howard University in Washington, D.C., recall their initial incredulity upon learning that African Americans' origins are in Israel:

> BATYA: I had been impressed with the Bible as history, but ME? I didn't see any connection. Israel? Isn't that in the Middle East? Africa was our homeland.
>
> TUMAYA: It was somewhat of a mind transition that I had to go through because I had grown up so much hearing that my connections only went as far back as the African, and not knowing that the African had a root in the Bible.

But once convinced, they, like all of the men and women of the AHIC with whom I have spoken over the years, came to accept their origins and destiny in Israel-as-Africa as self-evident (Markowitz 1996).[10] Tumaya clarifies:

> The more I heard and understood about our people, and how we came to be in the different slaveries that we were in, what was the reason for it, and how we were dispersed throughout Africa, and the building of the Suez Canal, and the separation of Africa from Israel, all of those things began to make all of that clear for me.

Having embraced that truth, the Black Hebrews are perplexed that so many African Americans reject this knowledge and refuse to change their lifestyle. But since they themselves had once been incredulous, they are also understanding of their neighbors' reluctance to give up the American dream. In Chicago, Atlanta, and Washington D.C., the AHIC's attractive and clean establishments, as well as the friendly people themselves, exemplify the healthy, life-affirming, holistic lifestyle upon which their Hebrew identity is based and offer an in situ alternative to the self-destructive existence of the diaspora (see Markowitz, forthcoming).

As Ben Ammi, the community's messianic leader, explains, one of the reasons why it is difficult to convince black Christian Americans that they are indeed Hebrews is that, "The Europeans have destroyed the ancient wisdom of African theology and the vision of African people.... The truth concerning this matter cannot be found in the history and religious books of Europe or America" (1990: 29). Having painstakingly discovered the truth of their origins and the significance of their destiny in Israel, the Black Hebrews are hardly concerned with the Eurogentiles'—or white Christians'—rejection of their identity. Much more disturbing is the refusal of the state of Israel to include them within the Jewish nation and accept their homecoming.

HOMECOMINGS

More than thirty years have passed since the first Black Hebrew trailblazers entered Israel and asserted their rights to residence and protection through the Law of Return. That law, formalized in 1952, grants Israeli citizenship to any and all Jews from throughout the world.[11] In 1969 and 1970 when young black Americans proclaiming themselves Hebrews initially entered Israel, immigration officials were stunned. They never imagined that anyone who was not a Jew would want to become part of their beleaguered country. Faced with the options of deporting or accepting these newcomers, the state of Israel granted to them three years of temporary residence rights while deliberating their status. During these deliberations it was ascertained that the self-proclaimed Hebrews were not Jews; they had been born into Christian families and never converted. Moreover, several of their beliefs and practices transgressed the boundaries of Judaism. The Israelis offered a solution to the ambiguity of non-Jewish Hebrews by assigning a rabbi to instruct them in Judaism and prepare them for conversion so that they would be eligible to be absorbed into the citizenry along with all the other new immigrants (cf. Anteby-Yemini; Levy, this volume). But Ben Ammi, who was still in Liberia waiting for the right moment to return to the Holy Land, invoked the "power to define who we are as a people" and ordered his followers to cease their studies.

Ben Ammi's insistence that he and his people be accepted on their own terms was and remains a key component of the rectitude of their return from diaspora. But it disregards the realpolitik of nations and defies states' rights to define "bounded populations, with a specific set of rights and duties, excluding 'others' on the grounds of nationality" (Soysal 1994: 2). Having rejected the state of Israel's requirements for belonging, the Black Hebrews found that when their temporary visas expired they had become illegal aliens in the Holy Land that they had come home to.

During the 1970s and 1980s Ben Ammi and his followers responded by declaring themselves the Original Hebrew Israelite Community and Nation and staged demonstrations in Jerusalem and Tel Aviv. Dubbing the Jews usurpers of *their* land of Israel, they vowed to overthrow the state's government and replace it with their princes and ministers, with Ben Ammi at the helm. Preoccupied with much larger problems, the Israeli government hardly took this rhetoric seriously, but it certainly did nothing to soften the state's resolve to deny the Hebrews legal recognition, to say nothing of citizenship.

Today some one thousand five hundred long-term residents of the Dimona Hebrew Israelite Community (of some two to three thousand) hold Israeli identification cards and all the rights that these documents confer. In 1992 they obtained temporary residence status, which was renewed several times, and in August 2003 they were granted permanent residence status (see Shadmi and Rotem 2003). The Black Hebrews are hopeful that full citizenship will quickly follow. Then, after thirty years in the Land, they will have made Israel their incontrovertible home.

Some analysts might point to the interventions made by the U.S. government to explain Israel's change in policy toward the Black Hebrews. But in addition to pressure applied by Israel's strongest patron, it should also be noted that from the late 1980s onward the AHIC had shifted its rhetoric from black exclusivity to stressing the diversity among all of the various Jewish people who returned home to Israel after two thousand years of diaspora. By placing themselves as one—albeit a distinct—cultural community among and alongside all other Jewish cultural communities, the Black Hebrews have conformed to Israel's dominant discourse of the ingathering of the Jews (Markowitz, Helman and Shir-Vertesh 2003; Michaeli 2000). Today, centered in the peripheral desert town of Dimona, the Hebrew Israelites' Village of Peace is bustling with activity as home to hundreds of men, women, and especially children. But what Virginia Dominguez wrote of the Black Hebrews' status in 1989 (p. 178) remains true today: "The rabbinate rejects them completely and the government denies them the right to immigrate under the Law of Return." Despite thirty years in the land, the Black Hebrews' homecoming remains suspect in the eyes of many Israeli government officials, Orthodox Jewish clergy, and, I daresay, most Jewish citizens of Israel.

The Black Hebrews respond to such skepticism by pointing to their steadfast, nonviolent presence as total commitment to the state of Israel, while narrating a seamless history, liberally sprinkled with citations of Biblical text, of their factual and prophetic connections to the land of Israel.[12] Similar tactics are used when reaching out to diasporic blacks in America: "We are Israel." Almost every year, during its unique New World Passover holiday that commemorates the exodus of Ben Ammi and his followers from America-as-Babylon in 1967, the community guides African Americans across the Holy Land, pointing out the sites of "our history" and connecting the patriarchs and prophets of the Bible to the present situation of black people around the world.

In August 2000 the community staged a gala ten-day Unity Conference. Prince Immanuel, who heads the African Hebrew Israelites' mission in Washington, D.C., officially opened the conference. Over a hundred delegates representing a score of sites from throughout the Black Diaspora mingled with their Israel-based brothers and sisters for what was billed as "the experience of a lifetime."[13] "You're not here on a tour," Prince Immanuel admonished them. "You've all come home to the Holy Land. You're not a guest. . . . We have come home to the home of our father. Family has come back home to the home of our father from sojourns in Chicago, Atlanta, Washington," and so on.

Unlike other Christian, Muslim, or Jewish pilgrims to the Holy Land, who may make temporary visits to pray at major religious sites and see where *it* all happened, Prince Immanuel told his audience that this is the place where *they* all happened and where they should be happening. The goal of the Unity Conference was to reconnect lost black bodies and souls to the land and law of Israel that is by rights theirs, even if they did not know of this connection until recently (Ben Ammi 1990).[14] Unlike the pioneers who exited America in the mid-1960s and had no home awaiting them in the homeland, today's diasporic blacks can end their exile by coming home to the Village of Peace—at least for a while. Every holder of a U.S. passport is granted a three-month tourist visa upon entering Israel, and the Hebrews and their potential recruits are no exception. But since self-declared Hebrews are excluded from the Law of Return, should they stay in Israel beyond the expiration date of their visas, they, like those who struggled throughout the 1970s and 1980s for the right to a home in the homeland, do so illegally.[15]

During the ten days of the conference, the delegates participated in seminars, workshops, worship services, and cultural events in an atmosphere free of urban stress, drugs, alcohol, and tobacco. They were offered a taste of what awaits when they accept the truth of their past and the mandate for their future and leave the painful exile of Babylon to return to and redeem the promise of Israel (see Ben Ammi 1990, 1991; Markowitz 1996).

AT HOME IN THE PRESENT CONTINUOUS

Over the centuries of the Black Diaspora the biblical narrative of the Israelites' exodus from slavery in Egypt into the freedom of the Promised Land offered an alternate template for imagining what life could and should be. The contradiction of an unhomely home, where their bodies bore the violence of slavery and an identity based solely on color, fired—and continues to fire—the imagination of African Americans for freedom and a place to put it into practice. For many, Africa was that place; preceding exile, it could also supercede it and offer a more bounteous future (Lemelle and Kelley 1994). For others, a return to Africa was unimaginable and unwarranted. Pointing to all the lives and unrewarded labor that blacks invested in the building of America, in the 1960s, the Republic of New Africa, the Black Panthers, and the Black Muslims issued demands for racial separation, including an autonomous black homeland in the American South (Cunnigen 1999; Hall 1978; Van Deburg 1992).

The decision of some radicalized young black men and women in twentieth-century America to search for their origins beyond West Africa, to envision a social program that would provide them with a healthy and satisfying lifestyle and a home that responded to their yearnings for safety and fulfillment, rebuts optimistic postmodern theorizing that views in hybridity and diasporic consciousness the potential to deconstruct boundaries, transcend exclusionary racial and ethnic categories, and bust oppressive political practices (Bhabha 1990; Gilroy 2000; Mathews 2000; Rapport and Dawson 1998). Neither convinced that homes disconnected from the homeland could be rid of elements of anti-home, nor content with the unhomely in their urban American homeplaces, the Black Hebrews embraced what they viewed as a natural, even divine, connection between a land, language, and people.

While looking to the past as they planned for the future and refusing to limit their hopes for home to West Africa, the Black Hebrews worked hard at interpreting the texts of the Bible, heeding the quaint expressions of their elders, and exploring historical sources to establish their identity as the children of Israel. Not content with diasporic imaginings (Appadurai 1996), they fused together an inspiring biblical narrative with concerted social action, made their exodus out of the United States, and strove to establish themselves as rightful heirs to the legacy of Israel.

Exiting the United States and entering Israel proved easier, however, than gaining accolades and adherents from the wider Black Diaspora or acceptance by the Jewish inhabitants and government officials of the homeland. The power of discourse that incontrovertibly places black Americans' origins in West Africa, coupled with the internationally recognized right of states to define immigration policies and set exclusionary criteria for citizenship, made it difficult for the Black Hebrews to gain legitimacy in the wide world as they enacted their goal of closing the circle of diaspora. In spite of doubt, ridicule, threats of deportation, and the lack of social services, the African Hebrew Israelite community stayed steady and today they enjoy the fruits of their labor in the Village of Peace in Dimona. Indeed, they are convinced that resisting others' definitions of who they are and where their home is has resulted in God's favor. Despite all predictions to the contrary, their return to the Promised Land has resulted in a community of peace where not one murder or rape has occurred in thirty years, recognition and rights from the state of Israel, and admiration from a wide range of American blacks, including Christian pastors and the Reverend Louis Farrakhan of the Nation of Islam. The circle of the Black Diaspora is far from closed, and the Hebrew Israelite Community still remains an ambiguity in Israel: residents of the land, but not quite part of the polity. Yet for the Black Hebrews, each year that passes is one more sign of the rectitude of their rejection of exile for the hard but joyful journey of a contentious homecoming.

NOTES

Funding for much of the research upon which this chapter is based was provided by the U.S.-Israel Binational Science Foundation. I am very grateful to that institution for supporting my work. My utmost thanks go to all the brothers and sisters of the AHIC in Dimona, Chicago, Atlanta, and Washington for graciously hosting me over the years. My deepest gratitude goes to Prince Asiel, Crown Sister Yahfah, and my sister, Khasida. In the "ivory tower" I thank André Levy, my comrade-in-anthro at Ben-Gurion University for many stimulating conversations about diaspora, the state-as-homeland, and homecomings. Thanks too to Anders Stefansson for helpful comments that sharpened the analysis of this chapter.

1. Oftentimes, the homecoming is a traveler's greatest trial. When Odysseus, the prototypical heroic homecomer, returned to Ithaca he found his home despoiled by treacherous friends; his wife was surrounded by suitors, and his son was barely recognizable. In J. R. R. Tolkien's twentieth-century masterpiece, *The Lord of the Rings*, at the end of a long series of trials undertaken to save their world from annihilation by the forces of evil, heroes Frodo and Sam eagerly return to their once green and pleasant land to find it in the throes of destruction. While they were away from home, the very anti-home that they had been battling seeped into the home that they had left in order to save. Like Odysseus, Frodo and Sam face their greatest trial when returning and reclaiming their home.

2. Ben Ammi, who changed his name from Benjamin Carter, means "son of my people" in Hebrew. In 1967 he had a vision that the time had come to make an exodus out of the United States to West Africa, retrace the route of the Black Diaspora, and return to the original home in Israel.

3. Like other U.S. citizens, the Hebrews entered Israel with American passports and received three-month tourist visas. Once these visas expired, they simply stayed. Over the years many did return to the United States; several dozen were deported and others left of their own accord. Some remained affiliated with the AHIC. Many more reverted to the life-threatening practices of the American-Babylon anti-home, or at least those are the stories—of drug addicts, prostitutes, and criminals—that circulate throughout the community.

4. Beginning early in the eighteenth century, trickles of slaves who secured their freedom returned to Africa, but the first black missionary institution was not established until 1759. Founded by Rev. S. Hopkins, a former slaveowner of Newport, Rhode Island, the American Colonization Society "helped to forge a connecting link

between emigration, Christianity, and black nationalism" (Wilmore 1986: 101) and played a central role in the founding of Liberia in 1822. Controversial among blacks and whites alike, Wilmore (*ibid.*) writes that "it cannot be doubted that the society gave impetus to the idea that black Americans had a contribution to make to the awakening of Africa."

5. The African Methodist Episcopal Church, a black Protestant denomination founded in 1816, was heavily involved in missionizing in Africa. William Becker (1997: 188) observes, "The African mission provided a dramatic symbol of the Afro-American as man, as leader, as authoritative carrier of God's word to those racial brothers who do not possess it. . . . It was a symbol which sought to make some sense of the suffering of the slave past . . . and which held out high hopes for the future."

6. See www.nettilinja.fi/~hsaarist/kolmonen.htm.

7. See Markowitz 2002 for a discussion of the insider/outsider dilemmas of this long term fieldwork.

8. These, along with Ethiopianist cults, Moorish temples, and a whole slew of evangelical and holiness churches, might be understood as the results of searching further and wider within the diasporic imaginary for solutions to the increasing post-Emancipation tension between American Negroes' newly won constitutional freedom and the lingering, if not intensifying, social unfreedom that they experienced in the United States. (Fulop 1997; Gilroy 2000: 191–201).

9. Prince Gavriel ha-Gadol's 1993 *The Impregnable People* recounts how Ben Ammi arose as a leader of his people and in 1967 led some three hundred men, women, and children out of America to Liberia. Some three years later, more than half of the original group had returned to America while the others came home to Israel.

10. I should note that even those who left the group told me that while they objected to some of the practices demanded from the leadership, they remain convinced that they are Hebrews and that their fate is linked to Israel. One woman returned to the United States, converted to Judaism and re-returned to Israel under the Law of Return (Markowitz 2000). A young man who had spent his childhood in Israel but then left the community to sow his wild oats in America approached me in Chicago for the name of a rabbi who would be willing to give him conversion classes so that he could return to Israel as a Jew among Jews.

11. The definition of "who is a Jew" has been challenged—and reaffirmed—throughout Israel's fifty-six-plus-year history. As the law now stands, Jews are defined through *halakha* (Jewish law) as those individuals born of Jewish mothers and those who have converted to Judaism and renounced all other religions. The Law of Return also extends to those who are the spouses of Jews and those who are the children and grandchildren of Jews (even if not born of Jewish mothers).

12. See, for example, the community's 1992 Public Relations Department brochure, "The Historical Connection of the Hebrew Israelite Community to the Holy Land" and their website, www.kingdomofyah.com.

13. Along with those who define themselves as Hebrew Israelites, or supporters of the Hebrew Israelites, the invitees included a Chicago delegate from the Nation of Islam and a Korean representative of the Unification Church. Dafna Shir-Vertesh, who was assisting me with the project, and I were the only whites in the audience.

14. According to AHIC theology (or divine history, according to their leaders), Israel is located in the northeast corner of Africa, and the original Hebrew Israelites

were black Africans. True to the prophecy of Deuteronomy 28, they disobeyed (their) God, were scattered to the four corners of the earth, where they embraced idols of wood and stone, and then were kidnapped, enslaved, and taken by ships to toil in foreign lands. The sad history of African Americans cannot be corrected until the descendants of the Children of Israel recognize their history, reconnect with the God of Israel in the land of Israel, and practice his law. The AHIC has already established a beachhead for the Kingdom of God, which is destined to come about when all these conditions have been met.

15. It should be noted that the temporary residence status first granted to members of the AHIC in 1992, followed by the 2003 granting of permanent resident status, was awarded only to those adults—and their minor children—who could document long-term habitation in Israel. Thus, today in 2004 there are still several hundred, if not thousands, of Hebrews who are illegal aliens in Israel. It should also be mentioned that during the 1990s and early 2000s dozens of newcomers to the AHIC converted to Judaism while still in the United States, became new immigrants in Israel, and obtained citizenship.

REFERENCES

Appadurai, Arjun. *Modernity at Large: Cultural Dimensions of Globalization*. Minneapolis: University of Minnesota Press, 1996.

Apter, Andrew. "On African Origins: Creolization and Connaissance in Haitian Voudoo." *American Anthropologist* 29, no. 2 (2002): 233–60.

Baer, Hans and Merrill Singer. *African American Religion in the Twentieth Century: Varieties of Protest and Accommodation*. Knoxville: University of Tennessee Press, 1992.

Becker, William H. "The Black Church: Manhood and Mission." Pp. 177–99 in *African American Religion*, edited by Timothy E. Fulop & Albert J. Raboteau. New York: Routledge, 1997.

Ben Ammi. *God, the Black Man, and Truth*, 2d. rev. ed. Washington, DC: Communicators Press, 1990.

———. *The Messiah and the End of This World*. Washington, DC: Communicators Press, 1991.

Ben-Yehuda, Shaleak. *Black Hebrew Israelites: From America to the Promised Land*. New York: Vantage Press, 1975.

Bernal, Martin. *Black Athena: The Afroasiastic Roots of Classical Civilization*, vol. 1. New Brunswick: Rutgers University Press, 1987.

Bhabha, Homi. "Interview with Homi Bhabha: The Third Space." Pp 207–21 in *Identity, Community, Culture, Difference*, edited by Jonathan Rutherford. London: Lawrence & Wishart, 1990.

———. "The World and the Home." Pp. 445–55 in *Dangerous Liaisons: Gender, Nation and Post Colonial Perspectives*, edited by Anne McClintock, Aamir Mufti and Ella Shohat. Minneapolis: University of Minnesota Press, 1997.

Brotz, Howard. *The Black Jews of Harlem*. Glencoe, IL: Free Press, 1964.

Bruner, Edward M. "Tourism in Ghana: The Representation of Slavery and the Return of the Black Diaspora." *American Anthropologist* 98, no. 2 (1996): 290–304.

Budick, Emily. *Blacks and Jews in Literary Conversation.* Cambridge: Cambridge University Press, 1998.

Burkett, Randall K. *Garveyism as a Religious Movement.* Metuchen, NJ: Scarecrow Press, 1978.

Chireau, Yvonne. "Black Culture and Black Zion: African American Religious Encounters with Judaism, 1790–1930, An Overview." Pp.15–32 in *Black Zion: African American Religious Encounters with Judaism,* edited by Yvonne Chireau and Nathaniel Deutsch. New York: Oxford University Press, 2000.

Cunnigen, Donald. "Bringing the Revolution Down Home: The Republic of New Africa in Mississippi." *Sociological Spectrum* 19 (1999): 63–92.

Dominguez, Virginia. *People as Subjects, People as Objects.* Madison: University of Wisconsin Press, 1989.

Ebron, Paulla A. *Performing Africa.* Princeton: Princeton University Press, 2002.

Fauset, Arthur Huff. *Black Gods of the Metropolis.* New York: Octagon Books, 1974 (orig. 1944, University of Pennsylvania Press).

Fulop, Timothy E. "'The Future Golden Day of the Race:' Millennialism and Black Americans in the Nadir, 1877–1901." Pp. 227–54 in *African American Religion,* edited by Timothy E. Fulop and Albert J. Raboteau. New York: Routledge, 1997.

Gilroy, Paul. *Against Race.* Cambridge: Harvard University Press, 2000.

Hall, Raymond L. *Black Separatism in the United States.* Hanover, NH: University Press of New England, 1978.

hooks, bell. *Yearning: Race, Gender and Cultural Politics.* Boston: South End Press, 1990.

Howe, Stephen. *Afrocentrism: Mythical Pasts and Imagined Homes.* London: Verso, 1998.

Jenkins, David. *Black Zion: The Return of Afro-Americans and West Indians to Africa.* London: Wildwood House, 1975.

Lake, Obiagele. "Toward a Pan-African Identity: Diaspora African Repatriates in Ghana." *Anthropological Quarterly* 68, no. 1 (1995): 21–36.

Landes, Ruth. "Negro Jews in Harlem." *Jewish Journal of Sociology* 9, no. 2 (1967): 175–89.

Lawrence-McIntyre, Charshee C. "The Double Meanings of the Spirituals." *Journal of Black Studies* 17, no. 4 (1987): 379–401.

Lee, Martha F. *The Nation of Islam: An American Millenarian Movement.* Syracuse: Syracuse University Press, 1996.

Lemelle, Sidney J. and Robin D. G. Kelley, ed. *Imagining Home: Class, Culture, and Nationalism in the African Diaspora.* London: Verso, 1994.

Levine, Lawrence W. "Slave Songs and Slave Consciousness: An Exploration in Neglected Sources." Pp. 58–87 in *African American Religion,* edited by Timothy E. Fulop and Albert J. Raboteau. New York: Routledge, 1997.

Lotman, Yuri. *Universe of the Mind: A Semiotic Theory of Culture,* translated by Ann Shukman. Bloomington: Indiana University Press, 1990.

Markowitz, Fran. "Israel as Africa, Africa as Israel: 'Divine Geography' in the Personal Narratives and Community Identity of the Black Hebrew Israelites." *Anthropological Quarterly* 69, no. 4 (1996): 193–205.

———. "Millenarian Motherhood: Motives, Meanings and Practices among African Hebrew Israelite Women." *Nashim: A Journal of Jewish Women's Studies and Gender Issues* 3 (2000): 106–38.

———. "Creating Coalitions and Causing Conflicts: Confronting Race and Gender through Partnered Ethnography." *Ethnos* 57, no. 2 (2002): 201–22.

———. "Claiming the Pain, Making a Change: The African Hebrew Israelite Community's Alternative to the Black Diaspora." In *Homelands and Diasporas: Holy Lands and Other Places*, edited by André Levy and Alex Weingrod. Stanford University Press, forthcoming.

Markowitz, Fran, Sara Helman, and Dafna Shir-Vertesh. "Soul Citizenship: The Black Hebrews and the State of Israel." *American Anthropologist* 105, no. 2 (2003): 302–12.

Mathews, Gordon. *Global Culture/Individual Identity: Searching for Home in the Cultural Supermarket*. London: Routledge, 2000.

Michaeli, Ethan. "Another Exodus: The Hebrew Israelites from Chicago to Dimona." Pp. 73–87 in *Black Zion: African American Religious Encounters with Judaism*, edited by Yvonne Chireau and Nathaniel Deutsch. New York: Oxford University Press, 2000.

Nelson, Gersham A. "Rastafarians and Ethiopianism." Pp. 66–84 in *Imagining Home: Class, Culture, and Nationalism in the African Diaspora*, edited by Sidney J. Lemelle and Robin D. G. Kelley. London: Verso, 1994.

Prince Gavriel ha-Gadol and Odehyah B. Israel. *The Impregnable People: An Exodus of African Americans Back to Africa*. Washington, DC: Communicators Press, 1993.

Raboteau, Albert J. *A Fire in the Bones: Reflections on African American Religious History*. Boston: Beacon Press, 1995.

———. "The Black Experience in American Evangelism: The Meaning of Slavery." Pp. 89–106 in *African American Religion*, edited by Timothy E. Fulop and Albert J. Raboteau. New York: Routledge, 1997.

Rapport, Nigel and Andrew Dawson. "Home and Movement: A Polemic." Pp. 19–38 in *Migrants of Identity: Perceptions of Home in a World of Movement*, edited by Nigel Rapport and Andrew Dawson. Oxford: Berg, 1998.

Scott, David. "That Event, This Memory: Notes on the Anthropology of African Diasporas in the New World." *Diaspora* 1, no. 3 (1991): 261–84.

Shadmi, Haim and Tzahar Rotem. "Ahkrei 30 shana b'israel: Ha-kushim ha-ivriim yehiyu tshvei keva" [After Thirty years in Israel: The Black Hebrews Will Be Permanent Residents]. *Ha'aretz*, July 28 (2003): 8-A [Hebrew].

Singer, Merrill Charles. "Saints of the Kingdom: Group Emergence, Individual Affiliation and Social Change among the Black Hebrews of Israel." Ph.D. diss., University of Utah, 1979.

Soysal, Yasemin. *Limits of Citizenship: Migrants and Postnational Membership in Europe*. Chicago: University of Chicago Press, 1994.

Van Deburg, William. *New Day in Babylon—The Black Power Movement and American Culture, 1965–1975*. Chicago: University of Chicago Press, 1992.

Wilmore, Gayrand S. *Black Religion and Black Radicalism*, 2nd edition. Maryknoll, MD: Orbis Books, 1986.

Zagrando, Joanna Schneider and Robert L. Zangrando. "Black Protest: A Rejection of the American Dream." *Journal of Black Studies* 1, no. 2 (1970): 141–59.

12

While Waiting for the Ferry to Cuba: *Adio Kerida* and the Goodbye That Isn't a Farewell

Ruth Behar

In some ways you might say that my entire life was a kind of preparation for making my personal documentary *Adio Kerida* (*Goodbye, Dear Love*). After all, the film is about Cuban Jews and I am a Cuban Jew. Or, rather, I'm a Cuban-American Jew or a Jewish Cuban-American. Or, as they say in Miami, I'm a "Juban." I was born a Jew in Cuba and came to the United States as a child. I grew up in New York, where I spoke Spanish at home and learned to speak English in school, and have spent a large part of my life explaining how it is that I am both Cuban and Jewish, since this combination of identities has continually baffled people in the United States, though less so in recent years, thanks to the discovery, at last, of multiculturalism.

Certainly one of my most basic motivations in making *Adio Kerida* was to find my own identity reflected in other Jewish Cubans. I wanted to make visible the way a variety of people negotiate the mix of being Jewish and Cuban. But the story quickly grew more complex than that. In the process of conceiving *Adio Kerida*, I made a strategic political choice. I decided to focus on Cuba's Sephardic Jews, rather than looking at the whole Cuban Jewish community, which includes Ashkenazi as well as Sephardic Jews. In other words, rather than looking at Jewishness as a single, monolithic category, I chose to call attention to the diversity of the Jewish experience and to challenge the Ashkenazi-centered view of what it means to be a Jew.

In grant proposals I wrote to seek funding for the project, I explained who the Sephardic Jews are in the following way:

> Sephardic Jews view themselves as Hispanic people who are connected to both the Arab and African worlds because of their history of cultural and emotional

interpenetration with those worlds. They descend from the Jewish populations expelled by the Spanish Inquisition in the fifteenth century. After the expulsion, they settled in the countries of the Ottoman empire and northern Africa, which welcomed them and made it possible for them to live as Jews among Muslims. "Sepharad" means Spain in Hebrew. Sephardic Jews are notable for having clung with a passion to their nostalgia for Spain and their love for the Spanish language, despite having been forced to leave Spain because of their ethnic and religious identity. They are misunderstood and often discriminated against by the mainstream Eastern European Jewish-American world, which can only imagine Jewish identity in terms of the novels of Philip Roth and the movies of Woody Allen. Beyond the Jewish world, Sephardic Jews are virtually unknown as a community and they are almost invisible in the contemporary world of literature and the arts. The Cuban Sephardic community, both on and off the island, offers so rare a mix of cultural traditions—Spanish, Turkish, African, Jewish, Cuban, and American—that it remains a mystery and has not yet been portrayed in any depth in literature, art, or film.

My own autobiography motivated me to want to learn more about the Sephardic Jews. Although both my parents were born in Cuba, they brought to their marriage quite distinctly different Jewish traditions. To be less diplomatic about it, let's just say they argued a lot when I was growing up. It took me years to understand that their disagreements were rooted in the cultural split between my mother, the daughter of Ashkenazi immigrants from Poland and Byelorussia, and my father, the son of Sephardic immigrants from Turkey. In my mother's family, my father was known as "*el turco*," and this was not a term of endearment. Instead, it was a way of referring to my father's hot temper, unforgiving soul, and patriarchal dominance. The Ashkenazi side, who thought of themselves as more rational, tolerant, and modern, viewed those character flaws as elements of a primitive Turkish character. I learned this early in life, because whenever my mother got angry at me she'd say I was just like my father. And my mother's family, in which I largely grew up, always reminded me that with my dark, curly hair, my less than good temper, and my own inability to forgive, I too was more like my relatives on the other side, more like the *turcos*.

In retrospect, I realize that I was fortunate to have known more than one way of being Jewish. It allowed me to understand from an early age that Jews were a diasporic people and had always had to find ways to creatively mesh their Jewish identity with the culture of the people they lived among. On a more critical note, I learned early on that, for reasons that eluded me, the Ashkenazi Jews had gained the upper hand in defining what it meant to be a Jew. When I was growing up, on the first night of Passover we always held our first seder at the home of my maternal grandparents and ate gefilte fish, matzo ball soup, and boiled chicken. On the second night, always *the second night*, we went to the home of my paternal grandparents and we ate haroset made with raisins and dates, egg lemon soup, stuffed tomatoes, and a holiday almond cake dripping with honey; this cuisine, my mother always reminded me, was very delicious but very bad for our figures, and indeed my father's mother was quite fat. Finally, at the end of the eight days of Passover, as if trying to resolve the contradiction of our doubled Jewishness through gastronomic means, my father would insist on taking my mother, my brother and me to El Rincon Criollo on Junction Boulevard in Queens for Cuban black beans and palomilla steak with onions.

In short, the Sephardim were mysterious to me, even though as a "halfie" and an ill-tempered soul I was a part of them. I didn't really know who these people, "my people," were. It all came down to the basic fact that being my father's daughter and being Sephardic were inseparable things for me. Inheriting my Sephardic identity from my father was a vexed issue because for many years he and I were locked in a contest of wills. In our life together, my father had usually either been absolutely furious at me or not speaking to me at all. As a teenager I'd upset him by going to college against his will and as a grown women I'd upset him by writing stories about him and my mother that he thought shamed and dishonored them. When I began to travel regularly to Cuba in the 1990s, I further upset him by returning to the country from which he had fled at great risk in the early 1960s, and he viewed my desire to reconnect with Cuba as yet another manifestation of my ingratitude and disrespect.

So, given this history of heartbreak between my Sephardic father and me, I knew I had to make *Adio Kerida* and I had to make it for my father. Although I couldn't convince my father to go to Cuba with me, I would go and make this film for him. I would dedicate it to him, even if I had to do it against his will. I would show him what kind of people we are, we the Sephardic Jews, with our strong tempers and our inability to forgive. For, despite the years of conflict with my father, I had never given up my Behar last name, the name I inherited from my father, the Béjar that is still the name of a town in northwestern Spain. And as I embarked on the making of *Adio Kerida*, it is this name that I would find all over Cuba, both among the living Sephardic Jews I met and the many Sephardic Jews who have departed to the next world and whose tombs abound in the cemeteries of the island.

Once I realized that *Adio Kerida* would be for my father, I hoped that he would appear in the film. But he vehemently refused. So I began filming in Cuba, until I could convince him to cooperate (in other words, while waiting). One way or another, I was going to get him to be in my film, and this informed the other key strategic political choice I made. I decided that I would include in my film both Sephardic Jews who remain on the island and Sephardic Jews from Cuba who now reside in the United States. This meant that my film would create a bridge that doesn't yet exist in reality. The Sephardic Jewish community of Cuba is divided by the politics of revolution and exile, and many members of the community who live in the states are unwilling to return to Cuba or even be in touch with fellow Sephardic Jews on the island. In my film, these Cuban Sephardic Jews would be shown side by side, embracing their common Sephardic and Cuban heritage.

Adio Kerida was the culmination, for me, of a long process of reconnecting with Cuba and of forging ties with the literary, artistic, and intellectual communities of both the island and the Cuban-American left in the United States. I have traveled back and forth to Cuba since 1991, going three times a year for brief but intense visits.

I first returned to Cuba in 1979 as a graduate student, in hopes of gaining permission to carry out my dissertation fieldwork in anthropology on the island. This was during the famous moment of the thaw in U.S.-Cuba relations led by then president Jimmy Carter, when it appeared that normalization of relations would soon take place. After much internal debate, Cuba both released political prisoners and agreed to the family reunification program, which allowed over 100,000 Cuban-Americans who left the island in the 1960s to return to visit their families between 1978 and 1979. But then, in 1980, came the Mariel exodus, which took everyone by surprise, leading to the dramatic departure of 120,000 Cubans to the United States. Blame for the mass exodus was placed on the *gusanos*, the so-called worms of the revolution. The returning immigrants came to be viewed as a contaminating force who returned to Cuba to flaunt the wealth they had obtained as immigrants in the capitalist United States of America. Relations between the United States and Cuba returned to their previous freeze and Cuban-Americans were again viewed as suspect by the official island sectors. My desire as a Cuban-American to return to the island to do research was no longer looked upon with favor. Unable to return, I embarked on a long detour as an anthropologist, doing research in Spain and then Mexico, before finding myself in Cuba again in the 1990s.

In 1979 it had been impossible to leave the city of Havana without official government permission. Foreign visitors, especially from the United States, were carefully watched. As a Cuban-American I was especially suspect and was appointed my own personal spy. At the time I was too innocent to realize that the friendly young man who always sat next to me on the bus and wanted to know everything about me was monitoring my activities. When I returned in 1991, I discovered quite another Cuba, a country whose survival now depended upon tourists, including those who came from the great enemy to the north, maintaining its embargo against the naughty communist island, and making it illegal, in fact, for Americans to visit as tourists. This was a Cuba whose survival now also depended upon offering a new kind of welcome, including to those Cuban-Americans who were not the confident, idealistic Marxists who returned to Cuba with the Antonio Maceo Brigades of the 1970s. By the 1990s the island was extending its welcome even to those wishy-washily Cuban-Americans of the left, uncertain liberals who hadn't yet made up their minds about Cuba.

It was a painful era, when Cuba sought to maintain its revolutionary goals while making the transition from being dependent on the former Soviet Union to becoming an independent player in the new global economy. The country was badly in need of hard currency, mired by all accounts in an economic and moral crisis. On a Cuban television cooking show, women were shown how to make breaded grapefruit-rind "steaks" for their families to curb hunger pangs. Contradictions between socialist ideology and everyday social life grew ever more dissonant. By the mid-1990s the U.S. dollar became a legal currency in Cuba. Essential items like soap, detergent, and cooking oil could only be obtained with dollars, yet Cuban salaries continued to be paid in Cuban pesos. The informal economy expanded as more and more Cubans went hustling for dollars, and tourism—including sex tourism—became a major sector for economic growth.

At the same time, after three decades of suppressing religious observance, the government ceased to penalize any Cubans, including party members, who openly practiced religion. Increasing numbers of Cubans began to return to Catholicism, Protestantism, Judaism, and Santería, among other religions, in search of spiritual solace. With the return of God to Cuba, the island became safe again for Americans to visit. They began to come in record numbers, bolstered by the fact that the embargo permits Americans to travel to Cuba legally if they are traveling as part of a humanitarian mission to deliver religious assistance.

Not only was religion a legally open door for Americans to cross the border into Cuba, but so too was the larger category of cultural exchange. The charm that Cuba holds for so many American visitors has precisely to do with the fact that Cuba represents a form of utopian dreaming carried out in opposition to American political interests. By the late 1990s numerous Americans were traveling to Cuba in search of the unique independence of Cuban music, art, and literature. Ry Cooder's *Buena Vista Social Club* musical CD, followed by Wim Wender's documentary about Cooder's heroic discovery of the lost ancient Cuban mariners, brought new attention, and nostalgia, to bear on Cuba and suggested to Americans that their embargo was depriving them of the richness of Cuban culture.

The American market is now flooded with CDs of Cuban music (you can hear them in any Starbucks or Borders), new films about Cuba, novels and memoirs about Cuba, ethnographies of Cuban Santería, photography books about Cuba, and architectural studies of the island. A Cuban revolution is happening in the United States and it has created an insatiable desire for all things Cuban.

My own return journey to Cuba, which began over a decade ago and is still in progress, unfolded in the midst of all these 1990s developments. As the years passed, and I traveled back and forth to Cuba from Michigan for more than thirty visits, I began to recognize that my return journey, even though it was profoundly personal and spiritual and began long before what I call "the Cuba boom," could not be seen as more or less exalted than the Cuba journeys of Cooder, or the sex tourists, or the gallery curators, or Pastors for Peace, or Jewish Solidarity, not to mention the return visits of all the other Cuban-Americans who were embarking on their own personal and spiritual quests. I found myself unable to think of Cuba as merely a fieldsite and in my first emotional reencounters with the island I turned to poetry, one of my youthful passions. But the anthropologist in me wanted to know whether my experiences had any social foundation, and so I became involved in creating a collective tapestry of voices and visions of Cubans of the island and Cubans of the diaspora who were of my generation, likewise seeking a common culture and memory.

During these years of visits to Cuba I attended Jewish services at the synagogues in Havana and also took trips to the provinces to get to know the synagogues and Jewish communities in Cienfuegos, Camaguey, and Santiago de Cuba. But I wasn't in any way trying to study the Jews of Cuba. I myself was still uncertain about what my Jewishness meant to me. I'd spent years of my life studying Catholic cultures in Spain and Mexico and keeping my Jewish identity well hidden so as not to raise any eyebrows, especially since I was so readily accepted in the communities I studied because I am a native Spanish speaker. Although I took pleasure in meeting Jews in Cuba and found it moving to attend services at the Patronato synagogue in Havana, which is just down the street from where I lived as a child, I rarely snapped any pictures or carried out interviews.

I wanted simply to be a Jew in Cuba and not have to explain my identity to anyone. I found that the combination of Cuban pluralistic tolerance and revolutionary secularism made it easy to be a Jew in Cuba. I could openly say I was Jewish to any and every Cuban. This was immensely liberating after my years of *conversa*-like hiding of my Jewishness in Spain and Mexico. In turn, I felt comfortable among the Jews of the island because they were often as uncertain about their Jewishness as I was about mine. Not that Judaism was foreign to me. After all, I went to Hebrew School and can read liturgical Hebrew, and my family observed the major Jewish holidays.

But over the years I'd lost touch with my Jewish identity. I was no longer sure what kind of Jew I wanted to be. I found it reassuring to be among Jews in Cuba who didn't quite know what to say or do at Jewish services, to be among Jews who were learning how to be Jews. If there was hope for them, there was hope for me. Later, as my son Gabriel's bar mitzvah approached and I decided to learn how to chant Torah along with him, I took pleasure in seeing that the Jews in Cuba, whom I'd gotten to know over the years, were becoming more confident and knowledgeable about their Jewishness too.

The four synagogues in Havana—Chevet Ahim, Adath Israel, El Patronato, and el Centro Hebreo Sefaradí—had never been shut down (although the fifth, the American synagogue, had been allowed to fall into ruins). Yet Jewish services were largely attended by older people during the 1960s, 1970s, and 1980s. The Jewish community, once at least fifteen thousand strong, had been decimated by the Cuban revolution, which undertook to nationalize the many small businesses owned by Jewish Cubans, the majority of whom left in the early 1960s and resettled in Miami and New York. With only a few thousand Jews left on the island, a number that eventually declined to around a thousand, it was difficult to maintain a strong Jewish community. In addition, the Cuban revolution frowned upon religious observance of any kind. Jews weren't singled out for persecution because of their ethnicity or faith, but they chose like other Cubans to pull away from religion and to suppress any sense of their own ethnic difference in order to fully integrate themselves into the revolutionary process, which was firmly rooted in nationalism and unity.

But by the 1990s, in the new atmosphere of religious tolerance, Jewish families and Jewish young people began to flock to the synagogues. Most of these Jews were of mixed heritage and many were discovering their Jewishness for the first time. Motivations for coming out as Jews were diverse. Some were attracted by the possibility of exploring their spirituality because it had previously been taboo. Others were glad for the Sabbath meals that were offered after the services. Yet others, learning that the Israeli government would cover the voyage and resettlement of Jewish Cubans who wanted to leave the island, treated the synagogues as travel agencies that could yield a ticket out of Cuba and a new life in Israel.

Throughout the revolutionary period, Jewish life had been sustained on the island with the assistance of Jewish organizations in Canada and Latin America, which sent matzo and wine on Passover and provided other modest but essential help. But it wasn't until the 1990s that major support began to arrive through the American Joint Distribution Committee and B'nai Brith. Helping the Jews of Cuba to survive as Jews became a priority of these Jewish-American organizations, which set up "missions" to assist the Jews of Cuba through donations of food, medicine, clothes, and books, as well as through Jewish education, which is most desperately needed in a country where there is not even a single rabbi.

These "missions" had a very strong impact, indeed. By the end of the century, Jewish synagogue life in Cuba was beginning more closely to resemble standard Jewish practice in the United States. The Patronato synagogue, which I'd seen in the early 1990s with a leaking roof that let in the doves, had been restored to its former grandeur and updated with computers and a video screening room. Although the Jewish community appeared to be shrinking as a result of deaths and recent immigration to Israel, more and more Jewish-American visitors continued to arrive on the island on goodwill "missions" to save the last of the Jews who survived communism. Jewish-American visitors became so ubiquitous that it seemed as if every Jew in Cuba had at least ten Jewish-Americans who wanted to help him or her continue being a Jew in Cuba.

The Jews of Cuba, by the end of the century, had become an exotic tribe. To outsiders they had come to seem as rare as the !Kung of the Kalahari Desert, and as overstudied, overobserved, overphotographed, overanthropologized, and elusive.

In the midst of this largely Ashkenazi-American "discovery" of Jews on the island, I entered the scene with a video camera wanting to make *Adio Kerida*. But where was I to place myself as a Cuban-American Jew of mixed Ashkenazi-Sephardic heritage? It was December of 1999, the century was ending, and I felt an immense urgency to begin telling the story I knew about the Jews of Cuba. I thought of following in the footsteps of filmmaker Dennis O'Rourke and making a kind of Jewish-Cuban version of "Cannibal Tours," focusing my camera on the Jewish-American tourists who came on "missions" to see the Jews of Cuba. I knew I was, to an extent, complicit in their exoticizing gaze, for in the end I too would be returning to the United States. And yet, though I wanted to incorporate a strong touch of irony in my film, it wasn't a tonality I wanted to sustain for the entire piece. There were too many other sentiments, experiences, and forms of knowing I wanted to examine. So I opted instead to show how my own shifting identity, as a returning Cuban Jew, a cultural anthropologist, and a tourist in my native country, opened a window onto a range of diasporic identities and homecomings.

With minimal funds and little previous filmmaking experience (I'd studied photography and made a short 16mm film in graduate school), I jumped into the project of *Adio Kerida*, assisted by Gisela Fosado and Umi Vaughan, graduate students in anthropology at the University of Michigan, who were embarking on their own ethnographic research projects in Cuba, in themselves yet another phenomenon of the "Cuba boom." (For Anglo-American ethnography departed the island after the embargo, with the sole exception of Oscar Lewis's trilogy, which brought him much suffering. A new generation of young anthropologists is now doing ethnography in Cuba.)

I didn't have a script, and I had only a rough idea of who would be the main protagonists of the story. One thing I knew from the start: the documentary would be called *Adio Kerida*, which is the title of a popular Sephardic song of nineteenth-century origin. *Adio Kerida* was one of the few Sephardic songs I knew by heart and could actually sing. It was among the few remnants of Sephardic culture that had been passed on to me. And the song spoke of unforgiveness, the quality that my Ashkenazi family had seen as so strongly a Sephardic characteristic. It is, indeed, the bitter lament of a lover who utters an angry goodbye after a beloved's rejection.

I was drawn to the song because I felt it could reference many layers of goodbyes, from the bitter goodbyes of Sephardic Jews, who were forced to leave their beloved Spain in 1492, to the more recent goodbyes of Sephardic Jews who had left Cuba in the 1960s, and yet more poignantly, to the immediate goodbyes of those Sephardic Jews who were leaving the island for Israel even as I hurried to interview them. I also felt the song could reference the desire for return that is so often the other side of exilic departure and speak to my own desire to find a way to return to Cuba, in contrast to my father's definitive goodbye.

With the lyrics to the *Adio Kerida* song in my head, I went in search of Jewish spaces, the synagogues and Jewish cemeteries where Jews had left traces of their presence on the island. One of the most important epiphanies took place early in the process of filming. As José Levy Tur, the director of the Centro Hebreo Sefaradí, was showing us the nine Torah scrolls brought to Cuba from Turkey by the Sephardic Jews, I could hear live Afro-Cuban music and singing from some place close by. Interrupting the interview, I asked José Levy where the music was coming from and he casually told me it was coming from next door, from the space that had once been the main sanctuary of the synagogue. As he explained, the Jewish community was now so small that their religious services had been moved to what had once been the women's meeting room, the room we were in. But what had been the majestic main sanctuary was located next door. Moving to the back of the room, we discovered a peephole through which we could look to the other side and see the musicians, who turned out to be Síntesis, a well-known Afro-Cuban musical group. We then went outside and entered through the main door of the synagogue to the old sanctuary, which was now used as a rehearsal space by Síntesis. They were rehearsing the song "Obbatala," the name of a Santería deity, and I was struck by the way an Afro-Cuban working of spirit now inhabited what had once been a Jewish religious space.

This mutuality, the play of disparate identities, spiritualities, and histories within shared spaces, became central to the film. The reality of Jewish-Cuban and Afro-Cuban religiosity existing side by side was brought home to me in the relationship between José Levy and his daughter Danayda, who is Afro-Cuban and has been brought up by him as a Jew. Not long after, while observing the children in the Sunday Hebrew school at the Patronato synagogue, I met an Afro-Cuban boy, Miguelito, whose mother told me he liked to drum Afro-Cuban rhythms on the buckets he uses to take his bath. As soon as I saw him drumming passionately on the buckets, a Jewish star dangling from his neck, I knew that Miguelito had to be in my film. What I couldn't have predicted is that on my last filming trip in the summer of 2001, he would announce on camera his upcoming departure to Israel with his family.

Another differently painful goodbye story had already been told to me by Alberto Behar, whose name, curiously, is the same as my father's. Alberto's revolutionary father, who rejected religion throughout his adult life, asked his son on his deathbed to bury him in the Jewish cemetery outside Havana. Confronted with the need to say the mourner's Kaddish, Alberto discovered he didn't know what a Kaddish was. He refused simply to repeat the words senselessly and was haunted for years by his inability to bid his father a proper goodbye. Only by learning to chant Torah was Alberto finally able to bring peace to his heart. Telling this story was for Alberto such a transformative experience that he subsequently pulled together all of his savings and had a tombstone built for his father in the Jewish cemetery.

With these key stories in place, I began to look for other cultural fusions closer to home, in Miami. There, I was immediately attracted to Alberto and Elza Habif, sellers of Turkish good luck charms, whose mirrored store is full of protective eyes. SAMY, a flamboyant gay hairdresser who keeps both a Jewish *hamsa* and a pair of scissors from the Vatican in his salon and whose grandfather, Samuel Cohen, "was like a rabbi," offered some very necessary humor and bold honesty, while belly-dancer Myriam Eli, who merges flamenco, Afro-Cuban, and Turkish traditions in her dance, raised key questions about the "boxes" into which multiple identities have to fit in the United States.

For the closing fragments of the film's mosaic of Cuban Sephardic identity in the American diaspora, I came even closer to home, within my own extended family. My uncle Enrique, a nouveau street peddler, sells clothes from his truck on Miami streets in the tradition of my grandfather and other Sephardic street peddlers from Turkey. My aunt Fanny conserves a nightgown that belonged to her grandmother in Turkey and traveled with her mother, my grandmother, from Turkey to Cuba to the United States. And my cousin Isaquito uproariously remembers what it was like to grow up in a Havana tenement on Calle Oficios, where the Sephardic Jews, the *turcos*, lived upstairs looking out on the sea, above the prostitutes below, and where sometimes even the nicest of Sephardic Jewish boys succumbed to the temptation of visiting the ladies they delicately referred to in Turkish as *oruspu*.

Finally it came time to go to New York to see if my father would agree to be in my film. Although my father said he would only allow us to film him for fifteen minutes, he had clearly been preparing himself for his interview. He'd hunted down the lyrics to the *Adio Kerida* song and rehearsed his singing with my mother. When Gisela Fosado turned on the camera, he was clearly moved to be able to sing the song for us, and held his hand to his heart, trembling with emotion. Afterwards, he surprised me by walking around the house, giving a kind of tour and pointing out the signifance of different objects he'd brought home from his journeys over the years, including a Sephardic cookbook from Istanbul. And I was overjoyed when he agreed to allow us to film him in the Rincon Criollo Restaurant. This was the one setting in which I had dreamed of capturing him, because this is his "little Cuba" and he is always in a good mood there.

It was only later, in the last stages of the editing process, that I realized we needed to balance out the Cuban part of my father's scene with the Sephardic part. I also wanted to connect the Cuban cemetery clips, where the Behar name hauntingly surfaces in so many of the tombstones, with cemetery clips in the United States. With a bit of fear, I asked my father if we could film him in the Jewish cemetery in New Jersey where both his parents are buried and where he and my mother wish to be buried when their time comes. He willingly agreed and I went with Marc Drake, my other key camera person and editor, to be filmed with my parents there. It was, naturally, an eerie moment for me, one that reinforces the theme of goodbye, because my parents already know that their final resting place will not be in Cuba but in the United States.

From the beginning, I expected to include my brother Mori in the film. He is such a strong counterpoint to me and is one of the few people who can always make me laugh. When asked to think about being Sephardic, the first association that that comes to him is that all the women were very fat. This he then connects jokingly to his dedication to playing the bass, "the big old lady." He hates to travel and can't understand what this anthropology thing is all about. And yet he participates in my film by improvising beautiful piano music, most memorably around the *Adio Kerida* song, joining me in my journey through the medium he most adores.

In an early version of *Adio Kerida*, the movie ended with my brother and then cut to the ocean splashing wildly over the malecón of Havana. But when I showed this version to colleagues and students in Ann Arbor in the spring of 2001, I was told that I ought to add a concluding scene in Michigan. I decided to create a scene that would revolve around a poem I'd written called "Prayer," about fears I've experienced often, of getting lost and not finding my way home.

I thought this scene was finished when the Spanish-language version of *Adio Kerida* premiered in the Havana Film Festival in December of 2001. But as I watched it several times in Cuba, I realized it wasn't yet complete. I came back to a snowy January in Michigan and realized that this snow and the desolation it evoked for me needed to be added to that last section. I also realized that the story of my own "intermarriage" to my husband David needed to be told, even if briefly, at the end, so that viewers could see that I too, like the Jews still on the island, had married out, was that kind of Jew who had crossed the border.

After working on it for over two years, I tell myself that *Adio Kerida* is done. It has been enthusiastically received by the Jewish-Cuban community in Havana and Miami, and most crucially of all, my father likes it. My mother's eating of the mango on camera (my father calls it her "Mango 101") is now part of the folklore of the Jewish-Cuban community, as is my father's line about how he'll return to Cuba when the ferry from Key West is operating again.

It's unusual to see a film that is so thoroughly Cuban and Latino, and yet focuses on Jewish identity. As a film that is mostly spoken in Spanish, it has a broad appeal for Latinos. The film has been shown already in two important Latino film festivals, in San Antonio and San Diego, and there is continuing interest in the film among Latino viewers. It hasn't been picked up quite so readily yet by Jewish film festivals (though it was shown in the Detroit Jewish film festival and will be shown in the Boston Jewish film festival), and I can only speculate as to whether this has to do with the Sephardic theme (always of lesser interest to Ashkenazi Jewish-Americans, who run the festivals, than films about Israel, the Holocaust, and the ultra-Orthodox Lubavitch), or my touch of irony about Jewish-American visits to Cuba, or the inclusion of Afro-Cubans and other Jews of mixed heritage in a film about Jews.

Or perhaps, my film is Jewish without being quite Jewish enough. It ends on a decidedly Cuban note, with the trio of Cuban musicians on the famous Habana malecón improvising a song about the split persona of Ruti/Ruth saying goodbye to Cuba, but returning every year to visit the island home she left behind before she was old enough to remember it. Maybe this desire for Cuba is something only Jewish-Cubans can fully understand. The *kerida*, after all, is Cuba, but "beloved" is spelled in Ladino with a "k" rather than the correct Spanish *querida*, to emphasize that the beloved Cuba is always a fiction, always an imaginary homeland. And I expect that will still be true even if the ferry from Key West to Cuba ever starts operating again.

NOTE

An earlier version of this essay was originally published in *Michigan Quarterly Review* 41, no. 4 (fall 2002): 651–67.

Index

Africa, 25, 151, 183–87, 189, 193, 194n2, 194n4, 195n5, 195n14, 200
African Americans, 9–10, 26, 166–80*ff*., 183, 186, 188–89, 192, 196
African Hebrew Israelite Community, 185, 188, 192–93. *See also* Black Hebrews
Afro-Cubans, 207–8
American Hungarians, 78, 81, 88
ancestors, 11, 23, 28, 37, 45, 49, 170–75, 187, 189
antiessentialism, 3, 13n12
anti-home, 183–86, 193, 194n1, 194n3
Armenia/Armenians, 9, 11, 26, 109–23*ff*.
assimilation, 5–6, 118, 173
authenticity, 25, 27, 93, 99, 103–4, 168

Babylon, 184–87, 189, 191–92, 194n3
belongings, 3, 5, 11, 22–23, 29, 41, 46, 50, 56, 94, 96, 104, 112–13, 168, 190
Bible, 153, 161n9, 185–86, 188–89, 192–94
Black Diaspora, 147, 149, 183, 187, 192–93
Black Hebrews, 26, 185–86, 188–91, 193–94
Bosnia and Herzegovina, 2, 54–71*ff*.

Bosniacs (Bosnian Muslims), 2–3, 57, 71n7, 71n13; Bosnian Croats, 57
Bosnians, 9, 54–71*ff*.
Bosnian Serbs, 2, 57, 71n7, 71n13, 71n14
Brazil/Brazilians, 10, 26, 126–42*ff*.

children, 28, 49, 64, 71n10, 134, 136, 146, 150–51, 153–54, 156, 161n1, 178, 188–89, 191, 195n9
Christian/Christians, 25, 148–49, 185, 187–88, 190, 192, 194
Christianity, 186–88, 195n4
citizenship, 23, 27–28, 30n2, 44, 139, 142n1, 147, 156–57, 184, 187, 190–91, 193, 196n15
Cold War, the, 6, 111
Cuba/Cubans, 10, 199–210*ff*.
Cuban revolution, 203, 205

deterritorialization, 3, 22, 29, 71n12, 125, 140–41, 177
diaspora, 4, 13n11, 24–25, 27, 29, 56, 71n12, 94–95, 100, 103–5, 111, 125, 140, 147, 151, 158–59, 161,184, 188, 190, 193–94, 204, 208; in the homeland, 10; research on, 5–6; return to, 4, 10–11, 173

diaspora tourism, 167–80*ff*.
discrimination, 26, 58, 95, 97, 117, 132, 157, 160
displaced persons (DPs), 77

Egypt, 100, 102, 106n14, 147, 185, 187–88, 192
elderly, 2–3, 47, 81–82, 142n10, 206
elders, 148, 153, 156
emplacement, 40, 46, 52n3, 93
Ethiopia/Ethiopians, 11, 36–52*ff*., 148, 150–56, 158–59, 161, 185, 187–88
ethnic cleansing, 2, 57
ethnic return migrants, 125–26, 141
Europe, 25, 147, 150, 190
exile, 4, 9, 11, 37–38, 56, 60, 67–68, 102, 104, 114, 121n8, 158, 185–87, 192–94, 202

Falashas, 146–52, 155, 160. See also Jews, Ethiopian
family, 21, 23, 28–29, 49, 83, 116, 134–37, 156, 158, 185, 200, 202, 208
fixity, 3

Ghana/Ghanaians, 9, 11, 166–80*ff*.
globalization, 3–5
Greece, 25

home, 2, 7, 22–29, 56, 93–94, 105, 125–26, 132, 140–41, 147, 154–56, 158–61, 167–68, 177, 179, 184–86, 188–94, 199, 208–10; change of, 10–11, 56–57; as dwelling, 7, 57; as primary place, 3, 6, 10–11, 37, 41–42, 47, 51; separation from, 4, 11, 12n1, 62; terms to define, 40–41, 43–46
homecomers. See returnees
homecoming, 25–28, 94, 126, 142, 147, 153, 159–60, 185–86, 188, 190–91, 194, 206; complexity of, 4, 7–8, 13n10; critique of, 78, 84–86; and death, 2–3, 78, 82–84; dream of, 2, 6, 77; the imagination of, 8–9, 77–79; impossibility of, 4, 10–12, 78; positive aspects of, 4, 10–12, 13n12, 69; problems of, 4, 8–9, 13n11,
55–57, 62–63; and retirement, 78, 82; in sedentary thinking, 5, 8, 69; studies of, 3–8, 12n6, 12n7, 42, 55–57, 69; as theme in literature, 13n11, 24, 194n1
homeland, 5, 22–23, 25–29, 30n3, 56, 77, 94–95, 101, 103–4, 110–12, 114, 123n6, 125–26, 132, 140–41, 147–49, 153, 156–61, 168, 184, 187–89, 192–94, 210; ancestral homeland, 126, 140, 147, 154, 159, 185, 187; historical homeland, 7, 28, 188; imagined homeland, 9, 10, 26, 77, 159–60, 168; natal homeland, 7, 10, 141; virtual homeland, 147, 159
homemaking, 12, 42–43, 46–47, 51, 69
homesickness, 13n11, 136, 142
hometown, 2
Hungarian Americans, 79, 83, 85, 87–88
Hungary, 76–89*ff*.; revolution in, 77–78, 80, 84, 87
hybridity, 3, 11, 23, 71n14, 141, 193

identity, 23, 41, 48–51, 66, 87, 93, 96, 110, 147–49, 151–52, 154, 156–57, 159–60, 171, 185–86, 188–89, 190, 192–93, 199–201, 204–06, 208, 210; diasporic identity, 7, 56; national identity, 38; returnee identity, 10, 63–66, 69, 71n13; transformation of, 4, 55, 70
immigrant communities, 135–39
immigrant settlement, 132–35
immigration, 7, 10, 22, 28–29, 102, 113, 147, 150–152, 187, 190, 193, 202, 206
integration, 6, 11, 55–56, 65–69, 118, 154–57, 185
Israel, 7, 9, 26, 27–29, 93–105*ff*., 146–61*ff*., 183–96*ff*., 205–8, 210
Israelis, 92–93, 96–98, 100, 101, 104–5, 153, 155–57, 186, 190; Ethiopian-Israelis, 158, 161n5, 161n6; Moroccan Israelis, 9, 93, 97–98, 101, 104

Japan, 10, 126–42*ff*.
Japanese Brazilians, 126–42*ff*.
Jerusalem, 146–50, 153, 155, 161n7, 191

Jewish Americans, 200, 205–6, 210
Jewish Cubans. *See* Jews, Cuban
Jews, 25, 30n2, 100–101, 103–5, 146–47, 149–55, 160, 189–91, 195n10, 195n11, 199–200, 204, 206–7, 210; Ashkenazi, 200; Cuban, 199–210*ff*.; Ethiopian, 9, 146–61*ff*., 146–47, 149–58, 160; Moroccan, 9, 93–94, 96–97, 101, 103, 105; Russian, 13n8, 28–29; Sephardic, 199–202, 207–8

Kessab (Syria), 109–123*ff*.

land, 28, 37, 39, 146–47, 149–53, 158–59, 183, 185–86, 189, 193; Promised Land, 114–15, 146–47, 149–52, 154–60, 188, 192–93
landscape, 92–93, 113

Maghreb, 25, 96, 101
memory, 26–27, 93, 106, 148, 150, 154, 170–77, 184
migration, 3, 5–7, 21–24, 26, 29, 113–14, 120, 151–52
minorities, 2–3, 25–26, 56–57, 71n14, 95
mobility, 3, 5, 7, 11, 141
Morocco, 7, 9, 92–106*ff*.
multiculturalism, 5–6, 199
Muslim/Muslims, 25, 52n7, 95, 103–4, 105n9, 118, 192. *See also* Bosnians; Bosnian Muslims

nationalism, long-distance, 78–79, 87
nation-state, 3, 22–23, 25–26, 28, 71n12, 93–94, 99, 101, 120, 139, 141
nikkeijin, 126–42*ff*.
nostalgia, 11, 23, 26–27, 56, 87, 96, 98, 122n12, 125, 142n7, 153, 200, 203

patriotism, 11, 44, 59–61, 114, 122n12
pilgrimage, 4, 93, 97, 101–2, 148, 158, 167, 177
place, 3, 4, 6, 11, 43–46, 68–69
postmodernism, 3, 140, 167–68

racism, 11, 132, 154, 157, 169, 173, 177, 183–85
reconciliation, 70

refugees, 3–6, 9, 25–27, 29, 38–39, 42, 48, 54–71*ff*., 77, 110, 120, 154, 159; in camps/centers, 24, 36, 49, 62, 152
reintegration. *See* integration
repatriation, 3–4, 6, 9, 11, 12n6, 12n7, 13n9, 13n10, 22, 25, 36–50*ff*., 55–71*ff*., 109–22*ff*., 150, 187–88
resettlement, 80, 147, 155, 185
reterritorialization, 3, 141
return, 16, 22, 24, 27, 29, 57, 100–102, 148–51, 154, 156, 158–60, 188, 190, 192–93, 194n2, 202–4, 206–7, 210; ancestral return, 4, 7, 70n1; Law of Return, 146, 190–92, 195n10, 195n11; myth of return, 5–6, 8, 22, 146–147, 186; return visit, 7, 10, 57, 77. *See also* homecoming
returnees, 4, 8, 13n12, 68; invisibility of, 65; in the media, 65; relationships with stayee population, 9–10, 54–71*ff*., 84, 87, 103, 175–78; resentment against, 9, 55–56, 58–66*ff*., 66, 69, 117; social alienation of, 9–10, 69, 116–18, 127–32, 136–39, 141
return migration. *See* homecoming
Roma, 25
roots, 4, 78, 81, 100, 112, 140, 160, 166, 168, 177, 186

Sarajevo, 9, 54–71*ff*.
slavery, 11, 167–80*ff*., 183, 187–88, 192
Spain, 200–202, 204, 207

transnationalism, 5, 7, 10, 26, 52n4, 56, 70n1, 88, 125, 139–41
tsaddiq, 92–93, 97, 106
Turkey, 25, 109, 112–13, 117, 122n17, 200, 207–8

United States of America (U.S.), 12, 28–29, 63, 65, 71n9, 76–86*ff*., 120, 122n17, 169–70, 174, 177–78, 183, 185, 193, 195n8, 195n10, 199, 201–2, 204, 206, 208–9

war, 13n11, 26, 38–39, 44, 57–63*ff*., 152

Yugoslavia, the former, 54–56, 72n15

About the Contributors

Lisa Anteby-Yemini is researcher for the Centre National de la Recherche Scientifique at the Institute of Mediterranean and Comparative Ethnology (IDEMEC) in Aix-en-Provence, France. She has written various articles on the Ethiopian Jews in Israel and has just published *Les juifs éthiopiens en Israël: paradoxes du paradis* (2004). She is coeditor of *2000 Years of Diasporas* (forthcoming) and is currently working on ethnicity and citizenship in Israel.

Ruth Behar is author of *Translated Woman: Crossing the Border with Esperanza's Story* (1993) and *The Vulnerable Observer: Anthropology That Breaks Your Heart* (1996), and is editor of *Bridges to Cuba* (1995) and coeditor of *Women Writing Culture* (1995). Her film *Adio Kerida* is available through her distributor, Women Make Movies (www.wmm.com). The film has since been shown in a wide range of international festivals (see www.adiokerida.com). She is professor of anthropology at the University of Michigan.

Laura Hammond is assistant professor in the Department of International Development, Community, and Environment at Clark University. She has worked as a relief and development consultant in the Horn of Africa (Ethiopia, Somalia/Somaliland, and Eritrea) since 1992. Her book *This Place Will Become Home: Refugee Repatriation to Ethiopia* will be published in 2004.

Bayo Holsey is assistant professor in the Program in African and African American Studies at Duke University. She is currently working on a manuscript based on her dissertation, "Routes of Remembrance: The Transatlantic Slave Trade in the Ghanaian Imagination" (2003), that examines the place of the transatlantic slave trade within Ghanaian collective memory and the impact of the diaspora tourism industry's elaboration of this history.

Éva V. Huseby-Darvas teaches part-time at the University of Michigan-Dearborn in the United States and gives mini-courses at the ELTE University in Budapest, Hungary. In addition to over forty articles and a number of encyclopedia entries, Huseby-Darvas's publications include *Hungarians in Michigan* (2003). She was born and raised in Hungary, but after the 1956 revolution she fled her homeland.

André Levy is senior lecturer of anthropology in the Department of Behavioral Sciences at Ben-Gurion University, Beersheva, Israel. His Ph.D. dissertation from the Hebrew University (1996) is "Jews among Muslims: Perceptions and Reactions to the End of Casablancan Jewish History." Levy is coeditor of *Homelands and Diasporas* (2004) and author of several book chapters and articles dealing with pilgrimages, diasporas, identities, and minority-majority relations.

Fran Markowitz teaches anthropology in the Department of Behavioral Sciences at Ben-Gurion University in Beersheva, Israel. Author of *A Community in Spite of Itself* (1993) and *Coming of Age in Post-Soviet Russia* (2000) and coeditor of *Sex, Sexuality, and the Anthropologist* (1999), she is currently researching the narratives and practices of Sarajevo's ethnic legacies while contemplating homecomings of her own.

Susan Pattie is senior research fellow at University College London and also teaches for Syracuse University Study Abroad. Author of *Faith in History: Armenians Rebuilding Community* (1997), she continues long-term research and writing on issues of living in diaspora and the dilemmas of return.

Anders H. Stefansson is assistant professor at the Institute of Anthropology, University of Copenhagen, Denmark. His Ph.D. dissertation is "Under My Own Sky? The Cultural Dynamics of Refugee Return and (Re)integration in Post-War Sarajevo" (2003). He is currently researching the interconnection between reconstruction, reconciliation, and refugee return in Bosnia and Herzegovina.

Takeyuki (Gaku) Tsuda is associate director at the Center for Comparative Immigration Studies at the University of California at San Diego. Author of *Strangers in the Ethnic Homeland: Japanese Brazilian Return Migration in Transnational Perspective* (2003), he has researched and written about comparative immigration policies, immigration to Japan, and ethnic return migration. He has taught at both the University of Chicago and the University of California at San Diego, has published numerous articles in anthropological and interdisciplinary journals, and is editor of two forthcoming collections.